MULTILEVEL GOVERNANCE AND EMERGENCY
MANAGEMENT IN CANADIAN MUNICIPALITIES

FIELDS OF GOVERNANCE:
POLICY MAKING IN CANADIAN MUNICIPALITIES
Series editor: Robert Young

Policy making in the modern world has become a complex matter. Much policy is formed through negotiations between governments at several different levels, because each has particular resources that can be brought to bear on problems. At the same time, non-governmental organizations make demands about policy and can help in policy formation and implementation. In this context, works in this series explore how policy is made within municipalities through processes of intergovernmental relations and with the involvement of social forces of all kinds.

The Fields of Governance series arises from a large research project, funded mainly by the Social Sciences and Humanities Research Council of Canada, entitled Multilevel Governance and Public Policy in Canadian Municipalities. This project has involved more than eighty scholars and a large number of student assistants. At its core are studies of several policy fields, each of which was examined in a variety of municipalities. Our objectives are not only to account for the nature of the policies but also to assess their quality and to suggest improvements in policy and in the policy-making process.

The Fields of Governance series is designed for scholars, practitioners, and interested readers from many backgrounds and places.

Multilevel Governance and Emergency Management in Canadian Municipalities

Edited by

DANIEL HENSTRA

McGill-Queen's University Press
Montreal & Kingston • London • Ithaca

© McGill-Queen's University Press 2013

ISBN 978-0-7735-4283-9 (cloth)
ISBN 978-0-7735-4284-6 (paper)
ISBN 978-0-7735-8953-7 (ePDF)
ISBN 978-0-7735-8954-4 (ePUB)

Legal deposit third quarter 2013
Bibliothèque nationale du Québec

Printed in Canada on acid-free paper that is 100% ancient forest free
(100% post-consumer recycled), processed chlorine free

McGill-Queen's University Press acknowledges the support of the
Canada Council for the Arts for our publishing program. We also
acknowledge the financial support of the Government of Canada
through the Canada Book Fund for our publishing activities.

Library and Archives Canada Cataloguing in Publication

Multilevel governance and emergency management in Canadian
municipalities / edited by Daniel Henstra.

(Fields of governance: policy making in Canadian municipalities; 6)
Includes bibliographical references and index.
Issued in print and electronic formats.
ISBN 978-0-7735-4283-9 (bound). – ISBN 978-0-7735-4284-6 (pbk.).
– ISBN 978-0-7735-8953-7 (ePDF). – ISBN 978-0-7735-8954-4 (ePUB)

1. Emergency management – Government policy – Canada.
2. Natural disasters – Government policy – Canada.
3. Intergovernmental cooperation – Canada. 4. Municipal
government – Canada. I. Henstra, Dan, editor of compilation
II. Series: Fields of governance; 6

HV551.5.C3M84 2013   363.3'480971   C2013-902694-0
                                        C2013-902695-9

Typeset by Jay Tee Graphics Ltd. in 10.5/13 Sabon

Contents

Foreword

This collection of papers about emergency management is a contribution to an important field of public policy, one that is relevant to all Canadians. It is also part of an intriguing field for anyone interested in policy-making more broadly. The researchers whose work is collected here have studied emergency management *in* municipalities, and not just policies enacted *by* local governments. This is an important distinction because the policies operative in municipal spaces are created by provincial governments and the federal government, as well as by municipal actors. This policy field is characterized by multilevel governance, as is the case in many other areas of policy.

Our focus is on two key determinants of policy. The first is the complex set of relations between officials and politicians from the municipal, provincial, and federal governments. Intergovernmental relations, we expected from the outset, are important in shaping the policies about emergency management that are implemented on the ground. The second factor, denoted by the term "governance," is the array of organized interests that are concerned with, or involved in, planning for emergencies and managing them. We expected that these interests would also help create the policies we explored.

Emergency management occasionally attracts huge public interest when tornadoes, hurricanes, floods, wildfires, epidemics, and human-caused disasters like chemical spills and industrial explosions damage property and claim lives. But then public attention soon wanes. This is a central characteristic of the policy field that those responsible for emergency management must cope with, as they seek resources and political support. Emergency management is also shaped by the fact that all disasters are local, with the result that municipal governments have a central role in preparedness and response. But disasters can have much broader geographical impacts, and they can demand measures and resources that are beyond the capacity of municipalities to deliver, so that there is intrinsically a part to be played by provincial governments and the federal government. We are concerned here with the roles of all governments in emergency management.

This collection of studies presents the results of original research that makes a significant contribution to a field that has been seriously understudied. The authors are experts, and the research is thorough. But their work is also part of a much larger project, one that explores more generally issues about multilevel governance and public policy in Canadian municipalities. This project includes several components, but most of the work has been done on six policy areas, of which emergency management is one. All the research covers various provinces and municipalities of different sizes, as in the studies in this volume. The objectives of the whole project are to document the policies that exist in the various fields and to explain their character by focusing on the processes of intergovernmental relations through which they were shaped, as well as on the "social forces" – organized interests of all kinds – that were involved (or not) in the policy process. We also aim to evaluate the quality of the policies and to make suggestions for improvements in policy and process. More information about the overall project can be found at http://www.ppm-ppm.ca.

Here it is appropriate to make some acknowledgements. We thank first the Social Sciences and Humanities Research Council of Canada for its support through the Major Collaborative Research Initiatives program. The University of Western Ontario and other universities have contributed generously to the project. We thank McGill-Queen's University Press for its continued interest in our research, and especially Philip Cercone and Jacqueline Mason for their help. Kelly McCarthy has served as manager for the larger project. She coordinated several meetings of the research team and helped with preparing the initial manuscript, and we are grateful for her efforts. Jen Lajoie also helped with this work, notably by preparing the index. We are grateful to Ron Curtis, whose copyediting improved the text. Finally, Professor Gordon McBean took the lead at the outset in animating the group of scholars engaged with emergency management. His experience and insights were invaluable to all of us.

MULTILEVEL GOVERNANCE AND EMERGENCY
MANAGEMENT IN CANADIAN MUNICIPALITIES

Introduction: Multilevel Governance and Canadian Emergency Management Policy

DANIEL HENSTRA

In the first decade of the twenty-first century, Canada experienced dozens of major emergencies that threatened public safety and disrupted critical infrastructure. Some were triggered by weather-related hazards such as Hurricane Juan, a tropical cyclone that struck near Halifax in September 2003, choking roadways with debris, severing power to thousands of households and causing extensive structural damage to buildings. Similarly, in December 2006 a series of powerful windstorms in British Columbia's Lower Mainland toppled thousands of trees, caused widespread power outages, and was responsible for more than $100 million in property losses. Other emergencies resulted from industrial accidents or technological failures, such as a massive explosion at a propane facility in Toronto in August 2008, which required the evacuation of thousands of nearby residents and closed Highway 401, one of the busiest traffic arteries in North America. Still others involved health-related threats: in 2003, for instance, hundreds of Canadians across six provinces were infected by severe acute respiratory syndrome (SARS), requiring a concerted national effort by health professionals to curb the spread of the virus. These events illustrate the diversity of hazards that Canadians face and underscore the importance of emergency management policies – courses of action designed to protect people and property from hazards and to respond effectively to emergencies and their impacts.

That "all emergencies are local" is a well-known and often-cited maxim among emergency planners. Regardless of the triggering agent, when an emergency occurs, it is local officials, such as firefighters, police, and emergency medical services personnel, who must manage response efforts in the critical early hours (Hightower and Coutu 1996). Canada's emergency management system is premised on the doctrine of tiered response, which holds that municipal governments respond first to emergencies, with support from higher-level governments when necessary (Scanlon 1995). Municipal governments in all provinces have a responsibility to plan to protect citizens and their property in emergencies (Kuban 1996).

Local officials are well positioned to spearhead emergency planning. Given their detailed knowledge of the community, local governments are best able to identify hazards, assess vulnerabilities, and design appropriate policies to reduce and manage risks (Newkirk 2001). Moreover, many practical measures can be implemented at the local level to ensure that emergencies are managed effectively (Henstra 2010a). For instance, a written emergency plan that designates authority and specifies operational procedures can provide valuable guidance for those coordinating response activities (Lindell and Perry 2007). Training for responders and decision makers prepares them for the roles they will be expected to play during an emergency and the difficulties they are likely to encounter (Daines 1991). Disaster simulation exercises help to detect and diagnose weaknesses in emergency plans, and foster stronger working relationships among responders (Perry 2004). Mutual aid agreements – contracts signed by two or more jurisdictions that obligate them to share equipment or personnel – allow communities to pool scarce resources in an emergency (McEntire and Myers 2004, 147).

But although municipalities bear primary functional responsibility for emergency management, local programs in this field are often weak and underfunded (GCSI 2004; Nirapuma and Etkin 2009; Wolensky and Wolensky 1990). Post-event analyses of responses to major Canadian emergencies document persistent problems with local emergency management (Haque 2000; Purcell and Fyfe 1998). In a national assessment conducted by the Standing Senate Committee on National Security and Defence, fewer than half of Canadian municipalities reported they were sufficiently prepared for even a minor emergency (Senate of Canada 2004, 86). Why? Every Canadian has witnessed, either personally or through media reports, the devastating impacts that an emergency or disaster can have on a community. Given the tremendous hardship these events can impose, planning for emergencies seems to be matter of prudent risk management.

Furthermore, emergency planning policies are meant to protect citizens and their property – a fundamental role of governments.

One problem appears to be perspective. From a national or provincial vantage point, localized emergencies appear to be frequent, and disasters probable, so planning for their impacts seems imperative. But at the local level, emergencies are rare and the likelihood of a disaster seems remote, so "the need for emergency management seems far less compelling and public support for disaster preparedness is very difficult to sustain" (Kreps 1992, 159–60). Beverly Cigler calls this the "intergovernmental paradox" of emergency management, whereby "the governments least likely to perceive emergency management as a key priority – local governments – are at centrestage in terms of responsibility for emergency management" (Cigler 1988, 10).

Another problem is capacity. Municipal governments operate with very tight budgets and face a wide range of demands from local residents, so they must selectively allocate resources to a limited set of problems. Whereas the costs of emergency management activities are immediate, the benefits of these efforts cannot be reaped until sometime in the future, if ever (Waugh 1990). As two analysts put it, "local governments – lacking both the political wherewithal to worry about events that may never occur and a clear rationale to expend limited dollars on technical expertise that may never be needed – prefer to shirk these costly responsibilities and concentrate on more pressing local problems" (Donahue and Joyce 2001, 733).

The limited interest and capacity among municipalities necessitates participation by higher-level governments, so governance of this policy field involves a wider network of relationships among officials at the local, regional, provincial, and federal levels. Because many hazards cross community boundaries and because emergencies can quickly exceed local coping capacity, the federal and provincial governments have programs and resources that support community-level emergency management. Furthermore, although governments play a crucial coordinating role, emergency management involves a broader community of interest populated by public administrators, private sector managers, non-profit agencies, military personnel, academics, and some interested members of the public, each of whom brings expertise and resources to the policy table.

The chapters collected here probe the structure and dynamics of interaction among Canada's levels of government and explore

the various social forces that influence policy-making in the field
of emergency management in Canada. The research reported here
is part of a Major Collaborative Research Initiative, funded by
the Social Sciences and Humanities Research Council of Canada,
which analyzes multilevel governance and public policy in Canada.
In addition to emergency planning, the project includes five other
policy fields: the management of federal property, municipal image-
building, immigrant settlement, infrastructure, and urban Aboriginal policy. Through comparative analysis, the researchers aim to
document existing policies in these domains and to determine what
patterns of intergovernmental interaction and forms of public participation are most conducive to good public policy in municipalities. In evaluating the quality of policy, the researchers consider
various criteria, including

- *speed* of policy development;
- *scale*: whether the scope of the policy is adequate to address the
  problem;
- *coherence*: the degree of complementarity among policy components;
- *effectiveness*: the degree to which the policy achieves its goals;
- *efficiency*: whether policy goals are achieved at a reasonable cost;
- *equity*: the distribution of benefits associated with the policy; and
- *optimality*: whether the policy is the best that can be achieved.

The three provincial case studies in this volume were chosen to
fulfill the methodological objectives of the broader research project. Two of the six policy fields were examined in each province.
To ensure that the findings were representative, the study design-
ers selected provinces to include those in which the policy field is
more visible and pertinent to policy-makers, as well as provinces
where the issue is less visible and salient. Some provinces that are
well known to have comprehensive emergency management policies,
such as British Columbia and Ontario, have commanded greater
attention from analysts than others, such as Alberta, whose policies in this field have evolved considerably in recent years. Once
the provinces were selected, the researchers were asked to analyze
policy-making in four municipalities of varying sizes, including the
largest city in the province. The broader project has produced a separate volume that contains studies of ten major Canadian cities, and

six of these include sections on emergency management (Horak and Young 2012).

This introductory chapter sets emergency management policy in a historical and analytical context. It begins by describing the evolution of emergency planning in Canada, including major events that have shaped policy objectives and instruments in this field over time. It then discusses the scope and nature of modern emergency management and identifies some significant defining features of the policy domain. The next section sets out an analytical framework based on the objectives of the broader research project and outlines the theoretical questions that guided the research in this collection. The final section provides a brief overview of the chapters.

THE HISTORICAL CONTEXT

Emergency management in Canada evolved out of civil defence initiatives started in the late 1940s that engaged all levels of government in planning to protect citizens from an armed enemy attack, particularly one involving nuclear weapons (Scanlon 1982). Civil defence planning required an intergovernmental partnership. The parameters were negotiated at a federal-provincial conference in 1950 whereby Ottawa established broad, national policy priorities, while the provinces coordinated and supported local planning (Timmerman 1980). The Civil Defence Financial Assistance Program was created in 1952, and it offered federal and provincial grants to local governments to pay for training, exercises, and equipment. Policy design centred on two primary objectives: protecting citizens from direct impacts of a nuclear attack and preserving government decision-making capacity and services. Operational priorities included mapping evacuation routes, surveying buildings that could serve as fallout shelters, and stockpiling items like radiological detection equipment and medical supplies.

The military nature of civil defence planning gradually eroded, as major emergencies throughout the 1950s and 1960s focused attention on domestic threats to public safety. By the 1970s, "peacetime" emergencies had ascended to primacy among emergency planners, prompted by events such as Hurricane Hazel, a massive tropical storm that devastated communities in the Toronto region in 1954 (Gifford 2004), and the Great Northeastern Blackout of 1965, in which a cascading system failure interrupted power to nearly thirty million people in Ontario, New York State, and New England (Friedlander 1976). At all levels of government the ethos and nomenclature of "civil defence" gave way to "emergency measures," as the policy design expanded to target natural hazards and incorporate new programmatic objectives, such as flood protection, public education, and backup power generation.

Industrial and technological hazards began to figure more prominently in Canadian emergency planning into the 1980s after a number of high-profile accidents raised questions about the adequacy of safety systems and response procedures. One was a partial core meltdown at the Three Mile Island nuclear power plant in Pennsylvania in 1979 that revealed significant weaknesses in emergency communication and evacuation protocols (Cantelon and Williams 1982). In the wake of the crisis, Canadian emergency planners turned their attention to risks associated with industrial accidents and emergencies involving hazardous materials. The policy focus on technological hazards was further reinforced by a lethal chemical gas release at a pesticide factory in Bhopal, India, in 1984 that killed nearly three thousand people and focused global attention on industrial risks (Shrivastava 1992). In Canada, the disaster was a catalyst for enhanced horizontal collaboration in emergency planning, embodied in the Major Industrial Accidents Council of Canada (MIACC), a non-profit association of public officials, industrial actors, trade unions, academics, and others, formed to integrate municipal and industrial planning in order to prevent and manage emergencies involving hazardous materials (Lacoursiere 2005). At its peak, MIACC had 106 members, including representatives from ten federal departments, eight provincial and territorial governments, seventeen major industry associations, and numerous municipalities, but it was eventually dissolved owing to a lack of funding.

In the early 1990s, a new paradigm of "integrated, all-hazards" emergency management had begun to take root, driven by an expanding body of research on disasters in the United States (Sylves 1991). The model advocated intergovernmental co-ordination directed at reducing the vulnerability of people and property to hazards and creating plans flexible enough to address any emergency, regardless of the triggering agent. It sought to expand the policy goals beyond a traditional focus on preparedness and response to include hazard mitigation – actions to prevent or reduce the impact of emergencies – and recovery, which involved planning to restore and rehabilitate a

community after an emergency (McLoughlin 1985). These objectives demanded a more systematic approach to emergency management, including the development of integrated plans to pull together
response resources, training and exercises for emergency responders,
and public education programs to inform citizens about hazards and
protective measures. The United Nations' declaration of the 1990s
as the International Decade for Natural Disaster Reduction served
to further diffuse these ideas through the international policy community, prompting governments in many countries, including Canada, to focus more attention on emergency management (Canadian
National Committee 1994).

The series of terrorist attacks in the United States on September
11, 2001 (9/11), had profound impacts on Canadian emergency
management, triggering significant changes to federal emergency
management policies and providing the catalyst for policy change
in a number of provinces as well (Henstra 2003). In Ontario, for
instance, a permissive policy framework based on persuasion and
cooperation was replaced by a prescriptive model in which legislation and regulations mandated specific standards for municipal
emergency management (Ontario 2006). Since 9/11, the federal and
provincial governments have prioritized measures to harden critical
infrastructure systems, such as water distribution networks and electricity grids, to protect them from both natural hazards and terrorist threats (Public Safety Canada 2009). Health emergency planning
has also developed significantly since the turn of the millennium,
driven by crises such as the SARS outbreak of 2003 and the H1N1
influenza pandemic of 2009. Operational experience and lessons
learned through post-event analyses have led to closer collaboration
between emergency managers and public health professionals.

MODERN EMERGENCY MANAGEMENT

Contemporary emergency management policy has a number of
distinct characteristics (Waugh 2007). First, it is comprehensive,
emphasizing readiness for all types of hazards and involving multiple dimensions, including mitigation, preparedness, response, and
recovery. Mitigation involves implementing anticipatory measures
to prevent or reduce the impacts of hazards, such as land-use regulations that prohibit residential construction on flood plains. Preparedness involves measures to increase a community's capability to

respond effectively to emergencies, such as planning for the evacuation of residents who are mobility-impaired. Response policies, such as search and rescue protocols and emergency shelter arrangements, are adopted to strengthen operations during an emergency and to assist victims. Recovery plans address issues such as debris management and psychological counselling for victims and are meant to aid in restoring and rehabilitating a community after emergencies.

Second, modern emergency management doctrine embraces the principles of risk management, which offer a logical and systematic framework for decision making. Risk-based emergency planning involves an assessment of the risks a community is likely to face and an estimation of the probable impacts associated with these risks over a specific period (Deyle et al. 1998; Ferrier and Haque 2003). This process of identifying, analyzing, and prioritizing risks is increasingly regarded as the optimal means to allocate scarce emergency management resources.

Third, emergency management is increasingly professionalized. Over the past decade, numerous communication networks have developed among practitioners, and several national and regional events targeted at emergency managers are organized annually, such as the Emergency Preparedness Conference in Vancouver, the Disaster Forum in Alberta, and the World Conference on Disaster Management in Toronto. Emergency management education programs offering knowledge and skills development have been established at a number of Canadian universities and colleges. Professional associations, such as the Ontario Association of Emergency Managers and the British Columbia Association of Emergency Managers, have formed to represent the interests of practitioners and to define and formalize the area of professional competence. In addition, in 2007 the International Association of Emergency Managers began offering a variant of the Certified Emergency Manager Program, providing a credential developed in the 1990s to designate those meeting professional criteria in this field.

Fourth, contemporary emergency management involves horizontal and vertical collaboration (Kapucu 2008; Waugh and Streib 2006). To be effective, municipal emergency planners must engage with actors who fulfill other functional responsibilities, such as water and waste-water management, transportation, public health, land-use planning and social services, actors who may be called upon to play a role in an emergency. In preparing a course of action to deal with a major ice storm, for instance, a municipal emergency manager must ensure that the local power utility is equipped to quickly recover from a system failure. Often the utility is a corporate entity, and although the municipality usually has influence as the sole shareholder, this is not the same as having direct control over service provision. Coordination with agencies in the non-profit sector is also crucial for effective emergency management, since these organizations often perform important response functions, such as providing first aid or organizing volunteers, and they assist with post-disaster recovery. The Canadian Red Cross, for example, provides emergency shelter and life necessities to evacuees and those whose homes have been destroyed in an emergency. Horizontal partnerships allow emergency planners, who generally operate with very limited budgets, to draw on a broader pool of expertise and resources.

Similarly, modern emergency management requires vertical collaboration with other levels of government. Some important public functions, including public health and social services, are administered by regional governments such as counties or districts. Municipal emergency planners must work with regional officials to ensure vital services will be available during and after an emergency. Furthermore, emergency managers in most communities operate with minimal resources and look to higher-level governments for information, equipment, money, and other forms of support. In these ways, Canada's emergency management system involves both formal and informal interaction among officials at the various levels of the state.

From its narrow, war-oriented roots in the civil defence efforts of the 1950s, Canadian emergency management policy has expanded into a comprehensive course of action involving all levels of government, the private sector, and non-profit organizations. The short historical account presented above suggests a pattern of disaster-driven evolutionary change, whereby the scope and substance of emergency management policy were incrementally adjusted in response to periodic emergencies that focused attention on natural, technological, and human-induced risks. However, this masks two important influences on public policy, which are the focus of the research in this volume. The first is the structure and dynamics of intergovernmental relations, which affect the distribution of resources in a policy field and the degree and quality of vertical collaboration. The second is the nature of interaction between state actors and various social forces – citizens, interest groups, business interests, voluntary associations, and so on – who make demands, participate in decision making, and sometimes play a role in policy implementation. These key factors are discussed below.

MULTILEVEL GOVERNANCE

A central objective of the research in this collection is to analyze the structure of intergovernmental relations in emergency management and its impact on public policies in this field. The authors seek to identify the roles and responsibilities of federal, provincial, and municipal authorities, assess the resources each level of government brings to the table, evaluate the degree of intergovernmental collaboration, and examine patterns of interaction between politicians and administrators based at different levels of the state. Of particular interest is the relationship between municipal governments and the federal government, since this connection varies across policy fields, is affected by the ideological and strategic interests of the governing party in Ottawa, and is influenced by the degree to which provincial governments resist federal "intrusion" into their constitutional domain. How do municipal officials perceive the federal government's contribution to emergency management? To what extent do federal initiatives shape municipal priorities and plans? In what ways do the provincial governments mediate federal-municipal interaction in this field?

The government of Canada has long played a role in emergency planning, but the structure and substance of its contribution has varied over time. The federal unit responsible for emergency management has changed frequently and has been shuffled between departments and cabinet portfolios half a dozen times over the past sixty years. Public Safety Canada, the current lead department in this area, is mandated to coordinate federal emergency management efforts and to provide support to provincial and municipal planning, which it extends through a number of programs and initiatives. First, under the Joint Emergency Preparedness Program, matching funds are available to support provincial and municipal investments in emergency preparedness (Public Safety Canada 2012). The money can be used to pay for activities such as training and exercises, or to purchase emergency response equipment. Second, the

Canadian Emergency Management College, a federal training facility in Ottawa, offers courses for provincial and municipal emergency planners who wish to strengthen their expertise in this area. Third, Ottawa produces and distributes printed materials to encourage citizens to take responsibility for emergency preparedness, in hopes of relieving some of the burden on public authorities. Fourth, the federal government sponsors conferences, workshops, and other venues that bring together public officials and stakeholders to share ideas and learn about emergency management. Finally, the federal government plays a key role in recovery after a disaster. Under the Disaster Financial Assistance Arrangements (DFAA), a cost-sharing program initiated in 1970, money is provided to provinces that request financial assistance to pay for response-related expenditures, damages to public infrastructure and personal property losses (Public Safety Canada 2011a).

Although mitigation is the least developed element of Canadian emergency management policy (Henstra and McBean 2005), in 2008 a federal-provincial-territorial initiative called the National Disaster Mitigation Strategy was launched, which commits governments to work together to support disaster mitigation (Public Safety Canada 2008). The strategy sets out a framework of shared principles, priorities, and action items that includes a commitment for a shared-cost program to fund disaster mitigation projects. As part of the Building Canada program, a major federal initiative aimed at renewing public infrastructure, matching funds are available for structural projects that reduce the vulnerability of communities to extreme events. For instance, a bilateral agreement between the governments of Canada and British Columbia committed $25 million to flood mitigation projects in 2008 (Building Canada 2008). In addition, the DFAA guidelines were revised in 2008 to allow up to 15 percent of the recovery funds to be devoted to "mitigative enhancements" that would reduce vulnerability to future emergencies (Public Safety Canada 2011b).

Constitutionally endowed with exclusive legislative jurisdiction over municipal institutions, provincial governments have a more central role in overseeing local emergency management. Every province has an institution – the British Columbia Provincial Emergency Program, the Manitoba Emergency Measures Organization, and so on – that leads the government's planning for emergencies. Ontario's approach can be used illustratively, since it is fairly typical of those found elsewhere in Canada. Policies are developed by Emergency Management Ontario, a branch of the Ministry of Community Safety and Correctional Services, and they are administered by regional field officers, who are assigned to specific geographic areas and are responsible for monitoring and reporting on the emergency planning activities of municipalities.

The chapters in this volume describe how various provincial governments have organized themselves to administer emergency management policies, the instruments they use to shape local emergency planning, and the nature of interaction between municipal and provincial officials. For instance, is the provincial-municipal relationship cooperative or coercive? How much autonomy do municipal policy-makers have in designing emergency management strategies? What provincial resources can local emergency managers draw upon to support their work? Moreover, the authors focus on both appointed and elected officials. Although the technical nature of emergency management suggests that policy is dominated by administrators, disasters impose immense pressure on politicians to meet public needs and assure affected citizens that measures will be taken to prevent a reoccurrence. What effect does this political attention have on the content and character of emergency management policy?

SOCIAL FORCES

The second broad area of inquiry addressed by the authors in this volume is whether and how municipal emergency management policies are influenced by the participation of social forces – more or less organized interests who have a stake in the policy issue and seek to shape the scope and character of a government's policy response. Policy-making typically involves a number of stages, each of which presents an opportunity for social forces to assert their interests and influence policy choices. For instance, organized interests are sometimes influential in setting the policy agenda: by making demands on governments, they can focus public and political attention on an issue and thus affect its priority relative to others under consideration by public authorities. Social forces can also have an influence at the decision-making stage, as interests likely to be affected by a particular policy outcome lobby decision makers in order to persuade them to adopt a preferred course of action. At the implementation stage, when authority and resources are mobilized to effect policy objectives, organized interests can sometimes be influential by participating as partners in policy delivery. This raises questions with respect to emergency management. What social forces are involved in emergency management policy-making? At what stage of the policy process are social forces likely to be influential? How does their involvement affect the character of public policy?

We are particularly interested in the influence of the business community, which has long been identified as a central actor in local policy debates. With budgets highly dependent on property taxes and development fees, municipal governments seek to encourage development and attract new business investment. Because of their desire for economic growth and their fear that mobile investors may go elsewhere, local governments are particularly susceptible to business pressure (Leo 2002). By lobbying policy-makers, organizations representing business interests, such as the chamber of commerce or the board of trade, can exert considerable influence on municipal policy priorities and choices. Many emergency management activities – protecting property, ensuring the continuity of infrastructure systems, and minimizing interruptions in public services, for example – clearly concern the business community. Moreover, some businesses have a greater stake in emergency management than others. In communities where there have been frequent hazard-related property losses, for instance, insurance companies might pressure governments to adopt policies to mitigate future losses. To what extent does the business community influence emergency management policy? Does business predominate in emergency management policy-making, as it appears to do in other policy fields?

Residents, and particularly property-owners, appear to have a direct interest in the quality of municipal emergency management and could reasonably be expected to demand a comprehensive course of action to protect them from hazards. To what extent are policies in this field shaped by public demands? Do individuals and groups form coalitions to increase their influence on public policy? On the one hand, analysts have long observed that emergency management is a low-salience political issue that generally attracts little public attention (Waugh and Hy 1990). Emergencies and disasters are generally perceived to be events that happen in faraway places, not in Hinton, Alberta, or Truro, Nova Scotia. Furthermore, since both the costs and benefits associated with emergency management are diffuse, there appears to be little impetus for individuals to mobilize and lobby in support of or in opposition to policies in this field.

On the other hand, citizens clearly *expect* governments to plan for emergencies and to be sufficiently prepared when disaster strikes. Beverly Cigler states: "under normal circumstances, few citizens place a high priority on emergency management. However, these same individuals expect their government leaders to effectively manage disasters that occur" (1988, 6). Public expectations are evidenced in the criticism that is directed at governments when emergency planning is perceived to have been inadequate. In a survey of people affected by a major power blackout in Ontario in 2003, for instance, roughly 40 percent of respondents felt that their local government had not responded effectively to the event, and about half stated that more effort should be made to prepare for emergencies (Murphy 2003). Thus, demand for emergency management is latent, but periodically it becomes manifest when public attention is focused on the "emergency problem."

Many policy scholars have demonstrated that a sudden, striking incident can act as a "triggering mechanism" that focuses public and political attention on a particular issue (Gerston 1997, 22–49). In his analysis of agenda-setting and alternative selection, for instance, Kingdon refers to a "focusing event" as a relatively rare occurrence that suddenly attracts attention to a problem, creating a critical moment in which political decision makers and the public are receptive to a new course of action (2003, 94–5). This short-lived "policy window" is an opportunity for a "policy entrepreneur" – a skilled advocate with political resources and access to decision makers – to propose a solution to the problem highlighted by the event (Henstra 2010b).

In this policy field, emergencies and disasters are the focusing events. In his extensive analysis of focusing events and the policy process, Birkland (1997) notes that the novel and unexpected character of disasters is inherently attractive for news media coverage, which in turn arouses the attention of a broader public and provokes questions about the adequacy of emergency management policies. The surge of attention in the post-disaster period temporarily elevates the salience of emergency planning, creating a political incentive for elected officials to propose or endorse new policies. Evidence of disasters as the catalyst for issue expansion and policy-making activity is found in various policy domains, such as flood management and earthquake protection (Johnson et al. 2005; Olson et al. 1998).

One such focusing event was the SARS crisis of 2003. In March of that year, then Ontario premier Ernie Eves declared a provincial state of emergency after dozens of people in Toronto were sickened by a highly contagious, but unidentified, illness (National Advisory Committee on SARS and Public Health 2003, 26–8). This health emergency was novel and presented challenges that had not been fully considered in provincial or municipal emergency planning. For instance, emergency responders experienced problems in communicating the threat to a frightened public, and government officials faced the difficulty of ordering infected people into quarantine. The event also revealed weaknesses in provincial emergency legislation. Afterward the government of Ontario passed a bill empowering the premier to make temporary emergency orders to provide assistance to victims and to facilitate recovery (Ontario 2003). The SARS experience underscored the importance of planning for an influenza pandemic, which inevitably requires collaboration among municipal, provincial, and federal officials and with non-governmental actors and organizations (Public Health Agency of Canada 2006).

A focusing event is an opportunity only; it does not automatically result in policy change. For change to occur, the policy window must be seized by a persuasive champion or an organized coalition of interests who promote an alternative proposal (Solecki and Michaels 1994). But as noted above, the low-salience world of emergency management offers little incentive for such concerted mobilization. A flurry of interest in the post-disaster period can motivate new actors to temporarily enter the policy milieu, but their attention quickly wanes as seemingly more pressing problems occupy the public agenda and emergency management is again relegated to the periphery (Birkland 1996). The issue-attention dynamics of the policy field, which results from the sudden and unexpected nature of emergencies, suggests a cyclical pattern of policy development, involving sporadic, repeated attempts to reshape emergency management, typically with a bias toward the most recent event (Waugh 2000, 154).

THE CONTRIBUTIONS

The chapters in this book analyze emergency management in Canada, including the actors, interests, and institutions involved in the

design and implementation of public policies in this field and the
factors that influence policy outputs and outcomes at the municipal
level. As noted above, of particular interest here are the relationship
between officials based in Canada's three levels of government and
the interaction between policy-makers and various social forces.

The contributions begin (in chapter 2) with an analysis of the
government of Canada's role in emergency management. Luc Juillet
and Junichiro Koji trace changes to federal policies over the last
decade, changes that have been driven by a number of high-profile
emergencies and by demands from municipalities for greater support and representation in national policy-making. Seeking to raise
the federal profile and to address perceived weaknesses in front-line
response, Ottawa initiated a number of legislative changes and targeted funding programs. The authors point out, however, that the
changes in federal policies do not appear to have secured a more
central role for municipal governments within Canada's national
emergency management framework.

The contribution by Malcolm Grieve and Lori Turnbull (chapter
3), which examines emergency planning in Nova Scotia, offers many
important insights. One is that several major emergencies, such as
Hurricane Juan in 2003, have prompted an increasingly prescriptive provincial policy framework, including legislation that mandates
specific requirements for local emergency management. Second, the
chapter highlights the importance of informal relationships between
municipal, provincial, and federal administrators. For instance,
informal contact with the regional federal and provincial representatives allows the local emergency manager in Halifax to assess the
feasibility of policy proposals before pursuing them through official
channels. Third, the study notes the important role played by non-
governmental organizations in implementing emergency management policies in Nova Scotia.

In chapter 4, Norm Catto and Stephen Tomblin document both
improvements and ongoing challenges in emergency planning in
the province of Newfoundland and Labrador. On the one hand,
significant crises have raised the profile of emergency management,
leading to the appointment of a deputy minister of emergency planning and increased provincial support for municipal efforts. On the
other hand, the provincial policy framework remains permissive:
local governments are permitted, but not required, to formulate and
implement emergency plans and procedures. Policies are primarily

targeted at preparedness and response, while less attention has been devoted to mitigating risks or ensuring a swift recovery after disasters. The authors conclude that emergency planning in Newfoundland and Labrador appears to be in transition from a model based on informal local networks and volunteerism to a more formalized, coordinated system better suited for the risks the province will face in the future.

Geoffrey Hale (chapter 5) examines emergency management in the province of Alberta. He notes some significant challenges in local emergency planning, including weak intermunicipal efforts to coordinate plans and resources and a significant disparity in response capacity between large urban municipalities and smaller rural communities. These problems appear to necessitate intervention from above, but the government of Alberta has traditionally followed a decentralized approach, providing guidelines and advice rather than imposing prescriptive regulations. Major emergencies have renewed these concerns, however, and the provincial emergency management agency has stepped up its efforts to encourage intermunicipal coordination and to centralize resource-intensive response capacities.

Together, the chapters offer a rich comparative analysis of the diverse hazards facing Canadian communities, the intergovernmental policy framework that has evolved to deal with emergencies, and the challenges associated with substantive reforms in this field. Municipal governments are key actors in Canada's emergency management system, and the quality of local emergency planning significantly influences the effectiveness of response efforts when disaster strikes. But emergency management is clearly a responsibility shared by all levels of government in Canada, and citizens expect governments to work together to protect public safety and meet the needs of people affected by disasters. These chapters show how and how well this coordination works in reality.

REFERENCES

Birkland, Thomas A. 1996. "Natural Disasters as Focusing Events: Policy Communities and Political Response." *International Journal of Mass Emergencies and Disasters* 14 (2): 221–43.
– 1997. *After Disaster: Agenda Setting, Public Policy, and Focusing Events*. Washington, DC: Georgetown University Press.

Building Canada. 2008. "$272 Million Invested in Smaller British Columbia Communities." http://www.infrastructure.gc.ca/media/news-nouvelles/2008/20080707victoria-eng.html.

Canadian National Committee for the International Decade for Natural Disaster Reduction. 1994. *Canadian National Report*. Ottawa: Royal Society of Canada and the Canadian Academy of Engineering.

Cantelon, Philip L., and Robert C. Williams. 1982. *Crisis Contained: The Department of Energy at Three Mile Island*. Carbondale, IL: Southern Illinois University Press.

Cigler, Beverly A. 1988. "Emergency Management and Public Administration." In *Crisis Management: A Casebook*, edited by Michael T. Charles and John Choon K. Kim, 5–22. Springfield, IL: Charles C. Thomas.

Daines, Guy E. 1991. "Planning, Training and Exercising." In *Emergency Management: Principles and Practice for Local Government*, edited by Thomas E. Drabek and Gerard J. Hoetmer, 161–200. Washington: International City Management Association.

Deyle, Robert E., Steven P. French, Robert B. Olshansky, and Robert G. Paterson. 1998. "Hazard Assessment: The Factual Basis for Planning and Mitigation." In *Cooperating with Nature: Confronting Natural Hazards with Land-use Planning and Sustainable Communities*, edited by Raymond J. Burby, 119–66. Washington, DC: Joseph Henry Press.

Donahue, Amy K., and Philip G. Joyce. 2001. "A Framework for Analyzing Emergency Management with an Application to Federal Budgeting." *Public Administration Review* 61 (6): 728–40.

Ferrier, Norman, and C. Emdad Haque. 2003. "Hazards Risk Assessment Methodology for Emergency Managers: A Standardized Framework for Application." *Natural Hazards* 28 (2): 271–90.

Friedlander, Gordon D. 1976. "What Went Wrong: The Great Blackout of '65." IEEE Spectrum October: 83–6.

Gerston, Larry N. 1997. *Public Policy Making: Process and Principles*. Armonk, NY: M.E. Sharpe.

Gifford, Jim. 2004. *Hurricane Hazel: Canada's Storm of the Century*. Toronto: Dundurn Press.

Global Change Strategies International (GCSI). 2004. *Municipal Emergency Preparedness and Management Costs: Issues and Resource Requirements*. Ottawa: Global Change Strategies International.

Haque, C. Emdad. 2000. "Risk Assessment, Emergency Preparedness and Response to Hazards: The Case of the 1997 Red River Valley Flood, Canada." *Natural Hazards* 21 (2–3): 225–45.

Henstra, Daniel. 2003. "Federal Emergency Management in Canada and the United States after 11 September 2001." *Canadian Public Administration* 46 (1): 103–16.

– 2010a. "Evaluating Local Government Emergency Management Programs: What Framework Should Public Managers Adopt?" *Public Administration Review* 70 (2): 236–46.

– 2010b. "Explaining Local Policy Choices: A Multiple Streams Analysis of Municipal Emergency Management." *Canadian Public Administration* 53 (2): 241–58.

Henstra, Daniel, and Gordon McBean. 2005. "Canadian Disaster Management Policy: Moving toward a Paradigm Shift?" *Canadian Public Policy* 31 (3): 303–18.

Hightower, Henry C., and Michel Coutu. 1996. "Coordinating Emergency Management: A Canadian Example." In *Disaster Management in the U.S. and Canada: The Politics, Policymaking, Administration, and Analysis of Emergency Management*. 2d ed. Edited by Richard T. Sylves and William L. Waugh, Jr, 69–98. Springfield, IL: Charles C. Thomas.

Horak, Martin, and Robert Young, eds. 2012. *Sites of Governance: Multilevel Governance and Policy Making in Canada's Big Cities*. Montreal and Kingston: McGill-Queen's University Press.

Johnson, Clare L., Sylvia M. Tunstall, and Edmund C. Penning-Rowsell. 2005. "Floods as Catalysts for Policy Change: Historical Lessons from England and Wales." *International Journal of Water Resources Development* 21 (4): 561–75.

Kapucu, Naim. 2008. "Collaborative Emergency Management: Better Community Organising, Better Public Preparedness and Response." *Disasters* 32 (2): 239–62.

Kingdon, John W. 2003. *Agendas, Alternatives and Public Policies*. New York: Longman.

Kreps, Gary. 1992. "Foundations and Principles of Emergency Planning and Management." In *Hazard Management and Emergency Planning: Perspectives on Britain*, edited by Dennis J. Parker and John W. Handmer, 159–74. London: James and James Science Publishers.

Kuban, Ron. 1996. "The Role of Government in Emergency Preparedness." *Canadian Public Administration* 39 (2): 239–44.

Lacoursiere, P.E. Jean-Paul. 2005. "Bhopal and its Effects on the Canadian Regulatory Framework." *Journal of Loss Prevention in the Process Industries* 18 (4–6): 353–9.

Leo, Christopher. 2002. "Urban Development: Planning Aspirations and Political Realities." In *Urban Policy Issues: Canadian Perspectives*. 2d ed. Edited by Edmund P. Fowler and David Siegel, 215–36. Toronto: Oxford University Press.

Lindell, Michael K., and Ronald W. Perry. 2007. "Planning and Preparedness." In *Emergency Management: Principles and Practice for Local Government.* 2d ed. Edited by William L. Waugh Jr. and Kathleen Tierney, 113–41. Washington, DC: International City/County Management Association.

McEntire, David A., and Amy Myers. 2004. "Preparing Communities for Disasters: Issues and Processes for Government Readiness." *Disaster Prevention and Management* 13 (2): 140–52.

McLoughlin, David. 1985. "A Framework for Integrated Emergency Management." *Public Administration Review* 45 (Special Issue): 165–72.

Murphy, Brenda L. 2003. *Emergency Management and the August 14th, 2003 Blackout.* Toronto: Institute for Catastrophic Loss Reduction.

National Advisory Committee on SARS and Public Health. 2003. *Learning from SARS: Renewal of Public Health in Canada.* Ottawa: Health Canada.

Newkirk, Ross T. 2001. "The Increasing Cost of Disasters in Developed Countries: A Challenge to Local Planning and Government." *Journal of Contingencies and Crisis Management* 9 (3): 159–70.

Nirupama, Niru, and David Etkin. 2009. "Emergency Managers in Ontario: An Exploratory Study of Their Perspectives." *Journal of Homeland Security and Emergency Management* 6 (1): Article 38.

Olson, Richard Stuart, Robert A. Olson, and Vincent T. Gawronski. 1998. "Night and Day: Mitigation Policymaking in Oakland, California before and after the Loma Prieta Disaster." *International Journal of Mass Emergencies and Disasters* 16 (2): 145–79.

Ontario. 2003. *SARS Assistance and Recovery Strategy Act.* S.O. 2003, C. 1, s. 14.

– 2006. *Emergency Management and Civil Protection Act.* R.S.O. 1990, c. E.9.

Perry, Ronald W. 2004. "Disaster Exercise Outcomes for Professional Emergency Personnel and Citizen Volunteers." *Journal of Contingencies and Crisis Management* 12 (2): 64–75.

Public Health Agency of Canada. 2006. *Canadian Pandemic Influenza Plan for the Health Sector.* Ottawa: Public Health Agency of Canada.

Public Safety Canada. 2008. "Canada's National Disaster Mitigation Strategy." 13 February 2008. http://www.publicsafety.gc.ca/prg/em/ndms/strategy-eng.aspx (accessed 12 March 2012).

- 2009. *National Strategy for Critical Infrastructure*. Ottawa: Federal-Provincial-Territorial Critical Infrastructure Working Group.
- 2011a. "Disaster Financial Assistance Arrangements (DFAA) – Revised Guidelines." http://www.publicsafety.gc.ca/prg/em/dfaa/index-eng.aspx.
- 2011b. "Interpretation Bulletin 3: Application of Mitigative Enhancements Cost Sharing." http://www.publicsafety.gc.ca/prg/em/dfaa/interp-bl-3-eng.aspx.
- 2012. "Joint Emergency Preparedness Program." http://www.publicsafety.gc.ca/prg/em/jepp/index-eng.aspx.
Purcell, Mary, and Stewart Fyfe. 1998. *Ice Storm 1998: Emergency Preparedness and Response Issues*. Ottawa: Emergency Preparedness Canada.
Scanlon, Joseph. 1982. "The Roller Coaster Story of Civil Defence Planning in Canada." *Emergency Preparedness Digest* 9 (2): 2–14.
- 1995. "Federalism and Canadian Emergency Response: Control, Co-operation and Conflict." *Australian Journal of Emergency Management* 10 (1): 18–24.
Senate of Canada. 2004. *National Emergencies: Canada's Fragile Front Lines*. Volume 1. Ottawa: Standing Senate Committee on National Security and Defence.
Shrivastava, Paul. 1992. *Bhopal: Anatomy of a Crisis*. 2d ed. London: Paul Chapman Publishing.
Solecki, William D., and Sarah Michaels. 1994. "Looking through the Post-Disaster Policy Window." *Environmental Management* 18 (4): 587–95.
Sylves, Richard T. 1991. "Adopting Integrated Emergency Management in the United States: Political and Organizational Challenges." *International Journal of Mass Emergencies and Disasters* 9 (3): 413–24.
Timmerman, Peter. 1980. *Emergency Planning in Ontario: A Critical History and Analysis*. Toronto: Institute for Environmental Studies, University of Toronto.
Waugh, William L. Jr. 1990. "Emergency Management and State and Local Government Capacity." In *Cities and Disaster: North American Studies in Emergency Management*, edited by Richard T. Sylves and William L. Waugh Jr, 221–37. Springfield, IL: Charles C. Thomas.
- 2000. *Living with Hazards, Dealing with Disasters: An Introduction to Emergency Management*. Armonk, NY: M.E. Sharpe.
- 2007. "Local Emergency Management in the Post-9/11 World." In *Emergency Management: Principles and Practice for Local Government*

2d ed. Edited by William L. Waugh Jr and Kathleen Tierney, 3–23. Washington, DC: International City/County Management Association.

Waugh, William L. Jr, and Gregory Streib. 2006. "Collaboration and Leadership for Effective Emergency Management." *Public Administration Review* 66 (S1): 131–40.

Waugh, William L. Jr, and Ronald John Hy. 1990. "Introduction to Emergency Management." In *Handbook of Emergency Management*, edited by William L. Waugh Jr and Ronald John Hy, 1–10. Westport, CT: Greenwood Publishing Group.

Wolensky, Robert P., and Kenneth C. Wolensky. 1990. "Local Government's Problem with Disaster Management: A Literature Review and Structural Analysis." *Policy Studies Review* 9 (4): 703–25.

2

Policy Change and Constitutional Order: Municipalities, Intergovernmental Relations, and the Recent Evolution of Canadian Emergency Management Policy

LUC JUILLET AND JUNICHIRO KOJI

INTRODUCTION

Designing effective organizational structures and processes to address natural and man-made catastrophes with potentially severe consequences for citizens is an important responsibility of democratic governments. Protecting the lives and property of citizens constitutes a fundamental role of the modern state, and in the aftermath of large-scale emergencies this vital mission frequently returns to centre stage in debates about state organization and public sector performance. As in many other Western democracies, the terrorist attacks in the United States on September 11, 2001, represented such an agenda-setting event for emergency management policy in Canada. However, over the last fifteen years, this epoch-making event has not been alone in bringing emergency preparedness policy under the spotlight. Indeed, Canada was also regularly exposed to significant weather or health-related emergencies over this period, including a major ice storm in central Canada in 1998, an outbreak of severe acute respiratory syndrome (SARS) in Toronto in 2003, a major electricity blackout in Ontario in 2003, and threats of an avian influenza pandemic in more recent years. Moreover, even though the country experienced other major emergencies of a national scale in its history, these recent emergencies seemed distinctive by their intensity, their scope, their cost, and the magnitude of the response that they required (Newkirk 2001; Federation of Canadian Municipalities 2006, 22–4).

Facing this new environment, over the last decade the federal government adopted major reforms to its organizational and policy frameworks for dealing with large-scale emergencies: it created a new federal department to take the lead in dealing with national emergencies, it adopted new legislation detailing its role and author-ities, it released new policy statements outlining a new approach to emergency management, and it put in place new structures and processes to deal with the coordination of emergency management policies across levels of government. In effect, from 2001 to 2010, the Canadian government completely revisited and significantly transformed its approach to dealing with large-scale emergencies at the levels of policy and organization.

During this period, the need for more extensive and effective coordination of policy and actions across levels of government became an important issue that needed to be addressed by these reforms. Recent experience with national emergencies and studies conducted on the state of Canadian preparedness for large-scale emergencies had shown that insufficient multilevel coordination often stood in the way of more effective emergency management, causing unnecessary delays or inadequate organization in times of emergency but also hindering the effectiveness of governmental planning and preparation between emergencies. In this respect, the role of municipalities in the multilevel governance of emergency management seemed particularly problematic to several of the key actors involved in this policy field: while local authorities play a key role in ensuring the first, and often main, line of response to most emergencies, they are also particularly disconnected from the multilevel processes and structures that are meant to ensure effective coordination in this policy area.

However, while the reforms implemented over the last decade led to a clear improvement of federal-provincial-territorial coordina-tion, they failed to bring municipalities into the multilevel govern-ance framework associated with emergency management policy. Given the presence of a significant coalition of actors pushing for greater integration of municipalities into multilevel governance arrangements and a strong conceptual case for their importance to effective emergency management, this outcome is somewhat puz-zling. In this chapter, we examine the politics that led to this choice by focusing mainly on the competing discourses that marked the debates about the reform of the policy and statutory framework for emergency management.

In particular, we attempt to show that the politics of reform were marked by a clash between two coalitions of actors, each framing the proper multilevel governance of emergency management in a distinct manner: one emphasizing the primacy of criteria of effectiveness in emergency measures and response over the respect of traditional administrative and political divisions, the other emphasizing the importance of respecting the historical divisions of authority for the conduct of legitimate and effective public action, including for the proper management of emergencies. We argue that the triumph of the latter coalition, and the resulting exclusion of municipalities from the reformed multilevel governance of emergency management, was mainly due to the congruence of its frame with the broader norms of the constitutional order in Canada, as well as to the institutional context of the legislative reforms, marked by a minority parliament that made the direct engagement of municipalities by the federal government politically difficult. In the end, the chapter illustrates how the enduring, overarching norms of state organization have made it difficult for Canada to restructure its governance processes to ensure a more effective emergency management framework.

The chapter is divided into five sections. The first briefly develops our analytical framework, which emphasizes the impact of discursive practices on policy decisions. Following the work of Ross (2000) on welfare reform and Hajer (1995) on environmental policy, we focus on three factors affecting the effectiveness of framing in policy debates: the resilience of pre-existing frames associated with the policy status quo; the credibility and trustworthiness of competing framers; and the impact of the institutional setting where the inter-frame conflict unfolds. The second section discusses the new emergency planning policy environment and the on-going shift in the paradigms associated with the field. It serves to highlight why municipalities are deemed to be increasingly important actors in emergency management. The third section provides a brief history of Canada's emergency planning policy: it explains how the dominant organization of multilevel coordination emerged out of constitutional and political constraints and how it worked to marginalize municipalities. The fourth section examines how the limited participation of municipalities in these multilevel processes increasingly came to be seen as a problem in the years that followed the turn of the millennium, and it describes how the coalition of actors working to increase their participation have framed their challenge to the status quo. Finally, the last section briefly discusses the recent federal initiatives to modernize Canada's emergency management policy, and it examines the discursive politics that affected the adoption of the new Emergency Management Act (EMA) in 2007, one of the key statutes underpinning the new framework.

REFRAMING PUBLIC POLICY

Over the last two decades, the policy studies literature has shown growing interest in the cognitive, normative, and discursive dimensions of policy processes as important variables for explaining policy decisions (Fischer 2003; Hajer 1995, 2006; Surel 2000). Questioning traditional approaches that focus mainly on the material resources and given interests of actors as explanatory variables, several scholars have sought to explore post-positivist approaches to the study of public policy, including in Canada (e.g., Orsini and Smith 2007). However, this approach has not been widely used in the analysis of emergency management policy, with the exception of a few studies in the United States (Prater and Lindell 2000; Wyatt-Nichol and Abel 2007). In this respect, the Canadian reforms examined in this study offer an opportunity to extend the use of this approach in this policy field as well as to the study of multilevel governance.

In the study of public policy, a "frame" is generally conceptualized as a filter through which actors define, interpret, and understand the social reality surrounding them. Social reality does not exist on its own. It needs to be cognitively processed by actors before acquiring a meaning as reality. In this process, actors adopt a frame to facilitate their understanding of their environment and to make sense of events or problems that they face. The frame is often derived from lessons drawn from personal experience, knowledge acquired through formal education, and religious or other convictions, and the mass media can play an important role in the adoption of particular frames by mass publics (Chong and Druckman 2007). But importantly for the study of politics and public policy, frames are also used strategically by political actors to advance a preferred interpretation of social reality and rationale for policy intervention that, if accepted as authoritative by key audiences – mass publics, opinion leaders, or decision makers – can shape policy outcomes (Fischer 2003; Polletta and Ho 2006). On this point, it should also be underscored that discursive frames are not purely instrumental – i.e., strategic tools used to advance some preset material interests, but that, by shaping actors' understanding of social reality, they can also affect how actors understand their own interests or how they can actually be furthered by various policies (Hajer 1995, 51).

To identify the frames competing in the reforms examined in this chapter, we examined the discourse of various actors involved in the policy process to uncover how they represented the political and spatial realities associated with emergency responses in Canada, as well as the policy prescriptions that they derived from these representations. For this purpose, we have analyzed a series of policy documents issued in relation to these reforms, the transcripts of hearings held by the Senate's Standing Committee on Public Safety and National Security on the state of emergency planning in Canada at various times between 2003 and 2008 and the answers provided by municipal respondents to a questionnaire used by the same Senate committee as part of its work, as well as the parliamentary debates that led to the adoption of the Emergency Management Act in 2007. Through content analysis, we worked to identify the two competing frames used in the analysis presented later in this chapter.

As Ross (2000, 173) points out, with the exception of new issues, framing really involves "reframing" an existing policy problem. We can therefore generally understand a conflict between two frames about public policy as the challenge to an existing frame by a new frame. Hence, discursive politics – the socio-political process through which conflicting frames compete for authoritativeness – constitutes "a struggle for discursive hegemony in which actors try to secure support for their definition of reality" (Hajer 1995, 59). While much work remains to be done to understand what makes for a strong and effective frame (Chong and Druckman 2007, 116–17), we focus here on three factors that have been considered significant in previous studies.

First, our attention goes to the resilience of existing frames that underpin the policy status quo. When policy entrepreneurs try to reframe policy issues, they need to confront existing frames that dominate the prevailing understanding of the issues at stake. Citizens, let alone decision makers, are not "empty vessels": they harbour existing conceptions and cognitively rely on long-standing referents that are not easily reconsidered in the face of alternative discourses. In the words of Ross (2000, 173–4), existing frames can work as "powerful defensive mechanisms" against new frames. Moreover, the resilience of existing frames can be particularly strong when they are institutionalized through legislation, policy directives, and statements, as well as through daily politico-administrative practices (Hajer 1995). Similarly, existing frames can gain further resilience when they are congruent or have a strong affinity with dominant norms and values in the social and political environment (Ross 2000, 174; Juillet 2007). As a result, alternative frames are likely to gain more influence and support if they can respond to other extant frames and demonstrate some congruence with dominant norms and values, especially those held by decision-making elites.

Second, the power of frames is also partly determined by some of their characteristics that will make them more or less plausible to decision makers and other policy actors. As Hajer argues, finding a policy frame convincing is not a narrowly cognitive process, since it involves much more than finding the arguments logically sound and empirically grounded (1995, 63). It is more properly conceived as a socio-cognitive process where, for example, the credibility or trustworthiness of its advocates (based on past record, institutional position, professional authority, etc.) is also assessed as a condition for the plausibility of their frames (Druckman 2001; Ross 2000, 174). Similarly, a frame can be found to be more plausible when it incorporates, or is seen to fit with, elements of common narratives widely used to make sense of the world. This is why, Hajer contends (1995, 63), analogies, historical references, metaphors, and even clichés are frequently used in political discourse: while they invariably oversimplify, even distort, arguments about complex policy problems, they can also increase the appeal and plausibility of frames by making them "sound right" (i.e., sound consistent with what is otherwise held to be true about the world) to different actors, especially in areas where technical knowledge is an important part of the policy debates.

Finally, we need to take into account the institutional settings affecting discursive politics. Policy actors have to operate within institutional constraints such as regulations, rules, and institutionalized practices that can both empower and constrain their capacity to further their preferred frames. This institutional setting can include, for example, the structure of the party system and the rules regulating venues of policy deliberations, including legislatures. For example, as Ross observes, European political systems that render coalition governments necessary call for consensus and may preclude significant reframing by some of the key institutional actors for certain periods of time. In contrast, two-party systems have created incentives and conditions that have been more conducive to the reframing of social policy (Ross 2000, 175). In sum, by providing, or denying, access to venues where policy positions can be advanced and affecting the manner in which discourse can be deployed, institutional features of the policy process can affect the outcome of inter-frame conflicts.

In the last sections of this chapter, we examine the evolution of the policy framework for emergency management in Canada and, relying on the analytical framework and the sets of factors discussed above, we attempt to shed some light on the inability of municipalities to significantly modify the traditional approach to multilevel governance in this area. However, before discussing this evolution, we look briefly at some of the reasons that have led municipalities and their advocates to claim a greater role in the making of emergency management policy in recent years.

MUNICIPALITIES AND EMERGENCY MANAGEMENT

The importance of local authorities in responding to emergencies has long been recognized in the Canadian emergency response framework. In fact, it has been estimated that, given the limited scope, about 80 percent of emergencies are handled solely at the local level. However, even in the case of large-scale adverse events, the primacy of local response has been a long-established principle of Canadian emergency policy. Local governments are often the first point of contact for many citizens dealing with disruptions of some essential services, such as water services, and local responsibilities for emergency services, such as firefighting and local policing, put them on the front line of many crises. Local public officials, both elected officials and municipal public servants, are generally best aware of conditions on the ground in their communities, and as result, they are often best positioned to ascertain what responses will likely work in addressing local problems. In this perspective, one of the central principles of Canadian emergency management has long been that local authorities should take the lead in responding to emergencies, progressively requesting the support and involvement of higher levels of government as they become overwhelmed by the situation at hand.

By itself, this "pyramidal" conception of emergency response systems calls for a considerable degree of multilevel coordination. For instance, speedy and effective communication among levels of government and sharing of resources in times of emergencies require established channels of communications, mutual awareness of potential needs, and the availability of resources, protocols, and equipment ensuring necessary levels of interoperability, and so on. Close collaboration between different levels of government is then required for an effective response both at local and national levels, but also to ensure that before emergencies present themselves, adequate preparation has been done at the local level to ensure an effective response by the authorities that the system conceives as its first line of defence. This is especially important since, as illustrated by recent cases of terrorist acts, local incidents can immediately provoke national security concerns and the performance of local governments and first responders can quickly have a great influence on national, even international, security (see Eisinger 2006).

However, going beyond this traditional conception of municipalities and their associated first responders (e.g., firefighting and local police services) as the "first line of defence," the recent literature on emergency management suggests that the importance of municipalities is growing, notably owing to the increasing concentration of people living in urban areas and the nature of contemporary urban living, which entail greater systemic risks (e.g., Britton 2001; Caruson et al. 2005; Caruson and MacManus 2007; Eisinger 2006; Gabriel 2003).

In particular, the considerable development of urban agglomerations has made cities crucial areas where man-made or natural emergencies can quickly create large numbers of casualties, significant hardship, and large-scale economic damage. In Canada, about 80 percent of the population lives in urban areas, and cities are clearly major drivers of economic activity. For example, the population of Toronto, Canada's largest city, is more than 2.6 million people, a number that reaches 5.5 million when the entire metropolitan area is counted (Canada 2012a, 13, 18; Canada 2012b, 4) . This number, which represents about 18 percent of the entire population of Canada, is larger than the population of most Canadian provinces. At the same time, the proximity and interconnectedness of urban lives create particular vulnerabilities to adverse events, such as large-scale reliance on common networks for electricity, water, or communication infrastructure and the easier spread of communicable diseases owing to physical proximity and urban mobility. Recent large-scale emergencies in metropolitan areas, such as Hurricane Katrina in New Orleans and the SARS epidemic in Toronto, not only revealed the vulnerability of urban infrastructure and the systemic risks associated with modern urban systems, but they also illustrated how such adverse events can pose a major challenge to metropolitan governments who have to deal with the evacuation and protection of citizens. It has become clear that the performance of metropolitan authorities is becoming crucial to the effective response to emergencies in a highly urbanized environment.

Another reason for the growing importance of local authorities for effective emergency management comes from a shift in paradigm in this policy field and the growing recognition that in addition to preparedness and response, the effective management of emergencies requires public authorities to devote more attention to prevention, mitigation, and recovery. In fact, in Canadian emergency policy circles, it is now common to speak of a move from "emergency preparedness" to "emergency management" in order to indicate the emergence of a new way of thinking about policy in this area. Emergency management is meant to represent a more proactive approach to emergencies, which stresses the role of preventive measures and the design of more resilient communities as a way of minimizing the costs resulting from unavoidable adverse events. In this perspective, the principal goal of emergency management is to build a sustainable and resilient society that is able to continue operating during emergencies, to minimize the likelihood that unavoidable hazards will turn into avoidable disasters, and to recover promptly after the emergency has subsided.

In this new perspective, community resilience is attainable only if local authorities are able to become fully fledged partners in emergency management because many of the key policy levers required for the development of resilient cities are under their control. For example, as Britton points out, the construction of resilient cities requires adequate territorial management, notably through urban planning and zoning regulations developed with potential risks in mind (2001, 44–5). Similarly, many of the critical infrastructures of communities, such as waterworks or electricity-distribution grids, are either fully under their control or are significantly affected by their policies. In sum, as prime actors in these matters, unless local governments are aware of the stakes, are knowledgeable about framework policies, standards, and best practices, and are consequently able to ensure such risk-based territorial management, their communities will remain unduly at risk in the event of a significant emergency. Thus, the full involvement of municipalities in emergency management at the policy development and implementation stages seems essential to the effective pursuit of an "emergency management" approach to this policy area.

On the whole, the traditional view of local authorities as first and main responders that should exercise leadership in times of emergencies as well as newer trends emphasizing their role in designing more resilient communities call for local governments to play a greater role in emergency management. They thus present a significant challenge to Canada's multilevel governance structures and processes in this area, which have historically limited their involvement and never considered them as full partners of provincial and federal governments. Taking note of these trends, some countries have moved to strengthen the role of municipalities in their security and emergency management systems. For example, the regional approach to emergency preparedness attempted in the United States in recent years constitutes a possible response to this reality. Recommended by the Government Accountability Office in a 2004 report on the state of homeland security, the approach seeks to build more effective emergency planning structures based on regions rather than on political and administrative jurisdictions in the hope of building strong networks of neighbouring localities able to share information and resources (Caruson et al. 2005; Caruson and MacManus 2007). However, as we will now see, while pursuing policy reforms that have strengthened federal-provincial collaboration and promise to improve performance in this area, Canada has been much less ambitious in addressing the role of municipalities in the multilevel governance of emergency management.

MULTILEVEL GOVERNANCE AND THE EVOLUTION OF EMERGENCY MANAGEMENT IN CANADA

Canada's federal emergency management policy originated in civil defence during World War II. In 1939, a few weeks before entering the war, the federal government adopted the Defence of Canada Regulations under the War Measures Act, which authorized government ministers to take steps, including the suspension of some civil liberties, in order to organize defence measures on its national territory. As part of these measures, instruments meant to prevent casualties in the event of air raids provided for exceptional authority to force evacuations and enforce curfews, which represented the beginning of a legal framework to deal with national emergencies. The context in which these early steps were taken provided the federal government with clear leadership responsibilities for emergency preparedness, since the military and war matters have always been unambiguously the constitutional purview of the federal government.

In the early 1950s, civil defence was progressively demilitarized, even if preparing for the threat of a nuclear war remained its central focus. Its responsibilities were transferred from the Department of National Defence to the Department of National Health and Welfare in 1951. In 1957, a new Emergency Measures Organization, which was a new administrative division of the Privy Council Office (the central agency supporting the cabinet), took on the responsibility of coordinating emergency management for the federal government. Over the following decades, responsibility for the office coordinating the federal government's response to national emergencies then shifted on a few occasions between the Department of National Defence and the Privy Council Office. In the 1960s, the scope of its activities was also broadened to include responding to large-scale natural disasters, even if the suspension of civil rights and the use of the military on Canadian soil in response to the terrorist acts of the Front de Libération du Québec (FLQ) in 1970 remain by far the most infamous use of emergency powers over this period.

The demilitarization of emergency management and the expansion of the scope of its responsibilities to include responding to natural disasters progressively raised significant political and constitutional issues. As stated above, the responsibility of the federal government for military and defence matters is unquestioned under the Canadian constitutional order. However, as emergency management came to be dissociated from defence policy and began to encroach more clearly on provincial matters such as health services and property and civil law, provincial governments began questioning the prominence of the federal government in this policy area. Because Canada's constitutional statute that sets the division of powers between levels of government was written in 1867, it does not explicitly address emergency management, and under the country's constitution, this policy field was soon interpreted to be a matter of shared responsibility between both levels of government. While the federal government could legitimately claim to have authority flowing from its responsibility for the "Peace, Order, and good Government of Canada" (section 91 of the Constitution Act, 1867), which the courts had already ruled could sustain legislative action taken to deal with national emergencies, the provincial governments could legitimately argue that their constitutional authority over property and civil rights, health care, and local matters (section 92, Constitution Act, 1867) gave them a central role to play in emergency management. In practice, as the development of a more sophisticated and comprehensive emergency management system required the collaboration of agencies widely spread across levels of government, from policing and firefighting to health care authorities and border services, shared jurisdiction and multilevel collaboration became essential.

However, this understanding of the shared nature of emergency management responsibilities simply did not account for municipalities: while already playing a key role as first responders, municipalities were never considered as fully fledged partners under the governance framework that developed during those years. In Canada, municipalities are not recognized as an autonomous level of government by the constitution. In fact, the Constitution Act, 1867, gives exclusive jurisdiction to provincial legislatures over "municipal institutions" (section 92(8)) and "local works and undertakings" (section 92(10)), as well as over "all matters of a merely local nature" (section 92(16)). As a result, as it is often put, municipalities are considered as "creatures of the provinces": constituted by provincial statutes, the extent of their authority and the scope of their responsibilities are largely limited by provincial governments. While they largely fund themselves through property taxes and user fees, they remain dependent on provincial transfers for part of their annual budget. As a result, while urban areas have grown over the century and many municipal governments have become ever larger and more complex administrations responsible for a wide range of important services, they have remained largely trapped in an unfavourable, constitutionally subservient position. Moreover, in the context of federal-provincial relations, provincial governments have jealously guarded their control over municipalities, generally resisting the development of direct federal-municipal contacts and refusing to consider municipalities as equals in intergovernmental processes.

Based on this constitutional and functional reality, the federal and provincial governments progressively developed a federal-provincial-territorial (FPT) collaboration framework that broadly conformed to standard Canadian practice over the 1970s and 1980s. In particular, an annual federal-provincial consultation process was established at the ministerial level and, in conformity with standard practice across policy fields in the federation, no provisions were adopted to provide for the inclusion of municipalities in this process. Coordination of emergency policy then essentially focused on the relationship between the federal and provincial governments. Between 1982 and 1988, the federal government signed bilateral memoranda of understanding with all the provinces and territories, with the exception of Quebec and Alberta. Fiscal transfers in support of emergency preparedness also developed in accordance with the conventional FPT framework. The Disaster Financial Assistance Arrangements (DFAA) and the Joint Emergency Preparedness Program (JEPP) are good examples. The DFAA was created in 1970 in order to provide financial assistance to the provinces and territories to cope with emergency-related damages, providing federal funding once the recovery costs from disasters exceeded about Can$1 per capita. The JEPP was established in 1980 as an FPT program to support emergency preparedness training and the purchase of equipment at the local level. However, the federal government provides funding to the provincial governments, which are then expected to support municipalities. There is no direct relationship between the federal government and municipalities.

In 1985, this FPT framework was entrenched in federal legislation. The Emergencies Act replaced the War Measures Act, and it provided legal foundations for the federal government to put in place measures needed to respond to four kinds of national emergencies: public welfare emergencies, public order emergencies, international emergencies, and war emergencies. Respecting the dominant understanding of intergovernmental relations, the statute required the federal government to consult with affected provinces and territories before declaring a national emergency. To the extent that municipalities were to be involved in those decisions, they were expected to transmit their demand for federal intervention and the declaration of a state of emergency through their provincial government. The same year, by enacting the Emergency Preparedness Act (EPA), the federal government created Emergency Preparedness Canada (EPC) as the lead federal agency in the field. The legislation gave powers to the minister responsible for the EPC to coordinate emergency preparedness measures within the federal government and to support the provinces and territories in developing their own emergency preparedness policies. The statute remained silent on its relationship with municipal authorities.

Hence, by the 1990s the dominant understanding of the appropriate and necessary approach to the multilevel governance of emergency preparedness and response was well entrenched in a set of norms, institutions, and intergovernmental practices that provided the framework for the formulation and implementation of Canadian emergency management policy. This approach to multilevel coordination is strongly congruent with a view of Canadian federalism that emphasizes a clear division of responsibilities between the two main levels of government and that values provincial jurisdictional autonomy, what some scholars have referred to as a "jurisdictional" form of federalism (Bakvis and Brown 2010). Under such an understanding of proper relationships between the federal and provincial governments, direct federal-municipal relations or even federal-provincial-municipal multilateral relations are considered violations of the norms of effective and legitimate multilevel governance. They are not illegal – there is no prohibition in constitutional law on the direct involvement of municipalities in multilevel policy processes or on the direct transfer of information between the federal government and municipalities – but they are understood as politically unacceptable, or at least problematic. As a result, the role of municipalities in the development of emergency management policy has been limited.

ATTEMPTING TO REFRAME THE MULTILEVEL GOVERNANCE OF EMERGENCY MANAGEMENT

The validity of this framework for multilevel governance has recently been questioned in the face of major emergencies calling for more integrated and seamless coordination between the three levels of government. In particular, municipalities themselves have strongly challenged this approach. Increasingly apprehensive in the light of what seems like the greater frequency of disasters and heightened security threats and taking stock of recent experiences with major emergencies, municipalities began to increasingly criticize the ineffectiveness of the traditional FPT framework. For example, pointing out that municipalities are the first responders in more than 90 percent of emergencies that occur in Canada, a recent report commissioned by the Federation of Canadian Municipalities (FCM) – a national body representing municipalities across Canada – decried the imbalance between such important responsibilities and the lack of direct municipal representation on the key instances dealing with emergency planning (FCM 2006, 5). As the report states, municipalities believe that "their concerns are not addressed [by federal and provincial governments] and ... extra costs and obligations are imposed on them through policies developed without their participation. Had they been consulted, they might have offered better solutions." The FCM then recommends a better "public safety dialogue" between the three levels of government with "a [municipal] voice at the national table" (11, 25). Speaking at the time of the report's release, the then FCM president, Gloria Kovach, fully endorsed this conclusion. As she put it, "We believe that the current situation, which leaves municipal first responders underfunded and left out of disaster planning, not only wastes resources but also threatens the well-being of Canadians" (3).

In addition to the FCM, which represents most of Canada's municipalities, the country's biggest cities also began to strongly criticize the traditional FPT framework. The Big City Mayors' Caucus (BCMC), a subgroup of the twenty-two largest municipalities, expressed their frustration over insufficient financial resources to deal with their increasing responsibilities in different policy areas, including emergency planning. "Municipal governments believe it is short sighted to download the implementation of a provincial/ territorial or federal policy/program to a municipality without first including them in the consultation process, and without ensuring that necessary resources are available" (BCMC 2006, 13). The BCMC, like the FCM, argues for "a true partnership" between the three levels of government that would give due recognition to municipal roles in the making and implementation of public policy in Canada (7).

Over this period, as the federal government was working on broader reforms of its approach to emergency management, officials from some important cities also challenged the dominant multilevel governance framework in this field. For example, speaking in 2006 before the Senate Committee on National Security and Defence, Toronto's Medical Officer of Health, Dr Sheela Basrur, who dealt with the SARS epidemic in 2003, expressed her dissatisfaction with the absence of municipalities at the intergovernmental table concerned with emergency management: "[M]any of the discussions occur at the federal-provincial-territorial level. There is no local, municipal or regional input in that paradigm. We are creatures of the provinces, and they include or exclude us at their sole whim. I think, frankly, that large urban centres ought to be treated as entities of national importance. It does not make sense to me that we should be treated as invisible and irrelevant on matters such as this" (Senate of Canada 2003b, 20).

Similarly, Barry Gutteridge, Toronto's commissioner at the Department of Works and Emergency Services, speaking before the same committee, argued for direct access to the federal government by municipal officials. According to the commissioner, "The lack of direct local access to federal agencies is an issue. We are aware of, and work with, the regional director. The provincial access protocols, however, tend to be enforced somewhat rigidly, even from a planning standpoint. A better design is needed, with provincial involvement. We are not trying to suggest that there should not be provincial involvement, but protocols for access and information flow should be improved, and more ability to work collectively is needed" (Senate of Canada 2003b, 45). This feeling of marginalization was also shared by other municipalities, such as St John's, Hamilton, Edmonton, and Regina (see Senate of Canada 2004, 67–75).

Like the FCM and the BCMC, these municipal officials who came to the Senate committee hearings often justified their arguments for a reformed multilevel governance framework by invoking the need for more effective and efficient operations at the street level during an emergency. The comments made by Randy Wolsey, Edmonton's fire chief at Fire Rescue Services, are representative in this regard: "Regardless of protocols, at the street level we really need to get the job done, and we are willing to do what it takes to get that job done" (Senate of Canada 2003a, 29). Again, speaking from his experience as the executive in charge of emergency services for Toronto, Barry Gutteridge put it even more forcefully: "There needs to be a way to make levels disappear in an emergency. For example, we at the responding level say, 'Here is what we need,' and it is provided directly to us. We must get past that 'I am provincial; you are municipal; you are federal.' We are all in this together. How can we collectively solve this? How can I bring my expertise and resources to the table? Then we can worry about the niceties later" (Senate of Canada 2003b, 50).

Over the course of those years, the work of the Senate Standing Committee on National Security and Defence contributed to placing emergency policy reform on the federal policy agenda, drawing significant media attention and serving as an important relay of municipalities' claims on the national stage. The committee started to review federal emergency policy in July 2001, even before the 9/11 terrorist attacks in the United States, and it subsequently published two reports on the issue that garnered significant public attention, partly because of the committee chairman's media profile and the strong language used in criticizing what was deemed a relatively poor state of emergency preparedness in the country (Senate of Canada 2004; 2008). Its work then gained even more momentum and prominence following the 9/11 terrorist attacks and the SARS public health crisis in 2003.

For municipalities, the work of the committee was particularly important because it provided an important institutional venue in which to make their case at the national level. The committee also became a significant institutional player providing credibility and visibility to their narrative – their frame – calling for important reforms of the multilevel governance of this area. It published reports containing recommendations that required an explicit response by the federal government (in accordance with the rules of the Canadian Parliament), and it had the institutional authority, which it used, to call federal officials to testify in public to answer questions on their approach to multilevel coordination. In sum, the Senate committee became an important part of the coalition of actors challenging the traditional understanding of multilevel governance in this area.

In this regard, the Senate committee's first report, *National Emergencies: Canada's Fragile Front Lines*, made pointed reference to the provinces as obstacles to effective and efficient emergency planning at the local level (Senate of Canada 2004, 42–3). Drawing lessons from the SARS crisis, it argued that Canada's emergency planning policy should not be fragmented by jurisdictional boundaries but designed first and foremost to protect Canadian citizens (38). While recognizing the importance of the constitution, the committee called for a new multilevel governance framework in which both federal and provincial/territorial governments could listen to municipalities and first line responders, who are considered to be more knowledgeable about the realities of dealing with disasters on the ground. For example, the report states: "The Committee understands that Canada's constitution assigns provinces exclusive control over the areas within their jurisdiction. But the federal and provincial governments need to get their acts together to respond to this very useful kind of initiative. The regions and municipalities have the best insights as to what they need, and when they come forward with a plan that makes sense within the context of national emergency preparedness, senior levels of government should do what this report is all about: *respond*" (71, emphasis in original).

A second report, issued by the Senate Committee in 2008 and simply titled *Emergency Preparedness in Canada*, also severely criticized the federal government for its sluggish progress in improving federal emergency preparedness in the years that followed its first report. As part of this critique, it continued to condemn the absence of direct communication channels between federal and municipal officials. For instance, the report qualifies as "a mind boggler" remarks by the federal chief public health officer, Dr David Butler-Jones, who told the committee that municipalities do not have to be informed about the location or contents of federal emergency caches (containing supplies needed in the event of disasters, such as antibiotics or medical equipment) because the information can be obtained through the provincial officials when necessary. As the committee report asks, "How can the federal government recognize that emergencies happen *locally*, but then hide vital tools like [emergency caches] from local first responders?" (Senate of Canada 2008, 28).

For senators on the committee, such adherence to a very traditional and rigid understanding of intergovernmental relations in this field clearly undermined the effectiveness of emergency management in the country. It recommended that the federal department of Public Safety establish a list of emergency managers in municipalities, provide them with security clearance, and start communicating directly with them whenever it had information that could improve local emergency responses (50).

Furthermore, concerning the limited inclusion of municipalities in intergovernmental processes, the Senate committee also made very critical remarks. While the federal government created a Domestic Group on Emergency Management in 2007 as a forum for discussion among federal bureaucrats from the department of Public Safety Canada and community organizations (such as the Red Cross, the association representing fire chiefs, and the Federation of Canadian Municipalities), the Senate committee noted, and criticized, the fact that municipalities remained excluded from higher-level political and policy discussions (Senate of Canada 2008, 59). In particular, it found that the absence of municipal representatives at the annual meetings of federal and provincial ministers responsible for emergency management did not make sense. As it put it, "It is revealing that the annual meeting of ministers responsible for emergency management does not include representatives from local governments. How can there be truly useful discussions about roles and responsibilities in emergency management without municipalities at the table? It is not surprising that our surveys show that municipal emergency managers are sometimes confused and frequently frustrated with federal government processes" (94).

In fact, the committee reiterated that it considered governance mechanisms allowing the three levels of government to meet together around the same table to be essential to the improvement of Canada's emergency preparedness. And it clearly did not consider the constitutional division of powers to be an insurmountable barrier to the creation of such a mechanism. As the committee stated,

> The Committee understands the constitutional division of responsibilities among jurisdictions. However, there is no jurisdictional impediment to sitting down with both municipal and provincial partners to hash out who does what, and how, nor should there be any impediment to having federal officials listening directly to municipal officials as to what their needs are on the ground. The provincial and territorial governments can sit in on the conversations if there is concern over jurisdictional niceties.

> The Committee strongly recommends that Public Safety Canada – as the lead federal agency responsible for national emergency preparedness – become better acquainted with the day-to-day responsibilities, challenges and needs facing Canada's first responder community through direct contact with municipal representatives. (Senate of Canada 2008, 96)

So, as we can see, the Senate committee devoted considerable efforts over this period to making the reform of federal emergency preparedness policy an important and pressing matter, notably by conducting studies on the issue, holding national hearings, and using its privileged institutional position to publicly call for changes. As it did so, it contributed to furthering an alternative way of framing the best manner to set up the multilevel governance of emergency management in Canada. By endorsing many of the views expressed by the FCM, the BCMC, and individual cities, it undoubtedly contributed to strengthening this alternative frame, including acting as a high-level advocate with no obvious self-interest in having municipalities treated as fully fledged partners. Unlike representatives of municipalities, it could not be dismissed as simply demanding more power and resources.

Overall, the statements quoted in this section should illustrate the core features of the competing frame that emerged over this period to challenge the dominant intergovernmental order of emergency management. Focused on the need for "effectiveness on the ground," as opposed to constitutional norms and the broader traditional understanding of the country that these norms embody, this frame emphasizing "street-level effectiveness" calls for a radical rethinking of the multilevel governance of emergency management, emphasizing speed, fluidity, and flexibility in the response to emergencies, as well as a more prominent role for municipalities in planning and policy formulation. On this view, ideally, "levels would disappear" in times of emergency and the emergency policy framework would treat municipalities as fully fledged partners because the effectiveness of the resulting policies demanded it. In particular, a reform of multilevel governance structures and processes would provide for more direct contact between the federal government and municipalities and for the integration of representatives from municipalities in what would become federal-provincial-municipal policy forums. However, as the next section will show, the challenge presented by this alternative frame was met with strong resistance from federal and provincial officials, who, in the end, held to a more traditional conception of intergovernmental relations.

REFORMING THE MULTILEVEL GOVERNANCE OF EMERGENCY MANAGEMENT

The years that followed the terrorist attacks in New York in 2001 saw many changes in how governments approached national security, including their management of eventual large-scale emergencies. In Canada, these events, as well as a string of public health and natural emergencies that occurred around the turn of the century, led the federal government to engage in a substantial revision of its national security policy. One of the key policy steps taken in this regard was the release in 2004 of a new national security statement entitled *Securing an Open Society: Canada's National Security Policy* by the Liberal government headed by Prime Minister Paul Martin (Privy Council Office 2004). It dedicated an entire chapter to emergency planning and management, and it launched a significant reform of how the federal government approaches emergency management.

This shift included a wide range of measures and was generally marked by a desire to increase the federal government's leadership in the area. To signal its political commitment, the prime minister had already appointed his deputy prime minister, Anne McLellan, as minister of public safety and emergency preparedness in December 2003. In this new portfolio, she headed several agencies related to national security, including the federal police force, the intelligence agency, and border controls, which were brought under a single umbrella in order to enhance the coordination of this file within the federal government.

The minister would also chair the new Cabinet Committee on Security, Public Health and Emergencies, which was established to strengthen the political attention to be paid to these matters. Following the new policy statement, a new department, eventually renamed Public Safety Canada, was also established through statute in March 2005 to provide the field with more affirmed leadership within the federal cabinet. The new department eventually established a new Government Operations Centre to strengthen its capacity to coordinate the federal response to national emergencies. The new centre replaced a much more modest Office of Critical Infrastructure and Emergency Preparedness (OCIPEP).

These very significant changes underscore the importance attributed to more extensive political and bureaucratic leadership in this area by the federal government. They also illustrate how the government believed that inadequate coordination within the federal bureaucracy was one of the key challenges for ensuring the effectiveness of national security and emergency management. From this perspective, it may not be surprising that the Martin government also emphasized multilevel coordination as a key determinant of effective emergency management in Canada. As the national security policy paper stated: "Major emergencies require extremely close co-operation between the federal government, provinces and territories, communities, first line responders and the private sector. National emergency co-ordination currently suffers from the absence of both an effective federal-provincial-territorial governance regime, and from the absence of commonly agreed standards and priorities for the national emergency management system" (Privy Council Office 2004, 25). In its policy statement, the government went so far as to argue that first line responders are "at the heart of our emergency management system" (Privy Council Office 2004, 22).

Yet, despite the broader reference to "communities" and the emphasis on first line responders, the absence of an explicit reference to municipalities or local authorities in this call for closer coordination among actors involved in emergency management is clearly noticeable. In fact, as its key reform measure, the Martin government promised to propose to provincial governments to create a more "permanent, high-level forum on emergencies in order to allow for regular strategic discussion of emergency management issues among key national players" (Privy Council Office 2004, 25). However, municipalities were not explicitly cited as such "key national players," and the extent of desired involvement by municipalities in the multilevel governance of emergency management remained unclear.

This ambiguity was partly a reflection of the political difficulty that the federal government would face if it decided to engage municipalities more directly in the governance of emergency management. In particular, even federal officials who believed that more direct engagement was necessary to improve the effectiveness of emergency management policy had to worry about the negative reaction of provincial governments. In a context where the ultimate objective was to improve multilevel governance, including by significantly improving federal-provincial coordination, any policy shift that might turn provincial governments against the reforms would likely yield failure or a disappointing outcome. If greater recognition of municipalities came at the price of dysfunctional federal-provincial relations, it might defeat the purpose of the reforms. For such a shift to occur, the provincial governments would have to be brought on board, and a new conception of appropriate multilevel arrangements would have to be endorsed by those key actors.

In the years that followed the release of the new national security policy statement, the federal and provincial governments worked to

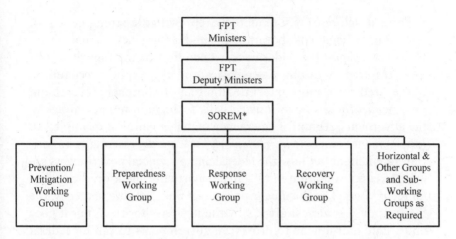

Figure 2.1   Reformed intergovernmental governance structure for emergency management

Source: Ministers Responsible for Emergency Management (2011). *Senior Officials Responsible for Emergency Management.

increase their cooperation. In January 2005 at a federal-provincial meeting, they agreed to "work together to improve and enhance the emergency response framework" of the country, and in 2007 a new formal framework entitled *An Emergency Management Framework for Canada* was adopted to specify the common principles, mechanisms, and instruments that would guide federal-provincial coordination in the future (Ministers Responsible for Emergency Management 2011, 1–2). In particular, as part of this agreement, a permanent federal-provincial structure, establishing a more elaborate and detailed set of intergovernmental committees at the political and administrative levels than had been seen in the past, was created (see figure 2.1). The new structure and processes are better-resourced, provide for more sustained intergovernmental interaction, and have already resulted in some joint policy statements or strategies on specific issues, such as dealing with certain types of hazards or ensuring the interoperability of communication during emergencies (Public Safety Canada 2011b). In parallel, bilateral federal-provincial memoranda of understanding were also concluded between the federal government and most provinces and territories, with the notable exception of Quebec, Alberta, and Nunavut (which together still represent about a third of the country's population) (Senate of Canada 2008, 46).

These developments undoubtedly represented a strengthening of federal-provincial collaboration around emergency management. However, despite the widespread recognition of the importance of local responders during emergencies and the explicit recognition of the need for a more integrated multilevel approach, federal and provincial officials have resisted calls to include municipalities in the governance regime of emergency management. For example, *An Emergency Management Framework for Canada*, essentially an official statement about how the federal and provincial governments see multilevel coordination in this area, is virtually silent on the role of municipalities. The document points out that "in an emergency, the first response is almost always by the local authorities," but it goes on to state that it is up to provincial governments to call for federal assistance when the situation warrants it. Similarly, while calling for an approach marked by partnerships with the key actors in emergency management, municipalities are mentioned only as part of a long list of potential partners that also includes universities, the private sector, and international organizations (Ministers Responsible for Emergency Management 2011, 6).

Similarly, the new *Federal Policy for Emergency Management* that came into effect in 2009 mostly ignored the role of local authorities. In the section describing the division of responsibilities between levels of government, it simply asserts that provincial governments are expected to deal with emergencies within their jurisdictions, "except where legislation allows for direct federal intervention or shared responsibility," and that the federal government can be involved only when a matter falls within its jurisdictions, a provincial government requests federal assistance, or an emergency is determined to have national implication (section 2.1). Municipalities and the possibility of direct federal-municipal involvement are not mentioned. Furthermore, when identifying the responsibilities of federal departments, the policy statement says only that they should include any measures to assist provincial governments in their emergency management plans, as well as measures offered to local authorities "*through the provincial and territorial governments.*" Finally, as we have seen, the high-level committees and processes created in the context of the new framework simply do not include municipalities. In sum, the new policies, structures, and processes adopted through the reforms of the last decade have strictly adhered to a very traditional conception of intergovernmental coordination in the Canadian federation, despite the sustained calls for new thinking and more engagement of local governments.

While most of the reforms described above were decided on and negotiated within the confines of the offices of ministers and senior executives in Ottawa and provincial capitals, the federal government's decision to modernize the key statute underpinning its authority in this area provided the opportunity for a more open and public debate about the role of municipalities in emergency management. Following a promise made in the 2004 policy statement on national security, the Liberal government tabled a bill to this effect, the Emergency Management Act (EMA), in the House of Commons in November 2005. While the bill soon died on the order paper because of the federal election of 2006, the incoming minority Conservative government led by Prime Minister Stephen Harper reintroduced the bill in the House of Commons soon after its arrival in power.

The bill's primary objective was to clarify the roles and responsibilities of federal ministers in relation to all aspects of emergency management, but it also sought to officially recognize, by entrenching them in legislation, the principles of multilevel collaboration and coordination as key features of the federal government's approach to emergency management. From this perspective, the new statute designates the minister of public safety and emergency preparedness as the minister "responsible for exercising leadership relating to emergency management in Canada by coordinating, among government institutions and in cooperation with the provinces and other entities, emergency management activities" (section 3).

In this regard, the minister for public safety and emergency preparedness, Stockwell Day, clearly stated at the time that a key objective of the new legislation was to improve intergovernmental coordination of emergency responses. As he said, "Emergency preparedness is a shared responsibility and everyone has an important role to play. Experience has taught us that leadership, coordination and collaboration across jurisdictions are essential to the Government of Canada's readiness for emergencies and more importantly – to saving lives. These principles are the foundation of the proposed *Emergency Management Act*" (Public Safety and Emergency Preparedness Canada 2006).

Similarly, speaking on the bill in the House of Commons, the parliamentary secretary to the minister of public safety, Dave MacKenzie, also emphasized improved coordination as the key

objective: "The emergency management act would set out the minister's responsibility to coordinate emergency management activities
across the federal government, with provincial governments, non-
governmental organizations and the private sector. In the same spirit
of cooperation, the minister would also be charged with promoting
a common approach to emergency preparedness" (House of Commons 2006b, 3072).

Clearly, the incoming Conservative government shared its pre-
decessor's objective for enhanced intergovernmental coordination
in this area. However, despite presenting enhanced intergovernmental coordination and collaboration as the "foundation" of good
emergency management and a fundamental principle animating
the legislative reform, the new Conservative government remained
largely silent on the role of local authorities. To the extent that the
bill itself mentioned municipalities, it clearly portrayed them as subservient to the provinces, and it expressed a conception of multilevel coordination that is essentially congruent with the traditional
federal-provincial framework. For instance, section 4(1)(f) of the
statute reads: "[The minister is responsible for] coordinating the
activities of government institutions relating to emergency management with those of the provinces – and supporting the emergency
management activities of the provinces – and *through the provinces,*
those of local authorities" (Canada 2006a, 2, emphasis added). In
this regard, the Conservative government also clearly aligned itself
with a traditional conception of multilevel governance.

While the issue might otherwise have continued to be ignored in
the legislative reform process, a lobbying campaign by municipalities
and some key allies within the House of Commons forced elected
officials to address more explicitly the role of municipalities in multilevel governance through the parliamentary debates on the adoption
of the bill. In particular, a small group of members of parliament
from the Liberal Party and the New Democratic Party (NDP), many
of them with previous experience at the local level, actively sought
to make the case for a more extensive integration of municipalities
in the national governance of emergency management.

Among several parliamentarians who spoke in its favour, Mark
Holland, a Liberal MP who had previously been the acting mayor
of Pickering, Ontario, was probably the most vocal advocate of
the greater recognition of municipalities during those debates. He
even tabled an amendment to the bill that would have explicitly

recognized, in the legislation, municipalities as fully fledged partners of the federal government in emergency management, on par
with the provinces and territories (House of Commons 2006d, 1).
Based on his experience, Holland stressed not only the importance
of municipal expertise in local emergency planning but also the need
for a new understanding of the country's urban reality *in spite of* the
prevailing constitutional order. As he argued in the House of Commons: "[T]he flaw I see in this bill, the thing that most concerns me,
is the lack of recognition of municipalities in the bill, and more specifically, the lack of representation of municipalities on some of the
committees that exist. I appreciate that municipalities are creatures
of the provinces, but I would think that our understanding of municipalities has evolved as our nation has become one of large cities
that are very complex and really true levels of government in their
own right" (House of Commons 2006c, 13). He even stated that the
absence of the word "municipalities" in the bill should be considered
"a slap in the face," an insult, by municipalities. "It's paternalistic,"
he added, "and in my opinion it's really missing the boat in terms of
how we will have to work with and treat municipalities" (House of
Commons 2006d, 4).

Other Liberal MPs defended similar positions (see, for example,
House of Commons 2006a, 3076), but some parliamentarians from
the NDP also spoke in favour of establishing direct federal-municipal
relations on emergency management and supported the inclusion of
municipalities in existing intergovernmental forums. For example,
Olivia Chow, a prominent NDP member and a former municipal
councillor in Toronto, raised the possibility of establishing mechanisms that would ensure direct federal-municipal contacts in the case
of emergencies (House of Commons 2006a, 3101). Another NDP
member, Joe Comartin, explicitly supported the Holland amendment, describing it as a simple reflection of the reality faced by first
line responders on the ground. He criticized the bill for its failure to
recognize municipalities as key players in this field, and he described
the legislation as unfair to municipalities. As he stated, "The legislation has a failing in this regard in that it does not adequately reflect
that key essential role that the local level of government provides
and I want to take this opportunity to acknowledge that" (House of
Commons 2006e, 5937).

Municipalities themselves, through the Federation of Canadian
Municipalities (FCM), also called for legislative amendments that

would result in a multilevel governance framework that would treat them as genuine partners. Speaking before the House Committee on Public Safety and National Security, James Knight, the FCM's CEO at the time, stated that "In our view, the bill as currently written will not lead to better coordination across jurisdictions because there's virtually no reference to the municipal order of government. We will suggest how that reference can be made explicit" (House of Commons 2006b, 1). Needless to say, the organization supported the Holland amendment as a necessary, formal first step toward rethinking traditional intergovernmental relations concerning emergency management.

However, the coalition of elected officials and municipal advocates that tried to reframe the dominant understanding of multilevel governance in this field faced considerable opposition from other legislators who defended the traditional understanding of multilevel coordination, with direct coordination strictly occurring between the federal and provincial governments and municipalities largely considered as implementing agents to be managed by provincial authorities. Their narrative about the need for more direct engagement of municipalities as a necessity for ensuring the effectiveness of emergency management on the ground was met by a narrative, a frame, that essentially espoused the traditional intergovernmental process and the consideration of municipalities as administrative entities coming under the sole authority of provincial governments as principles that remained crucial for the proper governance of the country.

In this respect, members of the Bloc Québécois (BQ), a sovereignist party defending the province of Quebec's interests in Parliament, expressed strong concerns about the implications of federal encroachment on provincial jurisdictions. Its MPs did not deny the crucial role played by municipal governments in emergency management, but they clearly thought that this reality, coupled with an understandable desire for greater effectiveness in emergency policy, should not be used to violate the fundamental norms underpinning the Canadian federation. For example, MP Réal Ménard called on the federal government to respect provincial jurisdictions and stated that "although the Bloc Québécois agrees with this bill in principle, we have some concerns. First is the issue of respecting provincial responsibilities. A national emergency should never mean there is just one government. We are long past the time of the Rowell-Sirois commission. We are not in an apprehended war situation. As elected members of the Bloc Québécois, as representatives of the people of Quebec, we must never act as though there were just one government" (House of Commons 2006a, 3077).

Similarly, Serge Ménard, another prominent MP for the BQ, who had previously served as a public safety minister in the Quebec government, argued for the pre-eminence of provincial responsibilities, advocating a bottom-up approach to emergency management, but one where the "local" is represented by the provincial government (House of Commons 2006a, 3102). Recalling his days with the provincial government, he argued that leadership in emergencies should really be assumed by provincial authorities: "The [federal] minister certainly has the right to exercise [authority] in areas of federal jurisdiction, but leadership roles must be the responsibility of local [i.e., provincial] authorities" (House of Commons 2006a, 3107). Later on he reiterated the same point: "I recognize that the federal government has a role to play, but that role is not to establish the rules for everyone. That is best done at the local [i.e., provincial] level" (House of Commons 2006a, 3110). Focused on the political and constitutional bickering opposing the federal and provincial governments, he simply ignored municipalities. In effect, he argued that the bill was going too far by implying a leadership role for the federal government in emergency management.

On the whole, parliamentarians sitting with the BQ opposed the development of more direct federal-municipal relations and the recognition of municipalities in the new act because they feared that it would result in the weakening of provincial autonomy. For them, the narrative calling for more extensive recognition and involvement of municipalities was not incoherent or implausible as much as it was politically unacceptable, because it would clash with more fundamental political norms and, as a frame, it was irreconcilable with some of their fundamental values and worldviews about the nature, and future, of the Canadian polity. In the end, those values and worldviews were more in tune with a traditional conception of federal-provincial relations, even if the legislative reforms being considered ran the risk of seeing the federal government asserting a stronger leadership role in emergency management.

While the Conservative members who spoke during the debates obviously held a different understanding of the country and were comfortable defending greater federal leadership in emergency management, they nevertheless saw the constitutional division of power as a legitimate and insurmountable barrier to more direct federal-municipal engagement or the inclusion of municipalities in multilevel collaboration forums. While defending the expansion of federal leadership as consistent with existing authority under the Peace, Order and Good Government clause of the constitution (House of Commons 2006a, 3110), they also stressed that the bill would not, and should not, change the status of municipalities in intergovernmental processes. For example, Dave MacKenzie, the parliamentary secretary to the minister of public safety, argued that "[The Emergency Management Act] is a federal piece of legislation dealing with the federal government's responsibility. Municipalities deal with the provinces. It flows up, down, sideways, but it would be a very difficult situation for the federal government to be directly involved with the municipalities, given that the provinces have their domain and jurisdiction" (House of Commons 2006c, 14).

Laurie Hawn, a Conservative MP from Edmonton, also defended the intergovernmental status quo, arguing that provincial governments could be "effective channels through which municipalities could access the federal government in times of emergency" (House of Commons 2006a, 3102). In sum, with respect to federal-municipal relations and the direct participation of municipalities in intergovernmental arenas, the Conservatives argued that the status quo worked sufficiently well and that, in any case, greater municipal involvement in multilevel coordination would be too difficult under the prevailing understanding of constitutional and political norms.

In the end, the amendment presented by Mark Holland was defeated, and the bill was unanimously adopted by the House of Commons. Under the minority conditions that existed in the House of Commons at the time, the combined support of the Conservative Party and the Bloc Québécois was sufficient to kill this change that would have led to the explicit legal recognition of municipalities as partners in multilevel governance. Once the amendment and others had been defeated, the bill was adopted with the unanimous consent of all parties in the House of Commons, since opposition parties were concerned to be seen as supportive of a stronger framework to address public safety. In any case, even legislative recognition of the importance of engaging local authorities more extensively in the multilevel governance of emergency management would have been a limited step forward: the substance of multilevel coordination would ultimately require a genuine commitment to this principle by federal and provincial cabinets and bureaucrats. Still, the debates in Parliament served to illustrate more visibly how there remained a strong coalition of political forces unwilling to rethink and move past the traditional norms of intergovernmental relations in the Canadian federation, regardless of the potential gains in effectiveness in addressing the growing risk of large-scale emergencies. While the Conservative government might also have feared the alienation of provincial governments if it had endorsed more engagement of municipalities, for its BQ allies in Parliament the conception of municipalities as entities under the sole control of the provincial government was obviously considered an immutable characteristic of the legitimate constitutional order of the Canadian polity.

Overall, the outcome of this legislative process, like the broader institutional and policy changes that occurred during the same period, shows that, despite its prominence in the debates, the alternative conception of effective multilevel governance did not gain sufficient support and did not succeed in fundamentally reframing how the essential decision makers involved in the policy process viewed emergency management policy. In the end, the dominant understanding of multilevel governance prevailed, and the reforms failed to provide for a more extensive role for municipalities in emergency management policy.

In the years since the adoption of the Emergency Management Act, the federal government made some further changes to its emergency management policies, but these new policy developments essentially confirmed its adherence to a traditional understanding of the constitutional order and its reluctance to consider municipalities as true partners in emergency management. For example, in January 2011 the government issued an official statement on Canada's *National Emergency Response System* (Public Safety Canada 2011a), which describes the principles, roles, responsibilities, and procedures to be followed in times of emergency in order to ensure an effective coordinated response. The statement was developed by a working group created as part of the FPT governance framework adopted in 2007, which was discussed earlier, and not surprisingly, the emergency response system described does not present municipalities as significant actors shaping coordinated emergency responses.

This policy statement does acknowledge at the outset that local authorities are the first responders in the vast majority of emergencies

and that effective emergency management calls for "good partnerships" among key stakeholders, including municipalities (Public
Safety Canada 2011a, 3). However, it also makes clear that municipalities are not included in intergovernmental discussions of emergency response integration and that in times of emergency any
request for federal assistance must come from provincial authorities
(3–6, 9). In fact, municipalities are not mentioned in the statement's
section addressing the roles and responsibilities of governments in
responding to emergencies, and they are not present in its descrip-
tion of the communication and activities that are deemed necessary
to ensure adequate situational awareness, risk assessment, or impact
analysis in the face of emergencies (8–9). The section on response
planning mentions only that provincial plans ought to address how
provincial authorities would provide support to municipalities when
they needed it (10). In sum, despite their acknowledged importance
in emergency response, municipalities remain largely ignored in the
official framework guiding emergency response. This observation
illustrates that the dominant frame for thinking about the multilevel
governance of emergencies continues to shape policy thinking years
after the debates that led to the adoption of the Emergency Management Act.

CONCLUSION

This chapter has examined the reforms of emergency management
that the Canadian government adopted over the last decade, with a
special focus on how they affected the evolution of multilevel governance in this area. Good multilevel coordination is widely seen as
a central condition for the effective management of emergencies in
contemporary federal states. In Canada its absence has frequently
been cited as a weakness of the national emergency management
system. Particular complaints and concerns have been expressed
about the lack of significant participation by municipalities in the
formulation of national emergency policy, as well as about impedi-
ments to direct federal-municipal communication during various
stages of emergency management.

Over the last decade, many representatives of local authorities and some federal politicians have argued for various changes
to intergovernmental processes and practices that in their view
could improve the multilevel coordination and, consequently, the

effectiveness of emergency management in Canada. For example, proposed reforms included the participation of municipal representatives on key FPT committees and a change in the norms and practices concerning the direct relationship between federal authorities and local governments. It is clear that identifying the specific mix of measures most likely to lead to improvements in emergency management remains a matter for debate among policy-makers and practitioners in the field. However, it is equally clear that a necessary precondition for any significant change in this direction remains a shift in the way the federal and provincial authorities think about the status of municipalities in the multilevel governance of emergency management. More specifically, it requires acknowledging municipalities as genuine partners in the multilevel governance of emergency management and moving away from traditional conceptions of Canadian intergovernmental relations. Nevertheless, as we have shown, despite the emergence of a political and conceptual case for improving multilevel governance mechanisms through more direct federal-municipal communication and the inclusion of municipalities in intergovernmental forums, the Canadian government has failed to move in this direction. To explain this outcome, we have tried to illustrate how the politics of reform have been significantly characterized by a clash between two distinctive frames about the proper organization of multilevel coordination in the Canadian federation.

Through this period, a coalition of actors, including municipalities, some members of parliament, and senators, succeeded in developing a frame justifying a significant rethinking of federal-provincial-municipal relations in the name of greater effectiveness in this area, as well as in giving this frame prominence in the national debates in this field. For this purpose, the institutional environment that shaped the reform process proved particularly important: the institutional leverage provided by parliamentary rules, whether those used by individual MPs during the legislative process or those used by the Senate Committee on National Security and Defence for the conduct of special studies, proved determinant in allowing this frame to become a significant part of the national policy debate.

However, despite its limited successes, the proponents of this alternative frame also faced significant opposition from advocates of a more traditional conception of federal-provincial relations in the Canadian federation. In the end, this latter frame, which benefited from its affinity with the established constitutional order, including the norms and processes already entrenched in the emergency management field, proved impossible to replace. While the Canadian government succeeded in strengthening multilevel governance in this policy field, these reforms took a very traditional approach, emphasizing conventional federal-provincial committees and eschewing a serious reconsideration of its relationship to municipalities.

In this respect, one of the conclusions that can be drawn for this case study of Canadian reforms is that the reorganization of state structures and processes to deal with catastrophic risks and large-scale adverse events is heavily mediated by politics and that in the struggles that ensue to modify state practices and organization in order to adapt them to the risk environment, historical norms and institutions significantly matter for reform outcomes. In other words, the politics of reform, in this area as in others, seem significantly "path dependent": historical choices get entrenched in structures, processes, and recognized norms that become very hard to alter as they come to reflect dominant ways of seeing the world, as well as patterns that serve important political interests.

However, as we have seen in the Canadian case, these historical norms and patterns of interaction are not necessarily congruent with best practices of emergency management. As a result, rethinking the organization of the state to face the heightened risks of adverse events may call for considerable political leadership in bringing political actors to rethink broader, more fundamental principles and norms underpinning political systems and bureaucracies.

REFERENCES

Bakvis, Herman, and Douglas Brown. 2010. "Policy Coordination in Federal Systems: Comparing Intergovernmental Processes and Outcomes in Canada and the United States." *Publius* 40 (3): 484–507.
Big City Mayors' Caucus (BCMC). 2006. *Our Cities, Our Future: Addressing the Fiscal Balance in Canada's City Today*. Ottawa: Federation of Canadian Municipalities.
Britton, Neil R. 2001. "A New Emergency Management for the Millennium?" *Australian Journal of Emergency Management* 16 (4): 44–54.
Canada. 2006a. *Bill C-12: An Act to Provide for Emergency Management and to Amend and Repeal Certain Acts*. First Reading, May 8.

- 2012a. *The Canadian Population in 2011: Population Counts and Growth*. Statistics Canada.
- 2012b. *Canada at a Glance*. Statistics Canada.
Caruson, Kiki, and Susan A. MacManus. 2007. "Designing Homeland Security Policy within a Regional Structure: A Needs Assessment of Local Security Concerns." *Journal of Homeland Security and Emergency Management* 4 (2), Article 7.
Caruson, Kiki, Susan A. MacManus, Matthew Kohen, and Thomas A. Watson. 2005. "Homeland Security Preparedness: The Rebirth of Regionalism." *Publius* 35 (1): 143–68.
Chong, Dennis, and James N. Druckman. 2007. "Framing Theory." *Annual Review of Political Science* 10 (1): 103–26.
Druckman, James. 2001. "On the Limits of Framing Effects: Who Can Frame?" *Journal of Politics* 63 (4): 1041–66.
Eisinger, Peter. 2006. "Imperfect Federalism: The Intergovernmental Partnership for Homeland Security." *Public Administration Review* 66 (4): 537–45.
Federation of Canadian Municipalities (FCM). 2006. *Emergency: Municipalities Missing from Disaster Planning*. A Report to the Federation of Canadian Municipalities (FCM) by the National Security Group. Ottawa: Federation of Canadian Municipalities.
Fischer, Frank. 2003. *Reframing Public Policy: Discursive Politics and Deliberative Practices*. New York: Oxford University Press.
Gabriel, Paul. 2003. "The Development of Municipal Emergency Management Planning in Victoria, Australia." *Australian Journal of Emergency Management* 18 (2): 74–80.
Hajer, Maarten. 1995. *The Politics of Environmental Discourse: Ecological Modernization and the Policy Process*. Oxford: Clarendon Press.
- 2006. "Doing Discourse Analysis: Coalitions, Practices, Meaning." In *Words Matter in Policy and Planning: Discourse Theory and Method in the Social Sciences*, edited by M. van den Brink and T. Metze. Utrecht: KNAG/Nethur.
House of Commons. 2006a. *House of Commons Debates*. Vol. 141, no. 050, 1st Session, 39th Parliament, 21 September.
- 2006b. *Evidence. Standing Committee on Public Safety and National Security*. 1st Session, 39th Parliament, no. 014, 19 October.
- 2006c. *Evidence. Standing Committee on Public Safety and National Security*. 1st Session, 39th Parliament, no. 020, 9 November.
- 2006d. *Evidence. Standing Committee on Public Safety and National Security*. 1st Session, 39th Parliament, no. 021, 21 November.

– 2006e. *House of Commons Debates.* Vol. 141, no. 095, 1st Session, 39th Parliament, 11 December.

Juillet, Luc. 2007. "Framing Environmental Policy: Aboriginal Rights and the Conservation of Migratory Birds." In *Critical Policy Studies: Contemporary Canadian Approaches,* edited by Michael Orsini and Miriam Smith, 257–75. Vancouver: UBC Press.

Ministers Responsible for Emergency Management. 2011. *An Emergency Management Framework for Canada.* 2d ed. Ottawa: Public Safety Canada.

Newkirk, Ross T. 2001. "The Increasing Cost of Disasters in Developed Countries: A Challenge to Local Planning and Government." *Journal of Contingencies and Crisis Management* 9 (3): 159–70.

Orsini, Michael, and Miriam Smith, eds. 2007. *Critical Policy Studies.* Vancouver: UBC Press.

Polletta, Francesca, and Kai Ho. 2006. "Frames and their Consequences." In *The Oxford Handbook of Contextual Political Studies,* edited by Robert Goodin and C. Tilly, 187–209. Oxford: Oxford University Press.

Prater, Carla S., and Michael K. Lindell. 2000. "Politics of Hazard Mitigation." *Natural Hazards Review* 1 (2): 73–82.

Privy Council Office. 2004. *Securing an Open Society: Canada's National Security Policy.* Ottawa: Her Majesty the Queen in Right of Canada.

Public Safety Canada. 2011a. *National Emergency Response System.* Ottawa: Her Majesty the Queen in Right of Canada.

– 2011b. *Communications Interoperability Strategy for Canada.* Ottawa: Her Majesty the Queen in Right of Canada.

Public Safety and Emergency Preparedness Canada. 2006. "Minister Day Launches Emergency Preparedness Week." Press release, 8 May.

Ross, Fiona. 2000. "Framing Welfare Reform in Affluent Societies: Rendering Restructuring More Palatable?" *Journal of Public Policy* 20 (2): 169–93.

Senate of Canada. 2003a. *Proceedings of the Standing Senate Committee on National Security and Defence.* No. 9, 28 January and 3 February.

– 2003b. *Proceedings of the Standing Senate Committee on National Security and Defence.* No. 26, 30 October.

– 2004. *National Emergencies: Canada's Fragile Front Lines.* Vol. 1. Ottawa: Standing Senate Committee on National Security and Defence.

– 2008. *Emergency Preparedness in Canada: Report of the Standing Senate Committee on National Security and Defence.* Vol. 1.

Surel, Yves. 2000. "The Role of Cognitive and Normative Frames in Policy-Making." *Journal of European Public Policy* 7 (4): 495–512.

Wyatt-Nichol, Heather, and Charles F. Abel. 2007. "A Critical Analysis of Emergency Management." *Administrative Theory & Praxis* 29 (4): 567–85.

3

Emergency Planning in Nova Scotia

MALCOLM GRIEVE AND LORI TURNBULL

INTRODUCTION

This chapter discusses emergency planning in Nova Scotia with reference to relationships among federal, provincial, and municipal governments, voluntary agencies, and other stakeholders. Interviews were conducted with municipal politicians, emergency planning officials, and associated non-governmental organizations (NGOs) in four municipalities, including Halifax Regional Municipality (HRM), the largest city in the province. The general conclusion drawn from these discussions is that emergency planning and the preparedness of municipalities in Nova Scotia is adequate and moving forward. Ad hoc but mostly effective lines of communication among emergency actors at each of three levels of government are being reinforced under the training and evaluation templates developed initially by the provincial Emergency Management Organization (EMO). In April of 2011, however, responsibility for emergency management was transferred to the Emergency Management Office, housed in the Department of Justice. The federal government is a distant actor for most municipal emergency planners, but it is more engaged in HRM exercises than it is in other jurisdictions.

The breakdown of this chapter is as follows. First, we identify the factors and events that have contributed to a higher profile for emergency planning in the province. Next, we explore the complex arena of intergovernmental relations in the field of emergency planning and management. In this part, we discuss the specific roles of the federal, provincial, and municipal governments and examine how the three orders of government collaborate in this policy sector.

Following this, we look to the presence of social forces in Nova Scotia, such as the business and voluntary sectors, to determine their influence on emergency policy. We end the chapter by evaluating the current policy framework and suggesting proposals for reform.

THE SIGNIFICANCE OF EMERGENCY PLANNING IN NOVA SCOTIA

Emergency planning gains more salience when floods, forest fires, or weather catastrophes are reported in the news. The perception of and increased risk of disaster is not merely media-fuelled, however. The Institute for Catastrophic Loss Reduction, a Toronto-based research unit funded by Canadian insurance companies, notes that there has been a significant increase in the number and costs of hazardous weather and weather-related events and that 80 percent of natural disasters are weather related (McBean and Henstra 2003, 1). As the climate changes, Atlantic Canada can expect to be exposed to more frequent hurricanes, as well as winter storms, so there will be steady and increasing meteorological pressures on emergency management in the region. This demand can be met by reactive measures, such as polishing procedures for providing shelter, or by more ambitious mitigation schemes to protect infrastructure and reduce proneness to flooding. In recent memory, Nova Scotians recall several severe weather events, such as Hurricane Juan in September 2003 and the White Juan blizzard of February 2004. The latter prompted Ernest Fage, as minister responsible for the Emergency Measures Organization at that time, to declare the first-ever provincial state of emergency. The power outages caused by these and lesser events have focused attention on the plight of those needing shelter, food, and communication and have led to improved emergency planning and communications. But while Nova Scotia Power has improved its emergency phone systems, transmission lines remain vulnerable to wind, as was demonstrated with power outages caused by "post-tropical storm" Noel in November 2007 and by "salty fog" in the fall of 2006 (CTV News 2006). More positively, emergency managers in the HRM found shelter for travellers stranded during the post 9/11 shutdown of airspace in 2001, and in 1998 they provided teams to conduct search and rescue operations in St Margaret's Bay, the crash site of Swiss Air Flight 111, followed by extensive trauma counselling services. These dramatic and highly publicized events injected political urgency, support, and salience into the otherwise mundane world of emergency planning. But the interest of the public in emergencies is sporadic and event-driven, which makes it difficult to sustain government resources for prevention and mitigation. Thus, the abiding legacy of major emergencies in recent years has been incremental changes to the process of developing, testing, and improving Nova Scotian emergency response plans rather than significant expenditures on preventing emergencies.

GENERAL PATTERNS OF EMERGENCY INTERGOVERNMENTAL RELATIONS

Emergency response begins at the periphery of government. A key policy principle of emergency planning is that emergencies are to be dealt with first and as far as possible by the lowest level. Responsibility for the first response to many emergencies is deemed to rest with the household. After these household preparations are overwhelmed, first response to emergencies becomes the responsibility of local government, with the province notified, but called on to help only as needed (Big City Mayor's Caucus 2005). In 2006, the Federation of Canadian Municipalities (FCM) published a report by the National Security Group, which found that only half the municipalities across Canada are in fact adequately prepared to deal with emergencies. They concluded that "many municipalities are not yet able to cope with significant emergencies to the detriment of Canadians, and that current federal emergency planning does not effectively respond to this major shortcoming" (2006, 11).

This gloomy conclusion is only partly true in Nova Scotia, since planning for emergencies, even in smaller municipalities, is improving thanks to the province's schedule of training and preparation. Two of the province's larger municipal units have amalgamated, and the province is encouraging regional emergency cooperation among non-amalgamated municipal units to help share emergency equipment such as generators and firefighting equipment. Nova Scotia has also established contractual arrangements with the Red Cross to provide emergency social services.

The Nova Scotian Emergency Management Office headquarters in HRM divides the province into three zones and uses the field officers in Kentville (Western Region), Truro (Central) and Sydney (Eastern) to "maintain close working relationships with local governments"

(Emergency Management Office 2008a). Provincial emergency officials in these three zones are included in the planning process at the municipal level along with HRM officials. In addition, the CEO of the EMO, who enjoys deputy minister status, tours the province to maintain interest in emergency planning among municipal officials and politicians, partly through presentations delivered at town council meetings.

In the 2006 Nova Scotia government, the deputy minister in the Emergency Management Office reported to the minister for natural resources. In 2008 he reported to Carolyn Bolivar-Getson, who was minister responsible for emergency management as well as for human resources, minister responsible for the public service commission, minister of seniors and chair of the seniors' secretariat, and minister responsible for the advisory council on the status of women. Until late 2007, this minister was also responsible for the Nova Scotia Liquor Corporation, and she was minister of immigration. Most members of the Nova Scotia cabinet have multiple portfolios, but this seems to be one of the broadest collections and speaks to the priority of emergency issues as compared to agriculture or natural resources, for example. As of 2012, the CEO reports to Ross Landry, who is also the attorney general and minister of justice.

Financial exigency may explain the combination of emergency roles with so many other functions for the minister responsible for emergency management. This is certainly true for most of the municipalities in Nova Scotia. The only two full-time municipal emergency managers in the province are in the Halifax and Cape Breton Regional Municipalities (the former since amalgamation and the latter since 2003).

A major part of managing an emergency is providing shelter, food, clothing, registration/inquiry, and personal services for those removed from their homes by some disaster. This goal brings into play departments of government not typically thought of in the array of emergency responders. The Nova Scotia Department of Community Services (DCS) is charged with developing plans to respond to the needs of those rendered homeless by emergencies. It undertakes to provide financial assistance in the event of "large-scale" emergencies – that is, those involving ten or more residential units, or twenty-five or more persons. The delivery of DCS assistance in Nova Scotia is formally contracted by the department to the Canadian Red Cross. Through the Red Cross, the DCS covers costs incurred by municipalities in managing emergencies. Municipalities do not approve or determine which social services or costs associated with social services are to be reimbursed; rather, these costs are met with the approval and authorization of the provincial DCS authority (Tyson 2005). Thus with the institution of this agreement, the DCS has contracted out emergency social services, rather than providing them directly.

INTERGOVERNMENTAL COLLABORATION

In the wake of major emergencies in Canada and other states, it is increasingly evident that effective emergency management requires collaboration among different levels of government. In a truly cooperative governance model, intergovernmental relations in emergency planning would facilitate training, standardize communications protocols, secure critical infrastructure, and achieve uniform minimum national standards of emergency response. In practice, the federal role seems most salient for the question of compensation for disasters. The government of Canada has two vehicles for transferring funds to the provinces on behalf of municipal claimants: the Disaster Financial Assistance Arrangements (DFAA) and JEPP. DFAA funds are subject to close bureaucratic review and are typically slow to arrive, which can be an irritant to the municipalities who incur costs in the front line of emergency response and who must field complaints from citizens waiting for reimbursement. In 2007, for example, HRM was still waiting for reimbursement of costs associated with managing the 9/11 emergency in 2001, when eight thousand passengers were stranded in Halifax as a result of the attacks (Tattrie 2010).

The policy field of emergency preparedness displays friction, as well as cooperation, among the three spheres of Canadian government. There is cooperation in federal compensation, mediated by the provinces, to municipalities for costs they incur in managing disasters such as floods. This is enshrined in a DFAA compensation formula based on the number of people affected and the population of the province. According to the program guidelines, "assistance is available when a province's eligible expenses incurred in carrying out its own disaster response and recovery program are above $1 per capita of the provincial population" (Public Safety Canada 2008b). There is some cooperation in sharing communication and training protocols to enhance regional responses to emergencies and to ensure minimum or uniform levels of preparedness. But governance models are predicated on the long-established practice of downloading emergency responsibilities to provincial and municipal levels of government and further tasking volunteers in fire departments, search and rescue organizations, and Red Cross emergency services.

The provision of security is a basic function of the highest level of government, yet while the government of Canada has become preoccupied with border and international security, other security subfields fall within the bailiwick of the provinces. The typical Nova Scotian emergency first responder operates at the municipal level under guidelines set by the province, and the federal government is perceived as a remote or irrelevant actor, providing (usually sluggishly) financial support for preparedness and disaster remediation but offering little policy guidance or coordination. To a degree, this delegation of security in emergency planning policy is rationalized by basic notions of subsidiarity, defined generally as the downloading of political responsibilities to the lowest level of government. It is politically expedient, as well as efficient, to assign responsibility for declaring and responding to local emergencies to the lowest level of government. Government services are also freed to cope with those in severe need if most citizens can provide their own essentials for the first seventy-two hours of an emergency.

One problem in applying the principle of subsidiarity is the tension between public expectations of federal support and the delayed action by the highest level of government. While citizens are exhorted in safety awareness campaigns, by official websites, and in the public media to equip themselves with a seventy-two-hour supply of food, water, and heat sources, in practice only a small proportion of households will be truly prepared for emergencies, and many will expect public succour almost immediately. A study of 594 households in Kingston, Ontario, with a response rate of 68 percent found that roughly half of all households had a five-day supply of drinking water and that only 7 percent had an alternate power source (Statistics Canada 2005, 8). Emergency planning is rarely a salient issue for citizens. Preparedness for emergencies is delegated to professionals and is largely conceptualized as a bureaucratic affair of contingency planning, testing of communications and other systems, and accounting for costs of remediation.

In emergencies, citizens expect their government to manage the emergency, as well as to help them claim reimbursement for damages and recovery costs. When there has been a breakdown in the supply of essential services and/or in communication during an emergency event, affected citizens may express discontent with the nearest public officials – those at the municipal level – followed by those at provincially owned or controlled utility companies. After a three-day power outage in November 2004, for example, the mayor of Truro found garbage strewn on his front yard in protest. In effect, the level of government with the weakest fiscal capacity to manage emergency events must field complaints from citizens who have experienced hardship during an emergency.

The Canadian emergency planning legislative framework mixes constitutional responsibilities with common sense. The Emergency Preparedness Act of 2005 was renamed the Emergency Management Act in 2007, perhaps to reflect faith in an "all-hazards" response plan applicable to any emergency. The act mandates all federal departments and agencies to develop programs to deal with risks related to their area of responsibility (Canada 2007). In addition to keeping the federal house in order, the act enables the cabinet to declare any provincial emergency to be of concern to the federal government and to provide funds and other assistance to manage emergencies. Although "emergency preparedness" has been dropped from the title of the portfolio, the minister of public safety is charged with "exercising leadership relating to emergency management in Canada by coordinating, among government institutions and in cooperation with the provinces and other entities, emergency management activities" (Canada 2007, s. 3). The act makes frequent reference to the responsibilities of the federal minister for coordinating and cooperating with the provinces. Provinces in turn can declare a state of emergency in order to trigger support enabled under the federal legislation.

The development and testing of emergency plans occurs mostly at the municipal level, where first responders are located. The preoccupation of the Canadian government with dealing with terrorist threats (prompted partly by the need to reassure the United States) has shifted attention from emergency management programs to high-profile border control initiatives, which are not the priority of provincial or municipal emergency planners in Nova Scotia. Emergency managers regard terrorist emergencies as they do any another hazard, yielding the same demands for shelter, food, and communications as weather or accident-related emergencies. There are no special efforts on behalf of local emergency planners to identify and mitigate human-caused emergencies of this sort (Interview 10).

Constitutionally, municipal governments are created by provincial legislation, which specifies the responsibilities and obligations of municipal officials regarding emergency planning. Provincial legislation in Nova Scotia requires all municipal governments to make plans to maintain order and restore peace during and after emergencies. In Nova Scotia the Emergency Management Act establishes rules for managing emergencies and charges municipalities to develop and test emergency response plans, with a detailed checklist of requirements for exercises and equipment (Nova Scotia 2005). Specifically, each municipality must establish an emergency bylaw and an emergency management organization, appoint a coordinator of the organization to prepare emergency plans, appoint a committee of the municipal council to keep council advised on the development of emergency plans, and finally, prepare and approve emergency plans. This legislation also expanded the scope of emergency planning in Nova Scotia to include preparedness, response, mitigation, and recovery, which is consistent with developments in other provinces. As well, it gave wide-ranging powers to the minister of justice to create regulations with respect to municipal emergency planning (Nova Scotia 2005).

An example of collaboration among municipalities to influence federal policy is the Federation of Canadian Municipalities' (FCM) Big City Mayor's Caucus Working Group on Public Safety, Security and Emergency Preparedness. This group of the twenty-two largest cities in Canada was chaired once by Peter Kelly, mayor of Halifax Regional Municipality (2000–12), who had a keen enthusiasm for emergency planning. On 25 November 2005, the working group produced a fifty-eight-page draft report with several hundred pages of detailed technical appendices. The report, titled "Emergency Response Management Model for Canadian Municipalities," notes many practical opportunities for municipalities to share resources and makes the case for more federal leadership in municipal emergency planning. Mayor Kelly's preface observes that less than half the municipalities in Canada believe that they are capable of responding effectively to major or even minor emergencies and notes that this is due, in part, to the absence of a Canada-wide emergency preparedness and response management standard. In particular, Mayor Kelly identified federal training for municipal emergency managers as a potential vehicle for a nationwide incident management system. To achieve national training standards for all responders, the report recommends that the FCM adopt the Emergency Response Management Model for Canadian Municipalities, a document meant to assist municipalities in the creation or revision of emergency preparedness and response plans, as the national standard for emergency preparedness and response (Big City Mayor's Caucus 2005, 3).

Horizontal intergovernmental relations – connections *among* municipalities – are progressing faster in Nova Scotia than are vertical relations *between* municipalities and the federal and provincial governments. Shared resources and training opportunities are possible after municipalities enter into regional emergency measures organizations (REMOS). REMOS have been negotiated in two of the municipalities covered in the present study: Truro and Kings County. Regional pooling and improved coordination of emergency response was an identifiable benefit of the amalgamation of municipal government in HRM and CBRM.

The HRM Emergency Coordinator's Office is located in the Dartmouth building, which houses the provincial Emergency Management Office and the federal representative of Public Safety Canada. This simple physical arrangement is credited by emergency planners with enhancing joint training, improving communication during emergencies, and speeding the release of supplies and equipment. Good public policy in emergency management realizes the importance of informal relationships, which are often created during training exercises. The physical proximity of officials representing the different spheres of government helps to smooth out the bureaucratic tangle of logistical, reporting, and accounting relationships among the three levels of government. Of course, the federal representative is a conduit to the Canadian government rather than a policy initiator, but this still helps to augment the regular federal-municipal links, which are exclusively mediated by the province. In the opinion of the emergency planners interviewed, the co-location of emergency offices puts Nova Scotia ahead of other Canadian provinces.

The executive director of the Nova Scotian provincial EMO enjoys deputy minister status in the provincial government, as previously mentioned. The incumbent interviewed felt that this status enhanced his ability to deal with the federal government. As deputy minister, the EMO director has implemented a project to upgrade the emergency capabilities of the municipalities, which the province encourages, in part with bi-annual tests. He sees the role of the provincial EMO as a hub providing guidance to the municipalities, along with evaluation of their emergency response plans. There are no explicit penalties for a lax emergency plan, but the publication of test scores seems to accomplish the upgrading of emergency preparedness across the province. The executive director/deputy minister also visits meetings of municipal councils in order to bolster their attention to emergency preparedness. He would prefer that each municipality have a full-time emergency management coordinator, but this is beyond the budget of many and is not necessary according to at least one emergency coordinator interviewed.

One policy innovation in emergency planning and response in the province is the increasing pooling of equipment and resources among mostly volunteer-based emergency services. Like Truro and Colchester County, Kings County emergency planners responded to the need for more cooperation among municipal units by moving (slowly) toward sharing resources under a regional emergency management organization (REMO). The REMO covers the towns of Berwick, Kentville, and Wolfville, together with the Municipality of Kings County. Similarly the Colchester County REMO saw Truro agree to share resources with the smaller communities such as Stewiacke and Bible Hill. These agreements are just common sense, according to interviewees, although the details of what resources are to be shared and under whose authority can require extensive bureaucratic negotiation.

Intergovernmental cooperation in emergency planning is strongest at the lower levels of government. REMO cooperation commits municipal governments to regular interaction in planning and responding to emergencies. Relations between municipalities and the provincial government are dominated by formal legislated requirements for mayors and CEOs to prepare for emergencies, but also by informal relations among emergency officials, especially in HRM. No municipal official or politician interviewed had made any attempt to bypass the province to expedite financial flows, for example under the DFAA arrangements. Only the mayor of HRM was seeking to change federal policies in concert with the Big City Mayors Group. The federal government long provided training of emergency managers and responders at the Canadian Emergency Management College at Arnprior and now offers courses in Ottawa. In Nova Scotia, training for heads of emergency measures organizations is mandated under the Emergency Management Act, 2005.

Generally, the federal government seems to be a remote player for municipal emergency planners and responders, except for the provincial emergency officials and the HRM emergency measures organization, thanks to their links to the federal representative in the Dartmouth headquarters.

CURRENT POLICIES IN FOUR MUNICIPALITIES

Perhaps because emergency planning at the municipal level is both mandated and regulated by the province, there is not much variation in emergency policy among the municipalities studied. There is, however, at least one difference between HRM as a "big city" and the other units studied. In HRM, the mayor actively seeks to influence federal policy by working with mayors of other big cities to achieve greater federal leadership in setting standards for training and communication. The mayors of smaller municipalities interviewed for this study are largely policy-takers rather than policy-makers in this field. They are aware of their responsibilities under the Emergency Management Act, and all of those interviewed had ready access to the bulky manual of practical emergency procedures generated by the provincial EMO. They are inclined to treat emergency management as a technical issue, for the most part, and to delegate responsibility to their chief administrative officers (CAOs), who direct emergency operations centres when necessary. The CAOs also advise when to declare a local state of emergency, so as to trigger support from the province.

Truro

Truro has a population of roughly twelve thousand and a broad commercial base including a textile factory and agricultural support businesses. It is the largest municipal unit in Colchester County, which itself has a population of roughly thirty-five thousand. Truro describes itself as the "hub" of Nova Scotia, since it is located on the Trans-Canada Highway and on the main rail link from Halifax to points west. Crashes and spills are thus among the most likely emergencies, along with hazards from light industry. The main challenge to emergency planners in Truro, however, is from the flooding of the Salmon River, which is linked to the night tides of the Bay of Fundy. Despite this threat, a flood plain study funded by the province and Town of Truro and the Municipality of Colchester County found that a "cut and fill" approach could be sustained and thus allow further development in the flood plain (Town of Truro 2000). Buildings in one of the town's shopping malls bear watermarks from floods in 1998 and 2003. The heavy spring rains in 2003 caused extensive damage, a state of emergency was declared by the mayor, and roads, schools, businesses, and government offices were closed. In March 2008 the town received the final installment of $96,344 from the province, totalling $1.3 million in compensation for the 2003 floods negotiated by the province under the federal Disaster Financial Assistance Arrangements. Mayor Bill Mills graciously noted that citizens value quick and decisive action to help those affected by disaster (Emergency Management Office 2008b). In contrast, the Truro Emergency Measures Coordinator was generally critical of the slowness of executing federal Disaster Financial Assistance Arrangements reimbursement.

The emergency measures coordinator in Truro is also responsible for the neighbouring town of Stewiacke and for Colchester County. A former fire chief, he performs duties on a part-time basis, as is the case with all emergency officials outside Halifax Regional Municipality and Cape Breton Regional Municipality and believes this part-time commitment is adequate for emergency planning purposes. He is enthusiastic about the benefits of regional emergency planning, a recent policy initiative in several parts of Nova Scotia and thinks that with regional cooperation, local resources are adequate to handle most emergencies. The Regional Emergency Measures Organization (REMO) facilitates communications and sharing of equipment such as generators.

Kings County

The Municipality of the County of Kings in the Annapolis Valley of Nova Scotia was incorporated in April 1879 and currently has a population of close to fifty-eight thousand, according to the 2006 census. The county headquarters are in Kentville, the largest town in the county and one that experiences periodic flooding of the Cornwallis River. The Municipality of Kings is in the primarily agricultural community of the Annapolis Valley, where emergency responders expect to encounter fire, flooding, highway accidents, and possible transport-related spills of hazardous goods. As in Truro, the municipal units of Kings County have agreed to work under a regional emergency management coordinator, who in 2007 was the emergency management coordinator for Kentville (Town of Kentville 2006). It took a few years of negotiation and amendments to each unit's bylaws to achieve this framework for cooperation. The CAO of Kings believes that regionalization helped with the coordination of physical and human resources and with setting priorities among other CAOs in the units. These preparations seemed satisfactory because, according to the Kings CAO, most public complaints have been about slow cost recovery after emergencies rather than inadequate preparedness.

As a question of governance applicable to both Truro-Colchester and Kings, we should note that the director of the provincial EMO encourages, but does not require, regionalization. He advocates for regional cooperation during regular tours of the various municipalities and in semi-annual (recently increased from annual) meetings of the province's emergency measures coordinators.

The Municipality of Kings County is fully engaged in the emergency management network, which is coordinated by the provincial EMO. The CAO reported frequent visits from the Western Zone controller and hosted a zone emergency coordinator's meeting in October 2006. In recent years, topics of concern to the administrators have included avian flu preparation and the availability of Department of National Defence resources from Camp Aldershot and the Greenwood base. The CAO was fully briefed on his role as head of an Emergency Operations Centre (EOC) in the event of an emergency and believed that the province was playing a helpful role in setting the pace for municipalities. He commented that the workload for emergency preparedness in the largest Nova Scotian rural municipality was high, including regular reviews of the emergency plan, on-site visits, and risk analyses. The process of regional coordination has helped to sensitize municipal politicians to the issues of emergency management, and each town in Kings County is engaged in emergency planning.

First responders are largely volunteers, and it is up to them to make decisions on managing an emergency – the EOC is there to support them, according to the Kings CAO. Overall the leadership of the province in this policy field received a positive rating from the Kings CAO and the emergency coordinator. The federal government in contrast was seen as largely "not there" for the Municipalities of Truro and Kings, and emergency management officials have made these concerns known to the regional representative of Public Safety Canada.

Cape Breton

Cape Breton Regional Municipality (CBRM) was formed in 1995, amalgamating eight former municipalities, boards, and agencies in the County of Cape Breton. CBRM has a population of approximately 106,000 and combines sparsely settled agricultural communities with industrial and post-industrial Sydney. Like all municipalities in Nova Scotia, CBRM is required in section 10 of the provincial Emergency Management Act to prepare emergency plans and to submit them to the provincial department to ensure their adequacy and their consistency with other plans in the province. This policy is formally implemented through the CBRM Emergency Measures By-law C2, which established a Municipal Emergency Measures Organization, an advisory committee, and a planning committee chaired by the emergency measures coordinator, John Dilny. CBRM is in the Eastern Zone of the province's coordinating structure. Quarterly meetings offer a valuable chance for emergency measures coordinators in the region to learn about available resources, to be briefed on standards, and to appreciate shortfalls in their plans and practices. In the opinion of the province's Eastern Zone controller, amalgamation greatly improved the implementation of emergency response policy in Cape Breton. Mutual aid agreements enhanced the capabilities of smaller units, even though some cling to the old regime rather than yielding control to regional authorities. Emergency services in CBRM are supported through a state-of-the art regional communication center, which provides for enhanced 9-1-1 call-taking and dispatching of municipal police and fire services (Cape Breton Regional Municipality 2008). There is a synergy between amalgamation and the provincial policy of evaluating municipal emergency planning every two years.

Planning for emergencies and coordinating emergency preparedness efforts in CBRM involves learning about the community and

the potential hazards it faces; developing informal and formal partnerships with other organizations; identifying needed resources
and skills; developing procedures at all levels of the response network; outlining the general roles, responsibilities, and duties of all
assigned emergency-related functions under the plan; and allowing
key personnel with related emergency response responsibilities to be
educated, trained, and involved in exercises to test the plan (Cape
Breton Regional Municipality 2009). Although CBRM emergency
preparedness has improved since amalgamation, one interviewee
believed that there was more work to be done, since the capabilities
of some smaller units are not able to meet demands.

Interviews in CBRM showed planning to cope with pandemics to
be well under way in 2006 but in need of more time and resources. A Health Services Emergency Preparedness Working Group
met monthly, including EMO Nova Scotia and representatives from
Public Health and from the District Health Authority. A strategic
planning committee including a Health Canada representative met
bi-monthly, but the Cape Breton representative interviewed believed
that the federal government was not effective in communicating on
pandemic issues and was worried that there would be a three- or
four-day delay in responding to an outbreak of infectious disease.
She noted that there were no federal guidelines on how to plan for
pandemic response.

Good public policy requires preparation for probable contingencies, and an infectious disease pandemic has a high enough probability in this regard. Planning requires measures to cope with an
expected casualty rate from disease, such as identifying key roles
and arranging for replacements in the event of widespread illness-
related absences. In addition the logistics of setting vaccination priorities and delivering the vaccines must be dealt with. Emergency
response workers, including volunteers, should be part of this protocol, no less than front line health workers. CBRM seems reasonably
advanced in this aspect of public policy, although our research found
that there were no major exercises to rehearse pandemic responses.
However, municipal officials seemed confident in emergency communications capabilities. More than other units researched for this
study, CBRM has links with Aboriginal authorities for planning purposes. The CBRM emergency measures coordinator noted that federal
jurisdiction complicates communication between First Nations communities and the municipality but that as an example of multilevel

governance, Aboriginal Affairs and Northern Development Canada has held emergency preparedness sessions for First Nations in Cape Breton in which the municipal emergency measures coordinator was a participant.

The Membertou First Nation is one of five Mi'Maw communities in Cape Breton and one of the thirteen in Nova Scotia. The Membertou budget has grown from $4 million to $65 million over the past ten years, and even a brief visit to the community impresses one with high-quality infrastructure such as a convention centre, a casino, a restaurant, and health facilities.

Membertou First Nation emergency planning operates independently of municipal government, since the community is not subject to the provincial Emergency Management Act. The Membertou have prepared for weather and other emergencies and cooperate with the provincial health services in CBRM regarding pandemic planning. The band has struck its own pandemic planning committee in which provincial public health officials participate. For regular emergency management the Membertou have a contract with CBRM to provide fire and water services. In 2007, the Cape Breton Regional Police Service (CBRPS) replaced the RCMP as the unit responsible for policing Membertou. They have constructed a second access road to the reservation and have emergency generators to provide heat in the shelter of the convention centre. The Membertou have communication instruments to inform the roughly eleven hundred band members of emergency procedures. In a community of this size, though, word of mouth may be more effective than community radio or newsletters. The situation is similar to municipal emergency planning, which is significantly enhanced by informal contacts and personal relationships among first responders and administrators.

Halifax Regional Municipality

The area now governed by HRM has experienced several emergencies attracting national media attention in recent years, and officials continue to look back on the major disaster of the Halifax explosion of 1917 for lessons in the challenges of sound emergency preparation. In particular, the city must prepare for the hazards associated with port, rail, and road transport. Weather emergencies entail demand for shelter, emergency power, and other social services. Pandemic planning is of special interest to HRM and the province, since the city houses the provincial government and several major hospitals. The urban core of Halifax itself is partly located on a peninsula, which poses challenges for any emergency evacuation, and even regular road works combined with a minor accident on one artery can paralyze commuter traffic. Across the harbour from Halifax, the twin city of Dartmouth is home to an oil refinery and an industrial park with an array of light industrial firms, many using hazardous chemicals, and the naval base in Halifax adds to traffic levels in the town and harbour and could also attract terrorist attention. For this reason, the facilities and the personnel of the military base are part of the HRM emergency planning inventories.

The HRM emergency measures coordinator is a full-time position involving much interaction with agencies from all spheres of government, as well as with volunteer groups. Until the creation of HRM, there were four part-time emergency measures coordinators for the Cities of Halifax and Dartmouth, the Town of Bedford, and the Municipality of the County of Halifax. Municipal amalgamation in 1995 led to the creation of a full-time role, whose present incumbent reports frequent contact with Public Safety Canada, as well as links with Environment Canada and Transport Canada. The creation of this role is one exception to the rule that amalgamation of HRM was "something dramatic that [Premier] Savage could do without affecting most people in any way" (Sancton 2004, 127). The EM coordinator sees the relationship with the regional federal representative as positive. Unlike emergency management personnel in the federal government, the regional representative understands the particular needs of the HRM, and relationships established during regular working hours and in training sessions make for more efficient communication during actual emergencies. The advantage of proximity is evident during an emergency: the HRM coordinator can tell his provincial and federal counterparts what resources are necessary to manage the event, and they can immediately tell him what is feasible, which he can then formally request through the protocol of a letter to the province, relayed in turn to the appropriate federal agencies. The alternative to this shortcut would be for the EM coordinator to convince HRM that outlays are required, after which he would be allowed to contact the province, which in turn would contact Public Safety and Emergency Preparedness Canada. If military, physical, or human resources are required, the federal minister would contact the Department of Defence, which in turn would approve the use of these capabilities. As long as the working relationship with the provincial EMO is good, the HRM coordinator can expedite responses to emergencies through informal working arrangements.

Despite the usefulness of informal contacts with governmental and NGO partners in emergency response, the HRM emergency measures coordinator noted that it was important that municipalities not try to bypass the provincial government, even though this mediation means inevitable delays in processing and releasing DFAA payments. However, he believed it would improve policy implementation if municipalities were present at meetings concerning the Joint Emergency Preparedness Program (JEPP), since first responders know best their specific needs for things like generators and fail-safe communications systems.

As a person close to the front line, the HRM emergency measures coordinator was interested in improving the management of emergency sites. There are two basic models for managing emergencies: "incident command" allows each department involved (fire, police, social services) to command its own resources, and "emergency site management" gives the coordinator temporary powers to manage resources for the duration of the emergency. The emergency measures coordinator felt that the federal government could do more to standardize the procedures for managing emergencies, initially focusing on site management and standards of training for managers. As noted earlier, this more active federal role was also advocated by Mayor Peter Kelly as part of the Big City Mayor's Caucus Working Group.

SOCIAL FORCES

Every element of society has some interest in emergency management policies, but there is little evidence that this latent interest has been actively influencing public policy in Nova Scotia. Apart from complaints about tardy restoration of power, public opinion seems relatively quiet on the subject. Society is, however, very involved in emergency management through the activity of volunteer firefighters and search and rescue personnel, without whom emergency management is too expensive for smaller municipalities to offer. Social actors are mainly involved as service delivery agents, rather than direct participants in policy formulation. The Red Cross, for example, channels volunteer activity when it provides beds, registration of displaced persons, and other services during emergency operations. But while it is present at planning exercises and operations management, the Red Cross does not advocate broader changes in policy priorities, for example, toward mitigation rather than response.

Volunteer capacity is being highly taxed by the demands on emergency response and by shrinkage in the volunteer base. Provincial fire marshal, Bob Cormier, hosted a meeting of volunteers in November 2007 that attracted coverage in local television, radio, and print media. The gist of his concerns focused on rural-urban migration and commuting patterns, both of which leave rural areas understaffed. As a result, he commented, "we are having difficulties maintaining basic services." The provincial government offers free vehicle registration (with distinctive license plates) and a $250 tax credit for volunteers, but Mark Parent, then the minister responsible for emergency services, noted that the limits on resources are "a major concern" (Simpson 2007).

Most businesses have a financial interest in reliable power supplies and swift responses to natural and man-made disasters. Yet the chambers of commerce in the province do not have emergency management in their portfolio of lobbying objectives, and businesses tend to be targets of emergency planning rather than shapers of policy. For example, one project of the provincial EMO is to persuade businesses to develop pandemic influenza contingency plans. The insurance industry is an exception to this generalization about involvement in policy. According to the Atlantic spokesperson for the Insurance Bureau of Canada (IBC), the insurance industry seeks to influence policy chiefly by raising awareness of the rising costs of disaster losses, which it achieves primarily through funding the Institute for Catastrophic Loss Reduction (ICLR). The IBC does not seek to influence or support emergency planning at the provincial or municipal level, except through the research disseminated by ICLR.

The Red Cross plays a major role in emergency response across Canada. In Nova Scotia, the organization enjoys a unique status. It plays a quasi-governmental role because of a formal contract with the province to provide services during a time of emergency. In return, the province provides modest financial support to the Red Cross for crisis preparation. This was initially negotiated in 2000 at sixty thousand dollars and was increased to eighty thousand dollars by 2006 and is subject to increase. The Red Cross performs a range of services during emergencies and is thus accorded a seat at the table when Emergency Operations Centres are activated. The DCS is the main partner, since the Red Cross undertakes to provide shelter and food to affected families and to emergency workers themselves. Thanks to donated resources, the Red Cross can provide financial assistance to pay for food, temporary rental expenses, transportation, medical supplies, and so on. The organization even undertakes to provide long-term recovery assistance "when other resources are not available or are inadequate" (Canadian Red Cross 2006).

Canadian Red Cross volunteers are recruited and trained to deal with a number of emergency management tasks, including computerized registration and inquiry systems for disaster victims, shelter management, and first aid. The community-based network of these volunteers is a valuable resource for Nova Scotia and one that needs to be constantly maintained, but predictably, the task of recruitment and training is easiest during and after a major emergency. Thus, when an extended, province-wide power outage in November 2005 tested the ability of the Red Cross to provide a large number of comfort shelters, Western regions of the province were not as well prepared as others (Interview 8). Although the general public has high expectations of the ability of the Red Cross to deliver services, most people appear to be unprepared to sacrifice their personal time to train for and to maintain emergency response skills.

The Canadian Council of Churches (CCC) is involved in emergency management in Nova Scotia through the vehicle of the Regional Advisory Group on Emergency Planning. The CCC established this body after the National Advisory Group was formed in 2002 in order to facilitate a role for the pastoral community in emergency response. The council signed a memorandum of understanding (MOU) with Nova Scotia's DCS that spells out the process by which pastoral services may be offered to victims and witnesses of disasters. Apart from providing spiritual comfort, the CCC shares resources to provide language translation, to meet special cultural or religious needs such as diet, to offer contacts with members of the church in other communities, and to provide referral services. The CCC does not typically have pastors with psychological training.

The MOU specifies that the CCC advisory group on emergency planning should wait to be called on by the provincial Emergency Measures Organization and to refer requests from other agencies to the EMO before acting (Canadian Council of Churches 2004). This MOU is not a binding contract, but it does illustrate how an organization with national resources can be networked with provincial and ultimately municipal emergency measures organizations.

The human resources available for emergency management clearly range wider than the celebrated skills of fire and rescue personnel. Psychological counselling is often valuable to victims, relatives, and witnesses and workers involved with major emergencies. A protocol of the emergency planning process in Nova Scotia provides that EMO staff can call on the psychological services organized by the Association of Psychologists of Nova Scotia through its Post-Trauma Services Committee. The protocol specifies that the services are provided free of charge in the short-term, roughly seventy-two hours from the conclusion of the emergency (APNS 1998).

Other coalitions of social forces are active in emergency social services. For example, an association of vulnerable groups such as seniors and disabled persons was formed in Nova Scotia after hurricane Juan in 2003 and the blizzard of 2004. A particularly specialized and professional NGO is the Special Care Emergency Preparedness Association of Nova Scotia (SCEPA). This group organized itself after the weather events of 2004 drew stark attention to the special plight of seniors and persons with disabilities during emergencies. The group has been welcomed into the emergency management and social services framework.

The SCEPA approached the director of emergency social services (DCS), John Webb, and asked what they could do to better prepare themselves for emergency situations. This cooperative venture struck a responsive chord in the DCS. One outcome was a brochure to inform target groups of general emergency preparation plans and the special preparations required by persons with disabilities – for example, attaching Braille or fluorescent labels to emergency supplies. The twenty-eight-page brochure was published on 28 April 2006 and was co-sponsored by phone provider Aliant and Nova Scotia Power. The SCEPA coalition aims to foster communication between members of the association, to provide training and educational programs in emergency management methodology, and to develop and promote standards for emergency management professionals (SCEPA 2008).

Another interesting example of civil society coalition building is the Nova Scotia Critical Incident Stress Management Network (NSCISMN). In its statement of understanding with the Canadian Red Cross, Nova Scotian Region, this network aims to support individuals and agencies interested in critical incident stress management. The network maintains a directory of member volunteers and assists in education and communication. The Nova Scotia Fire Officers Association has a Critical Incident Stress Management team (CISMT) made up of members and close associates of the Nova Scotia Fire Service. This team is a sub-committee of the Fire Service of Nova Scotia and on a volunteer basis it provides crisis intervention support primarily to the Fire Service in Nova Scotia. The team is registered with the International Critical Incident Stress Foundation (see http://www.icisf.org for more information), and it follows ICISF standards and policies (CISMT n.d.). The CISM network provided employee assistance services in the wake of the Swissair 111 crash at Peggy's Cove in 1998 (Health Canada 2007). The CISM networks are loosely linked to the federal level through Health Canada Employee Assistance Services.

In summary, emergency planning is enhanced by networks of social actors interlinked with government agencies. Professionals volunteer their time not only during emergencies but also during the interim periods of emergency preparation.

Business

The general business sector, although commercially interested in continuity of operations during emergencies, does not devote as much effort to emergency planning as do non-profit social actors. A policy analyst at the Halifax Chamber of Commerce commented that apart from a general concern about pandemic planning, the business community in HRM has not asked the Chamber of Commerce to take up the issue of emergency planning. This may be broadly indicative of the business community in general. For instance, the theme of business continuity plans topped the agenda for the 2007 World Conference on Disaster Management in Toronto. The primary sponsors of that conference were government agencies: Public Safety Canada, the province of Ontario and the City of Brampton. The only primary sponsor from the business sector was General Dynamics Information Technology, a company specializing in defence and intelligence systems (WCDM 2007).

Two exceptions to the general passivity of business toward emergency policy are Aliant and Nova Scotia Power. These corporations provide essential services and are thus consulted in Nova Scotian planning exercises and EMO proceedings. Aliant is present as the primary telecommunications company in the province. Its ability to maintain 9-1-1 services and landline telecommunication during a crisis is critical to preserving public confidence in government management of disasters. Nova Scotia Power is at the EMO operations table, since the maintenance or timely recovery of power to consumers and business is one of the key objectives for any emergency response operation.

Another exception to business passivity is the insurance industry, which has a special interest in ensuring that governments are able to take measures to reduce damage to private and public property. The insurance industry is a significant component of the Canadian economy, with registered annual sales of $40 billion (IBC 2012). The Insurance Bureau of Canada (IBC) can thus afford to support research at the Institute for Catastrophic Loss Reduction, which was founded by Canada's property and casualty insurers in 1998. The Atlantic vice-president of the IBC noted that the organization had made significant efforts to influence the federal government, in part through the House of Commons Federal Finance Committee and Senate Finance Committee in pre-budget submissions, but he observed that IBC contacts with Public Safety Canada declined after 2000, perhaps owing to the new focus on security against terrorism.

Disaster mitigation is a priority for the IBC, and it worked closely with Public Safety Canada on the National Disaster Mitigation Strategy (NDMS), originally announced by Prime Minister Jean Chrétien and implemented in 2008. In 1998 the IBC co-sponsored workshops on a national disaster reduction strategy in which all spheres of government participated. It was this initiative that led to the government's announcement of the NDMS. The strategy prioritizes efforts to reduce disaster impacts, including structural mitigation efforts such as floodways and dykes and non-structural mitigation efforts such as hazard mapping, public awareness, and building code enforcement. The Public Safety Canada website lists the Institute for Catastrophic Loss Reduction as one of the partners in the NDMS. Insurers are still working with Public Safety Canada, but the IBC expressed some frustration about the slowness of the process, which produced at least fifteen drafts of the strategy by late 2006.

The IBC also gives advice on emergency policy at the provincial level. Regional offices of the IBC have strong relationships with emergency managers across the country. The IBC has a Claims Emergency

Response Plan, which facilitates government communication with the insurance industry after emergencies. In the opinion of the IBC Atlantic vice-president, Nova Scotia does make emergency planning a priority, and "the province's emergency management authority is professional and competent." But the IBC questions whether enough resources are put into the mitigation aspect of emergency policy, since the focus is on preparedness to manage, rather than to prevent or mitigate, emergencies.

Politicians are attentive to emergencies for the most part during the event and in the aftermath. But in the interests of swift recovery, they tend to try to rebuild in disaster-prone areas, rather than to make the more difficult choices to relocate vulnerable communities. It is only recently that DFAA program funds can be used for mitigation purposes, in answer to a long-standing demand of advocates (Public Safety Canada 2012). Like other respondents, the IBC believes that the federal government is not playing enough of a leadership role, despite the financial resources it brings to bear through the DFAA and JEPP. Still, the IBC remains positively engaged in trying to improve public policy in this area, as one would expect from an institutionalized professional group with high stakes in better mitigation of disaster costs. We can expect to see continued attempts by the insurance industry to improve public policy on emergency planning in mitigation of disaster costs, an area singled out by the IBC as the chief source of friction in its lobbying and consultation efforts.

EVALUATION: WHAT IS GOOD EMERGENCY PLANNING POLICY IN NOVA SCOTIA AND HOW COULD IT BE FURTHER IMPROVED?

Good public policy can be measured in terms of efficiency and impact. We expect good policies to be well designed and to produce outcomes with a net public benefit. To equip every household with an emergency power generator would not be an efficient use of scarce resources, but to ensure that every municipality has a warming shelter with an adequate back-up generator is a good compromise. Emergency preparedness is in its essence an iterative policy field: lessons learned from each emergency event provide opportunities for practitioners to test and improve their response systems. Training for expected emergencies under an "all hazards" response plan is good public policy, and we expect all those involved, from firefighters to administrative officials, to practise their roles and test equipment and communications. We cannot judge emergency planning by the impact of events of large magnitude on affected populations. But if there had been no improvements in communication or infrastructure after the major power outage of November 2004, for example, there would have been good reason to criticize both the utilities and their public regulators. Good public policy would ensure a readiness to meet the needs for shelter and for infrastructure protection to prevent the emergency from becoming a disaster. Similarly, the practical goal of policy in pandemic planning is not to prevent any impact on the broader population – through mass vaccination, for example – but rather to prepare contingency plans for vaccination according to essential roles and to make quarantine plans to reduce transmission of disease.

The philosophy of emergency managers is to prepare and rehearse uniform responses to a variety of hazards. Thus, policy aims to make sure that there is a predictable and orderly series of responses, beginning with municipal emergency site management and drawing on resources from higher levels of government as needed. Subsidiarity in emergency response is efficient public policy, even though some politicians and public officials and the IBC seek more federal leadership regarding standards in training and communication and in mitigation measures.

Good public policy should not download all emergency response to citizens or to municipal government. As the Insurance Bureau of Canada emphasizes, major savings are to be realized both by governments and by insurers if steps are taken ahead of time to reduce vulnerability to weather hazards. This is the central objective of the National Disaster Mitigation Strategy (Public Safety Canada 2008a). In addition, fifteen percent of recovery funds reimbursed through the Disaster Financial Assistance Arrangements can now be earmarked for mitigating losses in the future. This policy recognizes the problem with previous DFAA rules, which did not reimburse municipalities who make improvements to floodways, dykes, and other infrastructure. The third part of the IBC plan is to make disaster preparedness part of the culture of public policy-makers, in the same sense that environmental impact assessments are now an expected part of public and private development projects (Baker 2004, 19–20).

Reducing the public and private costs of responding to emergencies makes sense. Each sphere of government would be keen to off-load the cost of mitigation, but since the current DFAA guidelines are specific about the federal contribution, one can envisage that a similar formula could be negotiated for mitigation programs. Improving infrastructure is one way to protect existing properties. Another way to mitigate losses would be to prohibit or penalize developments in areas statistically prone to various kinds of weather emergencies. Insurers and the federal government could exclude certain kinds of losses from reimbursement, and municipal governments could perhaps reinforce this with differential tax rates.

Emergency planning relies on volunteers to act as first responders and to provide comfort to displaced persons. Nova Scotia is fortunate to have well-trained emergency personnel under a framework of readiness established by a proactive provincial coordinator. It might be possible to strengthen this volunteer base through some kind of provincial or even federal tax credit. There is certainly room for improvement in the recognition of volunteers. In April 2007 the leader of the Nova Scotia New Democratic Party raised a question for the minister responsible for EMO about support for Nova Scotian volunteers' radio licensing fees. Industry Canada levies a $40 fee and was seeking payment for six radios from a search-and-rescue team in North Queens that was already in dire financial straits from a $3,000 repair bill for a bus used to transport it to emergency scenes. There are about one thousand search and rescue volunteers in the province organized into twenty-four teams (Valley Advertiser 2007). Would the federal government not be better served to forego the $40,000 from radio licenses in order to keep search and rescue volunteers well equipped? This issue, as much as the larger questions of allocating resources for emergency mitigation, illustrates the need for more multilevel collaboration in emergency planning.

CONCLUSION

The purpose of this chapter has been to show how federal, provincial, and municipal governments, as well as non-governmental actors, collaborate in emergency planning and management in Nova Scotia. The federal government's role is a distant but central one, since it is the order of government most responsible for financial relief and compensation. Most of the ground-level activities with respect to emergency management are carried out by local governments and the volunteer sector, while the provincial government mediates communications and relations between the federal and municipal governments. As well, the province relies on legislation to encourage emergency preparedness at the municipal level.

INTERVIEWS

1   Boutlier, Albert, Membertou Public Works, Sydney. 3 July 2007.
2   Boyd, Bill, chief administrative officer, Town of Kentville and acting emergency measures coordinator. 13 June 2005.
3   Brideau, Roy, chief administrative officer, Town of Wolfville. 21 June 2005.
4   Dilny, John, emergency measures coordinator, CBRM, Sydney. 15 June 2005.
5   Easterly, Lee, Health Services Emergency Preparedness Working Group, CBRM. 15 June 2005.
6   Forgeron, Don, Atlantic vice-president IBC, Personal correspondence, 16 January 2007.
7   Kelly, Peter, mayor HRM, Halifax. 7 June 2006.
8   Kersten, Catherine, Red Cross field associate, NS Region Western District, Kentville. 16 June 2005.
9   Lawlor, Joanne, Atlantic Canada Red Cross, July 2006.
10 MacLaughlan, Craig, Emergency Measures Office, Province of Nova Scotia, Halifax. 2 June 2005.
11 MacPherson, Crawford, director of community development, County of Colchester. 2 June 2005.
12 Manuel, Barry, emergency measures coordinator for Halifax Regional Municipality. 17 May 2005.
13 Mills, Bill, mayor of Truro. 1 June 2005.
14 Musgrave, Winston, eastern zone controller, Truro. 21 June 2005.
15 Shaw, Carl, emergency measures coordinator for REMO (Truro, Stewiacke, Colchester County). 2 June 2005.
16 Smith, Brian, chief administrative officer, Municipality of Kings County. September 2006.
17 Smith, Gary, emergency measures coordinator, Municipality of Kings County. September 2006.
18 Stead, Robert, mayor of Wolfville. 21 June 2005.
19 Webb, John, director of emergency services, Nova Scotia Department of Community Services. 19 July 2006.

REFERENCES

Association of Psychologists of Nova Scotia (APNS). 1998. "APNS-EMO Memorandum of Understanding for Post-Disaster Psychological Services." http://www.apns.ca/trauma_apnsmemo.html.

Baker, Mark. 2004. *Natural Hazards and the Canadian Insurance Industry.* Toronto: Institute for Catastrophic Loss Reduction.

Big City Mayor's Caucus Working Group on Public Safety, Security and Emergency Preparedness. 2005. *Emergency Response Management Model for Canadian Municipalities.* Unpublished draft report.

Canada. 2007. *Emergency Management Act.* S.C. 2007, c. 15.

Canadian Council of Churches. 2004. CCC-EMO *Memorandum of Understanding for Post-Disaster Pastoral Services.* Signed 4 June 2004.

Canadian Red Cross. 2006. "What We Do During Disasters." http://www.redcross.ca/article.asp?id=000302&tid=025.

Cape Breton Regional Municipality. 2008. "About CBRM." http://www.cbrm.ns.ca/portal/community/about/default.asp.

– 2009. "Public Safety." http://www.cbrm.ns.ca/public-safety.html.

Canada. 2007. *Emergency Management Act.* S.C. 2007, c. 15.

CTV News. 2006. "Salty Fog Cited for Nova Scotia Power Outages." 5 November. http://www.ctv.ca/servlet/ArticleNews/story/CTVNews/20061105/novascotia_fog_outage_061105?s_name=&no_ads.

Critical Incident Stress Management Team Nova Scotia (CISMT). n.d. "About Us." http://www.nsfirecism.ca/aboutus.asp.

Emergency Management Office. 2008a. "EMO Zones." http://emo.gov.ns.ca/content/emo-zones.

Emergency Management Office. 2008b. "Truro Receives Disaster Financial Assistance." http://www.gov.ns.ca/news/details.asp?id=20080317002.

Federation of Canadian Municipalities. 2006. *Emergency: Municipalities Missing from Disaster Planning.* Ottawa: Federation of Canadian Municipalities. http://www.fcm.ca/english/documents/emergency.pdf.

Health Canada. 2007. "Critical Incident Stress Management (CISM) Services." http://www.hc-sc.gc.ca/ewh-semt/occup-travail/empl/stress_e.html.

Insurance Bureau of Canada (IBC). 2012. "About IBC." http://www.ibc.ca/en/About_Us/index.asp.

McBean, Gordon, and Dan Henstra. 2003. *Climate Change, Natural Hazards and Cities.* Toronto: Institute for Catastrophic Loss Reduction.

Nova Scotia. 2005. *Emergency Management Act.*

Public Safety Canada. 2008a. "Canada's National Disaster Mitigation
     Strategy." 13 February 2008. http://www.publicsafety.gc.ca/prg/em/
     ndms/strategy-eng.aspx (accessed 12 March 2012).
– 2008b. "Guidelines for the Disaster Financial Assistance Arrangements."
     http://www.publicsafety.gc.ca/prg/em/dfaa/dfaa-guide–2008-eng.aspx.
– 2012. "Disaster Financial Assistance Arrangements (DFAA) – Revised
     Guidelines." http://www.publicsafety.gc.ca/prg/em/dfaa/index-eng.aspx.
Sancton, Andrew. 2004. "Why Municipal Amalgamations?" In *Canada:
     The State of the Federation, 2004 – Municipal-Federal-Provincial Rela-
     tions in Canada*, edited by Robert Young and Christian Leuprecht,
     119–37. Montreal and Kingston: McGill-Queen's University Press.
Simpson, Jeffrey. 2007. "'Woefully Under-funded' Fire Departments Strug-
     gling to Provide Basic Services." *Chronicle Herald*, 16 November.
Special Care Emergency Preparedness Association (SCEPA). 2008.
     "Bylaws." http://www.freewebs.com/scepa/BY-LAWS.pdf.
Statistics Canada. 2005. *Kingston Emergency Preparedness Survey.*
     Ottawa: Statistics Canada. http://www.cityofkingston.ca/pdf/emergency/
     SurveyResults_2005.pdf.
Tattrie, Jon. 2010. "The Master of Disaster." *Halifax Magazine*, 14 Sep-
     tember. http://halifaxmag.com/2010/09/cover/the-master-of-disaster/.
Town of Kentville. 2006. *Regional Emergency Management By-Law.* 12
     July. http://www.kentville.ca/documents/bylaws/remobylaw.pdf.
Town of Truro. 2000. *Truro-Colchester Inter-Municipal Land Use By-Law
     for Flood Risk Areas.* Truro, NS: Town of Truro and Municipality of
     Colchester.
Tyson, Marian F. 2005. Deputy Minister, Department of Community
     Services. *Memorandum to Nova Scotia Municipal Chief Administrative
     Officers re Emergency Social Services.*
Valley Advertiser. 2007. "Radio License Fee Burden." 24 April.
World Conference on Disaster Management (WCDM). 2007. "Emergency
     Management and Business Continuity: Working Together." Seventeenth
     World Conference on Disaster Management. http://www.wcdm.org/.

4

Multilevel Governance Challenges in Newfoundland and Labrador: A Case Study of Emergency Measures

NORM CATTO AND STEPHEN TOMBLIN

INTRODUCTION

Concern about emergency services and the need to work together across jurisdictions and policy fields, either in preventing unexpected emergencies or in dealing with them when they occur, has attracted much attention in multilevel policy discussions around the world. There has been a focus on conceptualizing the problem of "interdependence" and the factors and conditions that improve the prospects for bringing different institutions from various levels of government, civil society interests, resources, and knowledge innovation together in a way that might help promote more effective governance. A key challenge in multilevel governance is finding ways to pool problem-definition capacity and implement solutions based on common perceptions and experiences. In Canada, a diverse federal country with very different resources; local, provincial, and national police forces; and insular policy traditions and processes, there is much we still need to learn about the challenges associated with renewing governance based on common objectives and frameworks that may be more the result of an external crisis or pressures, than local needs.

Unless, or until, we map out these geographical, socio-economic, and institutional-political constraints across silos, there will be limited opportunities to construct common knowledge and new partnerships and to improve outcomes. Federalism as a model provides flexible ways for respecting diversities, but renewing governance requires mapping out key drivers and constraints for new reforms.

Our examination of the issues surrounding emergency measures in Newfoundland and Labrador (NL) is designed to generate new critical insights into the key informal and formal mechanisms that have been inherited and relied upon to adapt to new problems or challenges such as sudden emergencies. Among the differences that might explain certain responses in dissimilar provinces are factors such as capacity, political will, breadth of support, and the kind of political resources required to effect fundamental change.

At present, provincial government initiatives are under way to more fully involve municipalities in NL in emergency planning, response, and recovery. The requirement for all municipalities to generate an emergency response plan in order to be eligible for provincial funding is one manifestation of this. However, the variation in the comprehensiveness and currency of these plans and the requests by municipalities for assistance in their formulation are also manifestations of some of the challenges involved.

Our discussions with municipal, provincial, and federal stakeholders and diverse groups of social stakeholders captured the experiences, tensions, and problems of bringing together different interests and the struggle to deal with a new "interdependent problem." This has led to a clearer understanding of policy adjustments and the challenge of renewing governance in a province that has a strong tradition of relying on informal mechanisms for dealing with community emergencies. As discussed below, several central and interrelated themes emerged:

- *The relatively weak municipal policy capacity.* Many municipalities lack the personnel, technical expertise, and resources to implement emergency plans, assess hazards, or formulate effective policies.
- *The urban-rural divide.* The St John's metropolitan area (Northeast Avalon) represents approximately 40 percent of the population of NL and substantially greater proportions of both the economic resources and professional capacity for coping with emergencies and formulating policies and plans. Challenges within this urban agglomeration exist, but they are fundamentally different from those confronted by most other communities in NL. The historical division between "town" (St John's) and "the Bay" (all other areas

on the island of Newfoundland) remains significant in all matters of governance.

- *The asymmetrical treatment of communities.* Partly in response to the urban-rural divide and partly reflecting historical divisions, substantial asymmetry exists in the NL government's approach to communities of different size throughout the province.
- *Risk perception and demand for emergency measures policies and responses.* Substantial differences exist between the physical realities and associated costs (e.g., the types and frequencies of various natural hazardous events) and public and governmental perceptions of the likelihood and impacts of events.
- *The relatively weak federal presence.* The role of the government of Canada in emergency measures issues is perceived as limited; respondents note a tendency towards strictly reactive responses to individual events, rather than proactive planning or policy formulation.

Social and policy learning involves making incremental and sometimes "big bang" changes to old ideas, interests, and institutions connected with the status quo. Renewing governance and transformation are influenced by the levels of perceived crisis but also by the power of inherited processes and mechanisms when compared with new paradigms or visions. In small NL communities, without the expertise, personnel, financial resources, and institutional support required to effect major reforms, promote integration, construct a viable alternative to the status quo, or even to cope with events as they unfold, any reform will be slower than in places where the prospects for change are better. Declining and aging populations in almost all rural communities have led to the forced consolidation of provincial services ("regionalization"), which has resulted in the closure of small hospitals, local schools, and even garbage dumps. In the absence of any tradition of regional government, such as a county system, the political amalgamation of smaller communities may be economically desirable, but it is always contentious. Because the current distribution of legislative districts favours rural voters, it is more difficult to embed new reforms or to build the required coalition support. Despite certain industrial benefits of regionalization, in terms of equity there are also clear losers. In the end, this situation does affect the viability of any reform package.

Levels of industrialization, specialization, training, bureaucratic capacity, and rural-urban divisions, which are connected with geography and the political economy, must also be considered in our attempt to trace the history of the struggle to reform emergency services based on new external circumstances and pressures. Effecting change requires a sense of a problem (or crisis), a new vision that reflects core values and objectives, a coalition in support of new reforms, and institutions capable of getting the problem onto the radar screen and implemented.

While there may be increased support for an integrated vision for emergency services, there are bound to be key challenges in building social capital and promoting common priorities across a highly decentralized federation with much social diversity. In some regions, the lack of municipal government and a reluctance to embrace regional forms of governance has undermined knowledge construction and policy learning.

While the issue of coordinating across jurisdictional systems has been greatly influenced by new integrating theories, there are both drivers and constraints in any convergence call for transformation based on new interdependent realities. Insufficient focus has been placed on learning more about the inherited cultural and institutional constraints that make it more difficult, in practice, to build coalition support or to facilitate bringing different interests and institutions together to enable the building of common objectives and integrated approaches to policy initiatives. We still need to understand a great deal about how culture (informal), historical-institutional traditions, and policy traditions (or lack thereof) shape and influence the conditions required to promote new ways for conceptualizing and responding to new challenges. Our task is to recount the NL story in a way that better explains the challenges of social diversity in an era of interdependence and multilevel governance.

During the 1990s, New Public Management was embraced by boosters as a dynamic way to make government more transparent, build partnerships, and promote policy learning across departmental silos (Dunn 2002; Young and Leuprecht 2006). However, path-dependency theorists and other neo-institutionalists questioned whether such changes were likely or probable given inherited patterns of state-society relations (Pierson 1994). In the context of a divided NL, clear challenges emerged in building structures and processes that further reinforced urban-rural gaps and problems, and differences in rural and urban capacity created different opportunities and pressure to experiment. Not surprisingly, it was easier for the provincial government to adopt a more bilateral, incremental approach to emergency restructuring. Even with provincial government interest in regionalization and other attempts to strengthen emergency social-policy learning across policy silos and communities, clear cultural, economic, policy, geographical, and political forces were working against the push for new approaches to governance. Huge gaps in local government and social capacity remain across the province, and they are reflected in different views on centralization versus decentralization and state versus civil-society experiments in public policy. While urban areas appear to be more willing to play an active role in emergency planning and building coalitions, such a vision is not as popular, or embedded, in smaller community structures. There are substantially different perspectives on who should be responsible for constructing and implementing some key services and on whether the central government (in this case the province) should be working unilaterally, top-down, or as a banker. In our interviews, we were informed that it has been difficult to establish a common framework or policy approach for emergency services in NL. Rather, the tendency has been towards flexible policy, in order to ensure that when emergencies hit, they can be resolved by other stakeholders. In the meantime, every effort has been made to rely on an asymmetrical emergency system that encourages building knowledge and capacity where doing so is considered feasible, particularly in Northeast Avalon. Indeed, this form of restructuring goes back before 1949 and is very much part of the unique public policy history of NL.

CONTEXT MATTERS

Newfoundland and Labrador's perspective on emergency measures is shaped by several factors. Climate, meteorology, and terrain influence the majority of hazards and are contributing factors both in the occurrence of events and the responses to them. The economy of the province, which is dominated by resource-based activities and the necessary extraction, support, and distribution services, accentuates exposure to some natural hazards and restricts the occurrence of industrially related emergencies. As of May 2012, the province had a single petroleum refinery, one pulp-and-paper mill, and very limited amounts of other industrial activity that might lead to major chemical emissions or toxicological emergencies.

Positioned on the geographical and geo-political eastern margin of North America, Newfoundland and Labrador is not perceived by its residents as susceptible to politically motivated attacks. However, on September 11, 2001, centres throughout the province were confronted with the necessity of providing humanitarian aid to more than thirteen thousand stranded air travellers and flight crew. This event highlighted both strengths and areas requiring improvement in emergency response (Morrison 2003).

Civil strife and disobedience are extremely rare: the last significant incident occurred in March 1959 during a loggers' strike in Badger that resulted in one death. While the province was subjected to the ravages of the influenza epidemic of 1919–21, the lack of recent past experience is reflected in lowered public consciousness of potential biomedical emergencies, even though awareness among public health officials in the province is high.

The island of Newfoundland depends on ferry traffic across the Gulf of St Lawrence for most of its supplies, including food (Catto et al. 2006). Since it has an estimated five-day supply on hand (averaged across all foodstuffs), interruptions to water and ground transportation, including disruptions to highway traffic along the single route provided by the Trans-Canada Highway, are reflected almost instantly in empty shelves in food stores throughout the island. Air traffic is also frequently interrupted by weather events between December and April. In Labrador the somewhat tenuous links provided by the gravel-surfaced Trans-Labrador Highway, the coastal ferry service (operative only during the summer north of Cartwright), and air traffic are also subject to meteorological interruptions. Similarly, long transmission lines connecting hydroelectric plants in western and central Newfoundland to the main population centre in the northeast Avalon Peninsula, as well as to the Bonavista and Burin Peninsulas, are vulnerable to failure during ice storms accompanied by high winds (Catto 2012).

All groups of emergency measures responders in Newfoundland and Labrador have traditionally focused on events resulting from natural hazards. A plethora of meteorological and geological events since 2000 has necessitated intense activity by first responders and government agencies but has also spurred efforts by the provincial government to re-examine its emergency measures policies and response capabilities and to more accurately assess the socio-economic impacts. The emergencies that have resulted from human causes, including fires, commercial and industrial accidents, mishaps to aircraft and shipping, and the aircraft diversions of September 11, 2001, have also provided an impetus to reexamine the procedures. The investigation of preparedness and response by the government of Newfoundland and Labrador has been delegated to NL Municipal and Provincial Affairs through Emergency Measures. The positions of deputy minister of emergency planning and chief executive officer, fire and emergency services, have been created to address these issues (Interviews 11 and 12).

In May 2012, the processes of re-examination and formulation of technical and logistical responses were still ongoing, although with substantial progress. In order to assess the variety of perspectives involved in multilevel governance issues, discussions and semi-structured interviews were conducted with representatives of municipal governments of communities ranging in population from less than a hundred to more than a hundred thousand (St John's); with provincial government representatives from several ministries, including Municipal and Provincial Affairs, Environment and Conservation, Natural Resources, and Health and Community Services; with federal government representatives from Public Safety Canada; and with representatives from non-governmental organizations involved in emergency response throughout Newfoundland and Labrador. Additional perspectives were gathered during discussions of responses to climatological, geological, and meteorological hazards with representatives from the Newfoundland and Labrador ministries of Environment and Conservation, Natural Resources, and Transportation and Works; from the NL Rural Secretariat (Ministry of Innovation, Trade, and Rural Development); with representatives from Natural Resources Canada, Fisheries and Oceans Canada, and Transport Canada; and with numerous residents of Newfoundland and Labrador.

The Nature of Hazards and Emergencies

Most emergencies in Newfoundland and Labrador are triggered by natural phenomena, rather than by human activities. Since 2000, the province has seen a multiplicity of events, with significant economic impact (see Catto 2012). Between 2000 and 2009, direct economic costs resulting from natural hazards in NL exceeded $120 million. This total cost was surpassed by a the cost of a single event in 2010: Extratropical Transition Igor, which affected much of eastern Newfoundland on 20–21 September 2010, is currently estimated to have caused at least $160 million in direct damage to human property, and one human life was lost (Catto and Batterson 2011; Catto 2012). Allowing for additional indirect costs, the estimated impact of major natural hazards per resident of NL per year between 2000 and 2011 has exceeded $300.

Igor was not a unique storm for Newfoundland: hurricanes and extra-tropical cyclones and transitions are relatively common: two or three events occur in a typical year (Catto 2011; Catto 2012; Catto and Hickman 2004; Catto and Batterson 2011). More precipitation was recorded at St John's during Tropical Depression Gabrielle in September 2001 (Liverman et al. 2006), and higher totals were recorded at some stations during Tropical Storm Chantal in August 2007 (PIEVC 2008). However, the impact of Igor, extending across all of eastern Newfoundland, was unprecedented in comparison to other storm events since 1989.

Mid-latitude storms are significant natural hazards during the autumn, early winter, and spring (Catto 2011, 2012) that have involved repeated destruction and damage to dwellings and infrastructure at key installations, such as the ferry terminal at Channel-Port-aux-Basques. Readiness for hurricanes and storm surges was the focus of a 2006 emergency preparedness exercise held at Channel-Port-aux-Basques, which was coordinated by Health Canada and dubbed Operation Dolphin (see McMillan 2006; Seguin 2006). Flooding related to storm activity is also a serious problem in many areas (Catto and Hickman 2004; Liverman et al. 2006; Brake 2008; Catto 2011; Catto 2012), since the short fluvial systems typical of the island of Newfoundland are susceptible to storm-related flooding and the response time between precipitation and flooding is short. Precipitation from hurricanes is rapidly distributed to rivers and streams, triggering flooding within an hour after the initiation of heavy rainfall (Catto and Hickman 2004). Rain-on-snow events and rapid snowmelts are also significant occurences triggering flooding (Catto and Hickman 2004; Vasseur and Catto 2008). Ice jamming has caused serious flooding at Badger on several occasions, most recently in February 2003 (Picco et al. 2003; Peddle 2004), and at Rushoon, among other locations (Catto and Hickman 2004).

Slope failures, including avalanches, occur regularly in the province (Catto 2010; Catto 2012). More than fifty deaths have resulted from slope failures since 1823, in addition to more than thirty deaths from avalanches (Batterson et al. 1999; Liverman et al. 2003; Liverman et al. 2006; Liverman 2007). Investigations generally occur after an incident: there is usually no proactive mapping or anticipatory zoning and municipal planning (Interviews 11, 12, 14, 15, and 16). A slope failure in April 2007 at Daniels Harbour that destroyed one house necessitated the permanent evacuation of several others. Decisions and management of the efforts were largely the responsibility of the Newfoundland and Labrador Emergency Measures Organization (Interviews 11, 12, and 13). Subsequently, all the structures deemed at risk were purchased by the provincial government and destroyed. Slope movement had occurred in October–November 2006, so the failure in April 2007 was not surprising to the community. The residents in all the destroyed houses had been evacuated in November 2006, and although there had been some complaints and uncertainty concerning the necessity of the evacuation, the action proved to be appropriate.

Wildland fires pose another hazard for NL (Catto 2006; Catto 2010; Catto 2012). More than 90 percent of wildland fires in Newfoundland result from human activities. In Labrador, lightning-strike fires account for a larger proportion, but human-caused fires nevertheless represent the majority. Winter hazards include ice storms (Brake 2008; Vasseur and Catto 2008), snowstorms, blizzards, and prolonged winter accumulation.

Although industrially related emergencies are less common than those related to natural events, incidents have occurred. Recent emergencies necessitating a coordinated response and local evacuations have included the March 1998 North Atlantic Refinery Fire, Arnolds Cove (two-pile fire at Glenwood; no deaths), fires in Donovans Industrial Park, Mount Pearl (25 March 2005; no deaths), and the fibreglass plant fire at Holyrood (24 October 2007; no deaths).

Newfoundland and Labrador was directly affected by the events of September 11, 2001, when seventy-eight aircraft and thirteen thousand passengers and crew were diverted, initially to five airports. Subsequently, passengers and crew were accommodated in shelters and private homes in many communities, with an average stay of six days (Morrison 2003). Over 250,000 meals were provided, some 6,000 volunteers assisted in the relief effort, and 5,000 cots were provided for passengers stranded in St John's and Gander. The total cost of purchased services (accommodations, meals, telephone services, bus and vehicle rentals) exceeded $1 million, and $665,000 was subsequently reimbursed to health boards, municipalities, and school boards for expenses incurred. Much of the effort was voluntary, and in St John's the number of willing (but untrained) volunteers exceeded the available roles (Interviews 11, 12, and 13).

Perception of Risk

Because of the nature of the hazards, the general perception among Newfoundlanders and Labradorians is that the province has relatively few risks and hazards. The province lacks volcanoes and terrestrial focus earthquakes, two of the most commonly identified natural hazards affecting other jurisdictions. Events that occur more regularly and that have caused fatalities, such as avalanches, have been seen as random occurrences confined to particular areas, rather than as general hazards. Flooding, storm surges, and washouts have occurred commonly but are often perceived by residents to be a feature of the local environment to be endured, rather than a hazard to be combatted. Tragedies that result from combinations of weather events and human responsibility, such as the loss of the oil-drilling rig *Ocean Ranger* in February 1982, are also commonly considered to be human-induced rather than natural disasters (Catto 2012).

The fortunately limited death tolls of some of the largest natural disasters lessen the general profile and perception of risk among residents. The Burin Tsunami, which killed twenty-eight people had largely faded from public memory outside the affected areas until interest was revived by Alan Ruffman's efforts in 1994 to publicize the seventy-fifth anniversary of its occurrence (see Ruffman 1995a). Subsequent interest was maintained by the popular account by Hanrahan (2004). In the aftermath of the Banda Aceh Tsunami (26 December 2004), interest greatly increased. However, since 2006 both the interest in and the awareness of tsunami activity have declined in Newfoundland.

Hurricanes and winter storms are both common hazards, and both have resulted in significant death tolls. The Great Independence Hurricane of 12–16 September 1775 killed possibly as many as four thousand people in eastern Newfoundland and St-Pierre et Miquelon (Stevens and Staveley 1991; Ruffman 1995b; Stevens

1995; Liverman et al. 2006), which would rank it among the worst in the North Atlantic Ocean in the past four hundred years (Hyndman et al. 2008). However, the lack of documentation of the event has generally limited its visibility, even among professional hazard investigators.

On 27 September 2005, flooding triggered by an extratropical transition originating from Hurricane Rita destroyed several homes in Stephenville. The volume and intensity of rainfall was comparable to that generated by Extratropical Transition Hazel II in 1954, which resulted in more than eighty deaths in Toronto. In Stephenville, however, no loss of life or serious injuries occurred. The combination of better weather forecasting and prediction, effective warning, and the mid-day arrival of the storm (in contrast to Hazel II's unexpected arrival late at night over the Humber River) allowed pre-emptive evacuation of the area (Catto 2012). Subsequently, homeowners raised no objections to the purchase and eventual demolition of their flooded houses; indeed, some residents outside the flood-affected area and the designated flood plain requested that their houses be included in the relocation program. In Stephenville and elsewhere in Newfoundland and Labrador, people regard hurricanes, tropical storms, and extratropical transitions as manageable hazards. The reaction to the damage caused by Extratropical Transition Igor was similar: the difficulties were seen as the result of inadequate preparation (the failure to install large culverts, lack of maintenance), and it was assumed that better pre-storm management would have resolved most of the issues.

Winter storm events are routine in Newfoundland and Labrador, especially during years when La Niña conditions are combined with a positive phase of the North Atlantic Oscillation. During winter 2000–01, St John's Airport received 6.88 metres of snow, a relatively low total compared to communities in central and western Newfoundland and in Labrador. The repetitive nature of the events has effectively minimized sensitivity in communities, and adaptive capacity is high. Although complaints are endemic among many residents, the hazard is regarded as manageable, or it would be if snow-clearing policies and equipment were improved. Winter weather is seldom discussed as a significant hazard.

The combination of no recent large death tolls, the geographically limited nature of some of the events, and the resilience of the communities in the face of common hazards and events, including winter storms and disruptions to ferry traffic, influences the perception of risks and hazards from natural causes. To most residents and policy-makers in NL, human-related events, including the *Ocean Ranger* sinking, the aircraft diversions of September 11, 2001, and the 12 March 2009 offshore crash of Cougar Helicopters Flight 491 (seventeen fatalities), are more central to thoughts about "emergencies" and emergency measures. In NL, search-and-rescue is a high-profile, high-priority public policy and political issue, whereas emergency measures planning and preparation have a lower profile.

ORGANIZATION AND GOVERNANCE

Historical Influences on Governance Responses

NL has always found it difficult to promote convergence, bring different interests together, work across historical urban-rural structures, and transform governance practices based on universal frameworks. It is therefore not surprising that promoting a more integrated approach to emergency measures has not been a smooth process (Interviews 1, 3, 8, 11, 12, 13, and 16). From a historical perspective, policy reform has proved difficult in a place well known for insularity: for divergence, not convergence. NL has a tradition of both underdeveloped political institutions and fragmented political culture (Wilson 1974; Noel 1976; Elkins and Simeon 1980), which has constrained policy-political homogenization (Hillier and Neary 1980; Alexander 1983; Conrad 1988; Sinclair 1988; Blake 1994).

From a constitutional perspective, NL's historical roots began with a British-style cabinet-parliamentary government. However, in 1934 a British-appointed commission emerged as a result of the collapse of the old regime. Urban-rural conflicts over economic development priorities, an exploitive trucking system controlled by merchants in St John's, religious conflicts, and a corrupt party system all contributed to the rise of a commission government dominated by experts. It also created major socio-economic divisions that could not easily be transformed through political and policy actions.

In 1949, NL joined the Canadian federation, but only after a very divisive referendum and a narrow victory in favour of joining. It was not a period of celebration, and there was much resistance to change. For Joey Smallwood, the political operative who would become Newfoundland's first premier, it was a time of opportunity, when Newfoundland would move towards modernization. Several institutions were started anew or seriously upgraded in the quest to reinvent all major socio-economic processes and political institutions based on new modernization theories. However, promoting new forms of integration and interaction proved difficult. The new province was far behind the others in terms of socio-economic development. To make matters worse, the bureaucracy remained undeveloped until the 1970s. All of this added to the challenge of reversing fragmentation and the rural-urban divide. Within this context, formal public policy processes and mechanisms lacked the capacity and power necessary to remake society and to promote modern forms of integration.

Long-standing NL orientations to public policy debates and actions persist. A number of the people we interviewed suggested that there are huge differences between small and large communities in the province and that it has never been easy to establish a common perception of the needs and requirements for emergency services. Nor has it been easy to form common perceptions of the best way to develop more effective responses. There have also been efforts to encourage the municipal governments to embrace new regional partnerships and to bring different stakeholders (the RCMP, the Red Cross, the Salvation Army, fire services, and the City of St John's) into the policy exercise to a greater extent. Our interviews with non-governmental stakeholders suggested that coordination across networks was rare and that negotiations often took place on a bilateral basis, for example between the City of St John's and the province, making it difficult to get different interests together to agree on objectives, protocols, and priorities (Interviews 11, 12, and 16).

Within the Municipal Affairs department, emergency services have received more attention, and the establishment of regional emergency services sites in Clarenville, Grand Falls, Deer Lake, and St John's (with a partial "hybrid" site in Labrador) has clearly demonstrated the provincial push for capacity building and knowledge transfer on a regional basis. There have been several challenges for renewing governance and promoting new forms of integration among social forces and the defenders of the status quo (Tomblin 2007).

In municipal governance, there is no strong tradition of municipal engagement, which has precluded concerted efforts to build civic capacity or public support (Interviews 1, 3, 12, and 16). Outside

St John's, until recently there was little effort placed on promoting innovative systems of municipal governance. For the most part, small communities lack critical policy capacity, resources, and the kind of knowledge essential for good policy practice. Rural-urban divisions have remained salient since 1949, and political parties, the electoral system, the municipal system, and even patterns of federal-provincial conflicts have done little to reverse the status quo. Even today, St John's is seen as being unique in planning capacity: for example, it has a pandemic plan, but NL does not.

A number of people interviewed suggested that St John's was unique in having the capacity and social forces necessary for launching a new, more rational "emergency measures" game. However, from the perspective of the City of St John's, there has been no crisis or challenge big enough to warrant dramatic change (including Igor). As well, within a more integrated structure, there would be problems discussing planning issues, which would be perceived as more urban than rural. In practice, each event or problem reflected a unique context. St John's was granted much autonomy, and efforts were made to ensure that city officials and social forces were well prepared and informed. The province preferred to step in only when there was pressure to do so: for example, if a crisis or event required more resources. For middle-range problems, efforts were made to upgrade or construct emergency measures regions. Such an approach would reinforce and encourage new partnerships, policy learning, and innovation. Finally, small communities would not be forced to carry out policies that were not sustainable. Instead, there was clear support for pooling provincial partnerships and resources to ensure that when a crisis emerged, there was an emergency response (Interviews 11–16).

As argued by Dunn (2004, 297–332), the federal, provincial, and local governments have struggled with new regional forums and efforts to collaborate in dissimilar policy fields. In the case of regional development boards in NL, the federal and provincial governments had different ideas about community engagement, which complicated efforts to coordinate activities and build capacity within economic development zones. In the competitive federal-provincial context since 1990, sparked by a historic battle over equalization, it has been even more of a struggle to get federal, provincial, and local government decision makers and stakeholders to work cooperatively on economic development or on US-inspired security issues.

Several of the people we interviewed highlighted how politics shape outcomes and efforts to promote common objectives and values.

NL faces challenges similar to those of other provinces that are also operating in a knowledge/service-based economy: only about 10 percent of the labour force in any province is directly employed in the natural resource-based economy (Howlett 1996). Although NL has experienced common labour trends, it should not be assumed that convergence and inevitable changes occur in the same way everywhere. As indicated by Dunn (2004), while certain federal officials in community development have been keen about building regional capacity, the provincial government was concerned that regionalization and community building would improve urban (St John's) planning capacity while weakening rural independence and resources. The demands of operating emergency services in a place that is affected by and worries more about storms than terrorist attacks require making sure that efforts to build capacity, knowledge, and training also reflect local and provincial emergency preparedness requirements and preventive needs.

We were told in some of our interviews that there is not much empirical evidence to demonstrate that Joey Smallwood, the premier of Newfoundland from 1949 until 1972, was deeply committed to policy experimentation (Interviews 11 and 12). He operated in a period of fiscal federalism, when the province received generous transfers with few conditions attached. He was a dominant premier and failed to build a very sophisticated planning structure. Although Smallwood's transportation and resettlement policies reinforced the growth of "industrial areas," other government policies on taxation and transfer payments tended to have the opposite effect, by restraining the migration of people from the outports to the urban system (Economic Council of Canada 1980, 20). Since 1949, NL has been a laggard more than a leader with respect to most policy fields. Deeply embedded historical divisions, coupled with limited resources and a fragmented political economy made it difficult to build integrated policy networks (Brock 1996, 100–3). There has therefore been little opportunity for policy networks and interests to emerge or become important instruments of political communication.

Under Joey Smallwood, a clear preference emerged for a top-down, deferential approach to politics and public policy agenda setting and decision making, with the result that there was little opportunity to engage civil society in the process of transformation. In practice, most of the representatives in the legislature either came from or had commercial attachments to St John's, and little emphasis was placed on building a modern bureaucracy or constructing the kind of spatial-functional policy networks essential for bringing different interests together, working across boundaries, and constructing shared objectives and mental maps. Even the municipal system of government remained undeveloped. Between 1949 and 1971, NL was a poor province that featured strong executive dominance, but without the modern municipal or bureaucratic decision making normally associated with policy innovation.

Since joining Canada in 1949, NL has endeavoured to upgrade infrastructure, change the culture, and build market and state capacity. Historically, NL had a merchant-dominated economy ("trucking") and political system, and before Confederation there was much reliance on church, family, and other civil society mechanisms to define and solve problems. There were few municipal governments in the province, and only the city of St John's has a long history of defining and solving problems. Viewed comparatively, cultural, institutional, and rational policy traditions have little in common with other Canadian provincial contexts.

Before we compare and contrast emergency planning ideas, mechanisms, and experiences, we need to highlight both the drivers and the constraints that have always made it difficult to bridge rural and urban differences and priorities. Issues are propelled onto the public agenda by various forces, including a sudden crisis. But even with a crisis, different priorities or needs may work against achieving consensus on a course of action. For some, there may be clear benefits to pushing new joint ideas, interests, and institutions that promote more interdependent socio-economic realities. For others, adopting an integrated public policy approach may complicate matters. In the past, self-reliant rural communities have tended to be more suspicious of new policy initiatives that promote universal trends at the expense of diversity.

Emergency Management and Agenda Setting

Canada is not alone in dealing with the issue of emergency management. For various reasons, the issue of being prepared for anticipating, preventing, and dealing with disasters (whether human or natural) has been pushed onto the public agenda in many countries.

It is important to recognize that only certain events have shaped the policy discourse in a fundamental way. In Newfoundland and Labrador, the sinking of the *Ocean Ranger*, or the crash of Cougar Flight 491, were not pivotal events in the rise of emergency planning as a policy issue (as opposed to search and rescue). Nor have they had a significant impact on the conceptualization, visioning, or plans for implementation in policy debates. When viewed in this way, controlling the nature of the discourse or embracing new best practices associated with emergency preparedness is influenced by the power and independence of the state and the various societal actors involved. The evidence suggests that disaster events, including Igor, are not sufficient to induce marked policy change. However, in the aftermath of Igor, increased efforts have been made to engage communities. Emphasis has been placed on the preparation of municipal emergency plans and on the examination of the preparations for and responses of government departments to emergency events.

Critical events and periods of crisis may provide windows of opportunity for advancing new ideas, but whether they become institutionalized or not depends on the interplay of ideas, interests, and institutions. In the case of emergency preparedness, renewing governance required finding new incentives to encourage policy learning and the building of networks across jurisdictions. The push to keep emergency preparedness was greatly influenced by the goal of fighting terrorism, using the example of New York, to better coordinate across police, fire, public health, and other services. It was a powerful vision backed by the most powerful nation in the world.

According to the people we interviewed, there was little question that new efforts to promote emergency measures policy innovation and integration were greatly influenced by external events and actors (Interviews 1, 3, 5, 11, 12, and 16). However, the pace and direction of policy reform and the discovery of new ways to resolve internal differences and work across silos greatly depends on local conditions. Despite the crisis conditions in other places, it has been more difficult to convince NL communities to prioritize emergency measures. St John's and Mount Pearl were already well positioned to utilize new innovations and capable of dealing with new policy problems. From the provincial government's perspective, St John's was always well prepared for emergencies and even had a pandemic plan. With the support of Memorial University, the Eastern Health Authority, police, fire, NGOs, and other essential civil society organizations, there was much capacity and network support for pursuing an emergency measures policy agenda (Interviews 11, 12, and 16).

But this was not the case in rural areas. Smaller communities lacked the ability to initiate emergency preparedness or training. Without a strong rural-urban coalition in support of new policy innovation, it became difficult to continually stress the importance of emergency measures among communities that lacked interest in policy experimentation. Old practices continued, especially the tradition that each community (or its residents) should take care of its own emergencies: when this was not possible, others would be brought in to help. According to our interviews, there was a hier- archy of community responsibilities for emergencies, beginning with the individual, progressing to the local community, to adjacent communities in the region, to the province, and finally to the federal government (or military) if the emergency could not be contained (Interviews 1, 3, 5, 10, 11, 12, and 16). Neil Bradford argues that "policy innovation is the product of these interactions: ideas, institutions, and interests all matter. Each plays a part in the unfolding drama of large-scale policy change that begins with acceptance of the need for 'something different,' proceeds through confirmation of new conceptions of cause and effect relationships, and closes with consolidation of new administrative practices" (1998, 12).

With the terrorist attacks of September 11, 2001, the tsunami, Hurricane Katrina's devastation in New Orleans, ice storms in Montreal, floods in Stephenville, Mad Cow disease, SARS, and other disasters, there has been much political pressure for renewing governance, increasing capacity for dealing with disasters, policy learning, and making sure that problems are identified and dealt with. Similar shifts in agenda setting and restructuring have taken place in the past. For example, after the Great Depression old ideas and institutions appeared to be incapable of dealing with the challenges of industrialization; reform was required. The rise of the Keynesian welfare state created a different system of values, objectives, and market-state traditions. It was a period of nation-centred industrialization. By the early 1970s, conditions had changed, and the combination of high inflation and unemployment created a sense of crisis that was never resolved by incremental changes. The autonomy and power of established ideas, institutions, and interests weakened, and questions were raised about whether the status quo could survive in a new era. By the 1980s, free trade, globalization, continental-ism, and the decline of national powers became the norm both in Canada and around the world. The combination of the provincial governments of Alberta, British Columbia, and Quebec and the col-lapse of the National Energy Policy helped to propel the rise of a new model for restructuring, a model that sought to delist public services, reduce government regulation, reinforce globalization, and build new partnerships with civil society. It was an attempt to respond both to local diversity and to pressures for more local con-trol, while dealing with the challenges of globalization and the pre-dicted decline of the nation-state. The crisis spawned by September 11 created other questions about whether these kinds of relation-ships were capable of defending and protecting against the challenge of global terrorism.

The sense of crisis surrounding emergency preparedness is very much connected with the historical-policy context and the devices relied on to make sense of changing realties. In fact, the pace and direction of reform tells us a great deal about the impact of culture, capacity, institutions, and interests in the struggle to shift priorities, especially if they are being imposed externally.

September 11, 2001, reinforced the need to prepare for unexpected events. Having the ability to deal with emergencies has been further reinforced by a heightened sense that a local capacity to manage dif-ferent unpredictable events is absolutely essential in an era of "glocal-ization," where local and global are said to matter. However, there are clearly political challenges associated with cutting the embedded programs and services that may be necessary to pay for more effect-ive emergency responses. Since these emergencies frequently occur in areas with little human capacity, it is a political challenge for local governments to pay for emergency preparedness services that may or may not be needed. Aside from events such as September 11, there are few examples of public interest groups or parties lobbying for more investment in emergency services at the expense of health, for example. In Canada, local governments are not co-equals, and there are limits to the extent to which local emergency issues can domin-ate provincial or national agendas.

In order to understand the challenges of effecting policy change, it is important to see that emergency planning involves contestation, shifting priorities, building knowledge capacity, and merging policy and jurisdictional networks based on best practices. It requires renewing governance, coordinating, planning, collecting data, building infrastructure, and establishing a common vision where different interests can work together to promote common values and objectives. Yet emergency planning is difficult to reform based on a common vision, since the inherited formal and informal structures tend to be very complex local, provincial, national, and even international systems. Given these dissimilar interacting systems, it has been difficult to renew governance by establishing clear lines of authority and responsibility across jurisdictions.

It has also been difficult for groups outside government to support a process that is likely to diminish their influence. For example, whether volunteer firefighters should be able to drink beer in the firehall when not on duty (which has been a long tradition) has recently become an issue. Insurance issues, as well as a sense that more "professional" behaviour may be required, have led some communities to prohibit the practice. The fact that these volunteers promptly resigned rather than follow the no-beer guideline (CBC 2006) is one example of the challenge of promoting common practices across inherited systems. Establishing a standard framework and vision for emergency management is an important part of renewing governance, but there are few mechanisms for bringing different jurisdictional and stakeholder interests together to coordinate training and capacity-building and for evaluating effectiveness. In the past, various civil society organizations have played a significant role in helping communities and people in stress. In the new environment, they have needed to scramble to demonstrate that they are capable and willing to respond to new challenges. Emergency planning also requires developing a specific emergency response plan for the province, one that outlines who is in charge, what the protocols are, and how resources are to be shared or distributed. These are not easy questions to resolve even within unified hierarchical systems. Nor are they framed in a way that could be easily resolved in public debate.

As in most policy debates, Canada is compelled to pay attention to the US policy agenda. Reforms to emergency services are seen as a way to demonstrate Canadian support for America's campaign against terrorism. Since 1980 and the Joint Emergency Preparedness Program, provincial and local governments have received federal monies to improve emergency preparedness. In December 2003, a new federal department (now amalgamated with Public Safety) was established, linking emergency preparedness with national security.

By highlighting and strengthening emergency preparedness in this way, the federal government sent a clear signal that it was determined to keep the issue of emergency planning on the public agenda.

The approach reflected changes in internationalization, but the new agenda and discourse created both winners and losers. Given the power and responsibilities of provinces in this policy field, coupled with the diverse range of stakeholders involved, it has not been easy reaching a consensus on priorities or approaches. Part of the challenge in effecting change in emergency preparedness can be linked to different political-policy contexts. A major political-policy struggle in Newfoundland and Labrador is the challenge of managing rural-urban differences in capacity and perspective. While a province-centred, universal plan for disaster preparedness may make sense in St John's, questions are bound to be raised about its practicality for other areas (Interviews 1, 2, 11, 12, and 16).

Emergency management policy innovation involves making choices about priorities and resources, which may or may not serve the needs of different communities and interests. In discussions with various stakeholders, we were told repeatedly about the benefits of bringing different interests together, constructing common perceptions, and building new bridges across multilevel silos. There appears to be much interest in improving policy capacity, mapping out gaps in emergency preparedness, and finding ways to take advantage of new external funding to improve systems of delivery and policy learning across both territorial communities and functional policy networks. There was some interest (especially in Municipal Affairs) in upgrading key pieces of legislation, such as the Emergency Measures and the Fire Prevention Act, and facilitating new, more integrated and interactive approaches to fire services, police services, health professionals, and the like (Interviews 11, 12, and 16). Nevertheless, there has not been much opportunity to place emergency measures firmly on the public agenda: even the impact of Igor was insufficient.

At the provincial level, people within the Department of Municipal Affairs have been active making sense of current structures, processes, and gaps in emergency preparedness. In response, a regional strategy has emerged, financed by the provincial government, for upgrading and coordinating emergency services, policy learning, and cooperation. Clarenville, Grand Falls, Deer Lake, and St John's have been designated as regional emergency planning sites. There are also plans for adding Labrador as a regional site in the future. Although there has been a tradition of regionalization in health care, education, and municipal restructuring in NL, the concept of regionalization has not advanced very far among municipalities. Provincial government decision makers felt it was counter-productive for innovative policy planning in emergency preparedness and prevention among local governments.

Demographics and Community Stressors

Emergency measures policies and practices do not function in isolation. Any response is superimposed on a range of other socioeconomic and technological factors. The overall demographic pattern since 1990 has involved significantly decreasing and aging populations in Newfoundland (outside the urban St John's Census Metropolitan Area (CMA) and the Northeast Avalon), coupled with job losses in resource-based occupations. Similar trends, although less pronounced, have marked most communities in Labrador.

For emergency management and the organizations and individuals responsible, the accelerating differences in demography and socio-economic conditions between the St John's CMA and the rural areas pose challenges. The levels of service in the rural areas are subject to decline as the population decreases and ages. The recent phenomenon of an increasing transcontinental commuter workforce has also decreased the availability of community members to participate in emergency management organizations.

THE LEGISLATIVE AND REGULATORY FRAMEWORK

Overall responsibility for emergency planning in Newfoundland and Labrador rests with the NL Ministry of Municipal and Provincial Affairs (Interviews 11, 12, and 16). Fire and Emergency Services NL, including the Newfoundland and Labrador Emergency Measures Organization (NLEMO), has the legislative authority to act in cases of emergencies, whether caused by nature or human agency. The staff of Fire and Emergency Services has increased from less than five permanent staff positions in mid-2008 to twenty-seven in May 2012.

Traditionally, first responses to emergencies have most often been coordinated by the Office of the Fire Commissioner, whose importance stems from the effects of the Great Fire of 1892 in St John's, which destroyed most of the city core, as well as other serious fires, such as one that burned most of Harbour Grace in 1944. With the larger number of volunteer fire departments outside the major urban centres, responsibility effectively came to reside with the fire commissioner for coordination of response efforts, dissemination of information concerning the emergency, contacting persons with expertise relevant to containment and response, and efforts at recovery. As a result of the increased emphasis on emergency planning and response, the position of deputy minister of emergency planning was created in 2006. NLEMO, with its own director of emergency services since 2009, and the Fire Commissioner's Office are administrative components of Fire and Emergency Services NL.

Key legislation guiding emergency planning in the province includes three specific municipal acts (the City of Corner Brook Act, the City of Mount Pearl Act, and the City of St John's Act), the Emergency Measures Act, and the Evacuated Communities Act. Provision of policing services is covered under two pieces of legislation, the Agreement for Policing the Province Act and the Royal Newfoundland Constabulary Act. Specific emergencies are addressed in the Communicable Diseases Act and the Fire Prevention Act.

Three Municipal Acts Guiding Emergency Planning

The City of Corner Brook Act, the City of Mount Pearl Act, and the City of St John's Act formally incorporate the named cities and provide authority for each to exercise emergency powers. A city can unilaterally declare a state of emergency if in the judgment of the elected mayor (or councillors, if the mayor is incapacitated) it appears that the city is affected in whole or in part by an earthquake, a conflagration, an explosion, or a disaster; a riot, a civil commotion or an epidemic; a snowstorm or a flood; or a drought or a shortage of water. The state of emergency can be applied to the entire geographical area of the city or to a designated part. A declaration of a state of emergency takes force once it is signed by the mayor of the city and communicated to the public by means of radio, television, or other appropriate media. The declaration allows the closure or restriction of hours for businesses, shops, or places of entertainment; the suspension of shop-closing regulations (allowing vital services to remain open in excess of regularly legislated hours); the restriction or prohibition of the use of streets by vehicles; the imposition of a curfew; and the restriction or prohibition of the use of water in the city.

The intent and spirit of these acts allow municipal authorities to assess local situations and take immediate action without the necessity of prior consultation with other levels of government. Thus, they follow the general practice of initial local response to an emergency, followed only if deemed necessary by application to higher levels of government (Interviews 11–16). Local decision making can produce differences in perception and response: although the supply of municipal water for Mount Pearl and for the western part of St John's comes from the same source, the two cities have imposed different regulations for restrictions on domestic water usage during several years since 2000. No earthquakes, general conflagrations, explosions, riots, or epidemics have occurred in any of the cities since the enactment of these pieces of legislation, although numerous tropical storms, hurricanes, and winter storm events have.

The Emergency Measures Act

The Emergency Measures Act, which was most recently amended in 2008, outlines the procedures for proclaiming a state of emergency based on either a civil disaster (including natural disasters) or an act of war. The act continued the establishment of the Newfoundland and Labrador Emergency Measures Organization.

Under section 2g of the act, an emergency is defined as "a real or anticipated event or an unforeseen combination of circumstances which necessitates the immediate action or prompt co-ordination of action as declared or renewed by the Lieutenant-Governor in Council, the minister, a regional emergency management committee or a council." Emergency measures include the following:

• Preparing and executing all plans and measures that are required to ensure the survival and continuity of the civil government in the province in times of emergency;
• Preserving law and order;
• Controlling traffic, including movement of people, property, and the maintenance, clearance, and repair of roads;
• Establishing areas across the province and providing appropriate services in them for the reception, accommodation, and feeding of persons evacuated from areas;

- Organizing emergency medical services, public health, and welfare measures;
- Organizing firefighting, rescue, and salvage services, as well as radioactive-fallout detection services;
- Maintaining and repairing public utilities;
- Providing assistance to municipalities in the development of emergency measures within their jurisdictions;
- Liaising with the federal government, other provinces, and territories and municipalities that have entered into agreements on emergency matters; and
- Instituting training and public information programs to provide for the continuity of adequately trained and equipped forces to meet the emergency needs of the province.

The legislation requires municipalities to develop emergency plans to be submitted to the minister of municipal and provincial affairs for approval (through NLEMO), with the first version due on 1 May 2012. Approximately 95 percent of municipalities in the province, including all with populations in excess of about two hundred, have submitted plans. The legislation also authorizes municipalities to establish regional emergency management committees, which may consist of representatives of councils of municipalities, committees in local service districts, or other persons representing unincorporated areas. The regional emergency management committee is responsible for the development and implementation of the regional plan.

The legislation allows the minister of municipal and provincial affairs to declare a state of emergency encompassing all or any part of the province. Local consultation or a request from any affected municipality is not required. Although in principle the legislation could place the primary onus on the provincial government, in practice since 1994 the provincial government (through NLEMO) has acted only upon receiving either a formal or an informal request from a municipality. In the case of Igor (2010), an emergency encompassing a broad area of eastern Newfoundland was declared after initial contact with some affected municipalities. When a civil disaster is declared, the NL government has authority to

- Restrict or prohibit transportation and control vehicle access to affected areas;

- Acquire by purchase, lease, or through other methods goods, chattels, or lands;
- Provide relief of suffering by restoring the distribution of essential supplies and the provision of medical, welfare, and other essential services;
- Appoint persons, boards, and committees to perform duties as defined by the Lieutenant Governor, and establish compensation;
- Order evacuation of persons, livestock, goods, and chattels. The province is responsible for arrangements for adequate housing, feeding, care, and protection;
- Gain entry into a house, dwelling, building, or other private property for a purpose relating to a civil disaster or for the welfare and safety of the population;
- Demolish and remove trees, buildings, and other structures in order to reach the scene of a civil disaster or attempt to combat the progress of the disaster;
- Control the procurement, distribution, and maximum prices which can be charged for food, clothing, shelter, fuel, and other necessities of life; and
- Make any regulation that is considered necessary or advisable for the safety, health, and well-being of the population.

Newfoundland and Labrador Emergency Measures Organization (NLEMO)

Under the Emergency Measures Act, NLEMO is responsible for the development and maintenance of emergency preparedness and response and recovery measures to reduce the levels of human suffering and loss of property as a result of an actual or imminent emergency. NLEMO has the responsibility to coordinate and manage any emergency situation and is the only provincial agency that is authorized to control the activities of all police, fire, health, and social services, as well as other services in an area. The Planning and Operations Program is designed to raise the standard of emergency preparedness throughout the province to a point where all sorts of emergencies and disasters can be dealt with promptly and effectively. NLEMO is involved in joint contingency planning with all levels of government, the private sector, and the civilian population.

NLEMO also conducts training and education programs for emergency management and response personnel. The core course is the

Emergency Preparedness Program, periodically delivered by the director of education and training in several locations. Courses are targeted towards first-line responders (fire, police, ambulance personnel), municipal staff (clerks, managers, and maintenance staff), provincial government staff (in Municipal and Provincial Affairs, Natural Resources, Social Services, and Health), and volunteer and non-governmental organizations (ground search-and-rescue organizations, amateur radio operators, the Red Cross) involved in emergency situations. As well, the Emergency Air Services Program provides assistance to the RCMP and the Royal Newfoundland Constabulary (RNC) for search and rescue operations. Assistance is usually in the form of aircraft deployed to search for lost and missing persons.

Evacuated Communities Act

The Evacuated Communities Act primarily addresses issues of consequence in the NL government programs for relocating residents of isolated communities ("resettlement"), including property rights in the abandoned communities. Although not initially formulated to consider evacuations necessitated by disasters, the legislation does allow the NL cabinet to order an evacuation and to declare a community vacant if subsequent re-occupation is deemed to be undesirable.

Police Legislation

Responsibility for policing in NL is divided between the Royal Newfoundland Constabulary (RNC) and the RCMP. The RNC, established and governed by the Royal Newfoundland Constabulary Act, is responsible for policing the Northeast Avalon Peninsula (St John's CMA), Corner Brook, and Labrador City. All other areas are policed by the RCMP under the authority of the Agreement for Policing the Province Act. There are no municipal police forces in NL. Although cities have authority to engage officers to enforce municipal bylaws and parking regulations, they are not involved in policing or in official responses to emergencies.

The RCMP plays a key role in search and rescue efforts, generally taking the lead in terrestrial searches on the island of Newfoundland. It has formal written agreements with the Canadian Air Search

and Rescue Association (CASARA), the Canadian Marine Rescue
Association (CMRA), Parks Canada, and the National Search and
Rescue Secretariat. CASARA is a national not-for-profit organization that provides an organized and trained group of volunteers to
assist the Department of National Defence in carrying out search
and rescue operations. The organization also works with Transport
Canada to promote aviation safety, and 413 Squadron (Goose Bay)
has an excellent working relationship with CASARA. Members of
413 Squadron allow the use of both the Hercules and the Labrador
search and rescue aircraft for CASARA to train members as spot-
ters. The CASARA zone for Newfoundland and Labrador includes St
John's, Gander, Stephenville, Happy Valley–Goose Bay, and Wabush
(Interviews 1–9).

Communicable Diseases Act

The Communicable Diseases Act specifies illnesses and diseases that,
if present in the population, can result in the declaration of a state of
emergency. A long list of specified diseases is periodically updated.
Although some of the listed diseases have not been reported in NL
for many years and although other conditions, such as Creutzfeldt-
Jakob disease and food poisoning, cannot be transmitted between
humans, their inclusion is designed to facilitate emergency response.
Any disease that the minister of health and community services
declares by order to be communicable (in practice, one that could
create a widespread health emergency) can be added to the list.

Fire Services Legislation

In the context of emergency management, fire services are governed by the Fire Prevention Act, which established the Office of
the Fire Commissioner. Local fire prevention is the responsibility of
municipalities, through either professional or volunteer fire departments. The only regional fire department is the St John's Regional
Fire Department, which covers both St John's and Mount Pearl
through agreement between the respective city councils. A regional
fire services committee, consisting of four persons (two appointed
by the Councils of St John's and Mount Pearl, respectively) oversees
the administration of fire protection. In smaller communities, the

volunteer fire department is effectively the first line of response for many forms of emergency.

Staffing and financial support for volunteer fire departments have proven difficult in several smaller communities (Interviews 11–16). Declining and aging populations and shrinking tax bases have resulted in understaffed and under-supported fire departments. In cases where adjacent municipalities are expected to jointly support volunteer firefighting, disputes have arisen over finances. Unfortunately, withdrawals of firefighting services have resulted, with consequences for insurance and property losses owing to delays or refusals to combat fires.

Increasingly, residents of rural communities work on fly-in/fly-out (FIFO) multi-week commuter schedules at jobs based in Alberta and at distant mining operations. Although the FIFO commuters provide a needed tax base to the communities where their families continue to live, their work schedules are not conducive to full participation as "on-call" members of a volunteer fire department. Because most FIFO commuters are males twenty-to-fifty years of age, which is normally the demographic that comprises a volunteer force, the practical unavailability of this group for service creates stresses not fully evident in overall demographic statistics for the communities. In some communities, the scarcity of suitable volunteers has led to older residents forming the majority of the fire departments. High-school students without driver's licenses have also been accepted as volunteers, although they would require transportation to fire scenes.

The Office of the Fire Commissioner plays a critical role in fire prevention, training, and emergency response. Among numerous legislated responsibilities, those pertinent to emergency management include

• Fire Prevention and Life Safety Inspections,
• The establishment/organization and development of fire departments,
• Permitting and licensing individuals to service fire protection equipment and systems,
• Providing education and training to career and volunteer firefighters (in conjunction with NLEMO),
• Assisting in the development of regulations for use in all municipalities governing fire prevention and control,

- Providing emergency response assistance and guidance and fire ground control, and
- Engaging in firefighter training program curriculum development.

Public Safety Canada and Federal Programs

As it is elsewhere in Canada, Public Safety Canada (PSC) is responsible for coordinating federal emergency planning and preparedness for fourteen federal departments. In addition to the national office (Ottawa) and Atlantic regional office (Halifax), PSC maintains a Newfoundland and Labrador office in downtown St John's.

PSC administers the Joint Emergency Preparedness Program (JEPP), which provides funds for provinces and territories to prepare for emergencies (Wallace 2006), the costs of which are shared between the federal and provincial/territorial governments. Eligible projects for funding include emergency planning, emergency preparedness training, and the purchase of emergency equipment. The JEPP was created as a way of encouraging both the federal and the provincial governments to improve their capabilities in dealing with all kinds of emergencies, and its goal to create a uniform level of emergency services across the country. The projects funded under the JEPP must receive resources from both the federal and the provincial or territorial governments. Federal contributions are negotiated on a case-by-case basis. For example, in 1996 the federal government provided $269,320 to the province for several projects, including the purchase of a mobile training and a mass-casualty medical response vehicle for NLEMO. The funding has allowed the creation of a provincial emergency operations centre in St John's that supports a Provincial Emergency Response Team, assisting municipalities with the development of emergency plans and conducting emergency exercises. The town of Happy Valley–Goose Bay was provided with funding for an improved emergency communications system, while Channel-Port-aux-Basques was given funding to purchase an emergency response vehicle capable of handling hazardous-materials incidents for the volunteer fire department (Interviews 4–10, 16).

Since 1970, the government of Canada, through the Disaster Financial Assistance Arrangements, has provided funding to provincial and territorial governments when the cost of responding to, and dealing with, a disaster would place an undue burden on the provincial economy (Interviews 11, 12, and 16). Funding is allocated only for specific emergencies and disasters and only after the receipt of a request from the provincial government.

Summary

The assemblage of legislation, in combination with practice in recent years, has established a pattern of responsibilities and response in the face of an emergency. Initial response is the responsibility of local officials, organizations, and individuals, including volunteer fire departments, the RNC or local detachments of the RCMP, and municipal leaders. A state of emergency can be declared by the mayors of Corner Brook, Mount Pearl, or St John's, based on local information and without consultation with other levels of government. Municipalities are theoretically responsible for requesting provincial assistance, and in theory NLEMO and other provincial agencies cannot respond or intervene without a request, unless a state of emergency is declared by the minister of municipal affairs. In turn, federal government assistance depends on an application from the province. The chain of responsibility requires each successively higher level of government to receive a request for assistance from the government directly below.

The legislation does encompass some departures from this pattern, however. Terrestrial search-and-rescue operations are commonly undertaken directly by the RCMP (and its partners) without prior consultative approval by municipal authorities. Training is the responsibility of the provincial government, through NLEMO and the Fire Commissioner's Office, and the programs are initiated by the province, not by the municipalities (Interviews 11, 12, and 16). Medical emergencies are addressed through the Communicable Diseases Act, under which the designations and decisions are made by NL Health and Community Services; a declaration of a medical state of emergency would be executed by the province.

The various pieces of legislation do not address the role of nongovernmental organizations or civil society directly. In smaller communities, however, volunteer firefighters, union locals (notably the Food, Fisheries and Allied Workers, or FFAW), social and church groups, school councils, and community service groups are among the first responders to any event. Many individuals will serve simultaneously in several official and unofficial capacities. Outside the largest cities, elected municipal officials serve part-time for little compensation, continuing to work full-time at other occupations (potentially including FIFO commuter occupations).

DISCUSSION: PROBLEMS AND BARRIERS TO GOOD EMERGENCY MANAGEMENT

Diverse public policy processes and systems of communication are used to define, conceptualize, and solve problems in the area of emergency preparedness in a period of multilevel governance. This approach to public policy and governance pays close attention to both formal and informal mechanisms and processes, how they interact, cooperate, and work in isolation or in competition. Any area of public policy can be analyzed for its effectiveness in identifying a problem; getting it and keeping it on the public agenda; building political, bureaucratic, and public-coalition support for a new vision; and obtaining resources required for building capacity. For the issue of emergency services, both formal public policy responses and informal mechanisms and social forces are significant. In an era of multilevel governance, where problems are increasingly considered "interdependent" and require different state and social forces to come together to promote common objectives, there is much interest in exploring patterns of state-society communication and policy learning across inherited federal-provincial, provincial-municipal, and state-society silos of the past.

Before 1949 the role of government at all levels within Newfoundland and Labrador was limited compared to elsewhere in southern Canada. There were few municipal governments in Newfoundland prior to 1949, and they were confined largely to towns where forestry or mining were dominant. Only the City of St John's has a long history of defining and solving problems using the mechanisms and practices of municipal government and civic organizations and entities. As a result, a strong tradition of depending on informal mechanisms for dealing with community emergencies developed. The church, the family, and other civil-society mechanisms were relied on to define and solve problems. Until the 1990s, there was no public school system in the province, and the church and other civil society organizations played a major role in delivering health and welfare services.

A major political-policy struggle in Newfoundland and Labrador is the challenge of managing rural-urban differences in capacity and perspective. While a province-centred plan for disaster preparedness may make sense in the St John's CMA, questions are bound to be raised about the location for training, patterns of communication, capacity building, and implementation. Another challenge involves finding ways for professions to merge their protocols and train together. In the health services system, effecting changes in scope of practice has been difficult. Doctors have not always been keen about training with nurses, social workers, and others. However, with the support of Health Canada, medical schools around the country have been advancing new approaches to inter-professionalism.

The field of emergency management has emerged as a significant policy issue only in the last twenty years. It is also important to recognize that only certain events have shaped the policy discourse in a fundamental way. In NL, the 1982 sinking of the *Ocean Ranger* was not a pivotal event in the rise of emergency planning as a policy issue. Nor did it have a significant impact on the conceptualization or visioning of or plans for implementation in policy debates. The sinking was perceived to be primarily the result of human factors, rather than the result of a natural hazard, notwithstanding the final report of the royal commission (CBC 2012). Consequently, it was seen as the product of vessel design failure (shortcomings of people outside NL), inadequate training of the crew (not a municipal or provincial responsibility), uncertainties in weather prediction (a federal responsibility), and difficulties in response (by the Canadian Coast Guard), which occurred offshore. The problems posed by the *Ocean Ranger* sinking were seen as truly offshore issues, largely beyond the purview and mandates of the existing provincial legislation and out of reach of any response from municipalities. When viewed this way, controlling the nature of the discourse or embracing new best practices associated with emergency preparedness is influenced by the power and independence of the governmental and societal actors involved. The *Ocean Ranger* disaster failed to significantly influence emergency planning in NL, perhaps because there was no immediately apparent action that could be taken by those based in any of the levels of governance within the province.

Critical events and periods of crisis provide windows of opportunity for introducing new ideas. In the case of emergency preparedness, renewing governance required finding new incentives to integrate across jurisdictions and old state-society boundaries. The importance of emergency preparedness was reinforced by the events of

September 11, 2001, and the need to better coordinate across police, fire, public health, and other services. Successive events, notably the Okanagan Mountain Park fire and Hurricane Katrina, have further reinforced the necessity of coordination among agencies.

Emergency policy response in NL has been greatly influenced by these events. More attention, provincially and municipally, has been focused on the belief that emergencies can occur, that local response is both necessary and effective, and that the preparation and development of crisis management skills should become a higher priority. The coordination of emergency management and response is seen as a high priority by NLEMO, and exercises have been led by the Coast Guard in several areas and by Health Canada in Channel-Port-aux-Basques. There has been political pressure for renewing governance, increasing capacity, policy learning, and making sure that problems are identified and dealt with. Efforts have focused on preparation and response, but relatively less effort has been exerted on assessment and mitigation, particularly for natural hazards, and even less attention has been paid to the recovery phase that inevitably follows an emergency.

The extent of the direct impacts of September 11, 2001, on Newfoundland and Labrador produced a strong impetus to action. The presence of the thirteen thousand stranded passengers and crew throughout the province and the rapid response of the provincial government, municipalities, communities, and individuals exposed many to the realities of an emergency. In the St John's CMA, the departure of the last of the stranded passengers coincided with the arrival of Tropical Storm Gabrielle (18–19 September), which caused widespread flooding and property losses. Although no deaths or serious injuries resulted, the sequence of two emergencies over eight days further spurred efforts to assess preparation and response.

Public policies are not inevitable products of crisis events. They reflect differentials in power, capacity, and independence. All stakeholders may not share the same core values, and there may also be internal ideological or rural-urban divisions that shape patterns of agenda-setting, communication, and implementation. In NL, the divisions are largely between levels of governance, rather than within them. Urban-rural tensions are evident in all aspects of governance issues. In the context of emergency measures, they are commonly played out as discussions concerning resource allocation by the government of NL, with the factors of relative population size and perceived hazards balanced against a desire to allocate the available resources as evenly across the province as possible. The increasing availability of resources from the government of Canada following September 2001 and the recent improved budgetary situation for the provincial government have helped the distribution process and alleviated tensions to some degree.

A related issue is the relationship between the City of St John's (population 106,172 in 2011) and the other communities in the Northeast Avalon, particularly Mount Pearl (24,284), Conception Bay South, and Paradise. Firefighting in Paradise (population 17,695 in 2011), which is directly contiguous to St John's and Mount Pearl, is covered by agreement with the St John's Regional Fire Department. The regional fire service does not extend to the communities of Conception Bay South (population 24,848 in 2011) or Torbay (7,397), although both are directly contiguous to St John's. The Conception Bay South (CBS) Fire Department (sixty-one members in April 2012) is described as a "composite" organization, where volunteers outnumber professional firefighters by thirty-nine to twenty-two (Conception Bay South 2012). In April 2012, the Torbay Volunteer Fire Department consisted of thirty-six "very competent and reliable ... highly professional volunteer firefighters" (Power 2012). These fire departments would be the first responders to most emergencies.

The "volunteer" status of the CBS and Torbay fire departments does not accurately reflect their capacity to respond. Both departments are well-equipped and the personnel are well-trained. The "volunteer" designation more accurately reflects the state of municipal finances rather than the qualifications and capacities of the organizations. However, both communities continue to grow: Torbay is anticipated to have a population in excess of 23,000 by 2020 (Codnor 2012).

The increase in infrastructure, and particularly in commercial and possibly industrial infrastructure, may strain emergency response capacity. Questions of payment for regional services (such as water supply, sewage disposal, and waste management) and boundary disputes between Mount Pearl and St John's have complicated the relationships. Political pressure to amalgamate the Northeast Avalon into a single city (at least including Mount Pearl and Paradise) has remained significant in St John's since 1990, as has resistance to amalgamation in the other communities. The sharing of regional fire services between Mount Pearl and St John's, as governed by the Regional Services Act, was established only after considerable discussion.

Although the potential regional nature of emergencies has led to efforts at regional coordination of planning, preparation, and response, the desire of representatives of Mount Pearl and Paradise to maintain political autonomy has acted as a counterweight. Discussions concerning emergency measures continue between the communities of the Northeast Avalon, but truly integrated regional plans do not exist for either preparation or response. In practice, however, relationships between the organizations tasked as first responders (for example, firefighters) are strong, and collaboration in the event of an emergency is likely. The role of the Royal Newfoundland Constabulary as a common police force across the Northeast Avalon also would coordinate response.

Discussions with both provincial and municipal officials revealed matters of concern in their mutual relationships. Some municipal officials felt that cooperation between themselves and their elected members of the Legislative Assembly (MLAs) was good but that difficulties resulted from the actions raised by non-elected provincial officials. These concerns in part reflect the changes from the traditional relationship that developed between community and government since 1949 to the more technical requirements imposed by provincial civil servants in response to changing perceptions of emergency management. The model of "it's the MLA's responsibility to fight for his or her district in the House of Assembly" has partially been replaced by a model based on technical analysis and quantitative assessment, supported in part by outside investigations. Technical and professional advice from consultants under contract and from researchers from Memorial University of Newfoundland is increasingly sought by provincial civil servants seeking to make decisions related to hazard assessment and emergency management, particularly decisions pertaining to physical hazards (e.g., Catto 2011). This can create strains when the advice received and conclusions drawn are at variance with political instincts (Interviews 11, 12, 16).

The strength and experience of municipal officials charged with emergency response in rural communities must not be undervalued (Interviews 1, 3, 11, 12, 14, and 16). Even though the numerous positions are "voluntary" or "part-time," many of the individuals directly involved in emergency measures organizations (including all those interviewed during this research) are experienced, aware of recent technical developments, and cognizant of training opportunities. Many volunteers bring relevant past or current experience (for example, military or police service) to their responsibilities, and the skills and knowledge in the communities have contributed to the development of emergency response plans. The flow of resources for emergency management has substantially improved, with the consequence that the state of emergency response and management has improved in many communities, to the point where the available equipment and trained personnel are comparable to other Canadian jurisdictions.

The government of NL has recognized the importance of strengthening Fire and Emergency Services. Funding has been allocated for efforts at hazard assessment, and contingency plans have been or are being developed for responses to specific types of emergencies, including petroleum spills and pandemics. Administrative reorganization, including the appointment of a deputy minister specifically responsible, is indicative of the emphasis placed on emergency management. Increases in the personnel and budget for Fire and Emergency Services have occurred since 2008, with the construction of a dedicated facility in St John's and an increase in staffing from five (2008) to twenty-seven (2012).

Relationships between municipal and provincial representatives in NL and federal officials and departments have largely focused on financial matters. Provincial requests for compensation for previous disasters and emergencies, extending back to damages caused by Tropical Storm Gabrielle (2001), have not been entirely met, causing frustration at the provincial level and delays in compensation to municipalities and individuals. The municipal officials and residents interviewed all acknowledged the role of the government of Canada in providing financial support and compensation but felt that the processes involved could move more rapidly. The absence of a direct request-response relationship between the municipalities and the federal agencies (with the provincial government as a required intermediary) muted any direct tensions somewhat. In instances where municipal officials dealt directly with federal personnel (at, for example, St John's International Airport), personal relationships were good, and collaboration on emergency preparation exercises was effective.

Establishing a standard framework for emergency management is an important part of renewing governance. There are few mechanisms for bringing different jurisdictional and stakeholder interests together to coordinate training and capacity-building and to evaluate effectiveness. In the past, various civil society organizations have played a significant role in helping communities and people in stress. In the face of new challenges, the need to demonstrate that they are capable and willing to respond remains great.

CONCLUSION

Emergency planning requires developing an emergency response plan for the province that outlines who is in charge, what the protocols are, and how resources are to be shared or distributed. These are not easy questions to resolve even within unified hierarchical systems. Nor are they framed in a way that could be easily resolved in public debate. The approach currently taken by the government of NL, following examinations of existing structures, mandated procedures, and current de facto practice, is to strengthen NLEMO, provide additional resources to communities, continue to seek federal funding (both as compensation for previous events and for equipment and training), and emphasize emergency management as a political priority.

Emergency management in the provincial context is thus undergoing changes, driven both by changes in policies and by socioeconomic issues. In recent years, the range of potential emergencies has expanded. Concurrently, more resources have been allocated to municipalities, and training has increased significantly. Municipal capacity for responding to emergencies has thus increased in most instances, although local problems associated with community demographics have developed. The perception has grown that reliance on a few key inter-personal connections may prove inadequate in the future. Emergency measures policy, practice, and response in NL are all thus currently in a state of transition. But the pace and direction of policy reform will be determined by capacity, coalition support, and the opportunities available for bringing different interests together in a way that can produce common objectives. In a highly fragmented, incremental, territorially divided system of municipal government, the provincial government has struggled with the task of reworking key ideas, changing legislation, and building coalition support for a universal, best-practices framework (Interviews 11, 12, and 16).

Until debate in emergency measures focuses on constructing a common vision, instead of different rural-urban outcomes, renewing governance based on shared objectives will remain a problem. An alternative strategy might consist of adopting an asymmetrical approach to emergency measures based on federal policy experience. On the other hand, such an approach to accommodation is historical, and without a crisis more severe than those that have affected NL in recent years, it would be difficult to transform.

INTERVIEWS

1   Official, Argentia Management Authority, Placentia, 27 September 2007.
2   Provincial politician, Placentia, 27 September 2007.
3   Municipal official, Placentia, 17 and 18 October 2007.
4   Municipal official, Happy Valley–Goose Bay, 17 October 2007.
5   Municipal official, Happy Valley–Goose Bay, 17 October 2007.
6   Municipal official, Happy Valley–Goose Bay, 17 October 2007.
7   Officer #1, 5 Wing Goose Bay, 19 October 2007.
8   Officer #2, 5 Wing Goose Bay, 19 October 2007.
9   Officer #3, 5 Wing Goose Bay, 19 October 2007.
10 Official, Goose Bay Airport Corporation, 18 October 2007.
11 Group interview: NGO representatives, provincial government officials, federal officials, municipal official, St John's, October 2007.
12 Senior provincial government official in Emergency Management, October 2007.
13 Mayor of medium-sized town, September 2007.
14 Municipal emergency management official, St John's, October 2007.
15 Former city manager, St John's, October 2007.
16 Emergency measures official, St John's, April 2007.

REFERENCES

Alexander, D. 1983. *Atlantic and Confederation.* Toronto: University of Toronto Press.
Batterson, M.J., D.G.E. Liverman, J. Ryan, and D. Taylor. 1999. "The Assessment of Geological Hazards and Disasters in Newfoundland: An Update." *Current Research, Newfoundland Department of Mines and Energy* 99 (1): 95–123.

Blake, R. 1994. *Canadians at Last: Canada Integrates Newfoundland as a Province.* Toronto: University of Toronto Press.

Bradford, N. 1998. *Commissioning Ideas.* Toronto: Oxford University Press.

Brake, K.K. 2008. "An All-Hazard Assessment of the Marystown Area, Burin Peninsula, Newfoundland and Labrador." MA thesis, Memorial University of Newfoundland.

Brock, K. 1996. "Lifting Impressions: Interest Groups, the Provinces, and the Constitution." In *Provinces: Canadian Provincial Politics*, edited by C. Dunn, 95–122. Peterborough, ON: Broadview Press.

Canadian Broadcasting Corporation (CBC). 2006. "Booze Ban Sparks Mass Resignation at N.L. Fire Hall." CBC News, 13 June. http://www.cbc.ca/canada/newfoundland-labrador/story/2006/06/13/nf-fire-alcohol-20060613.html.

– 2012. "Ocean Ranger: Royal Commission; Wreck Examined; Lawsuits Filed." http://www.cbc.ca/archives/categories/environment/extreme-weather/the-ocean-ranger- disaster/ocean-ranger-royal-commission-wreck-examined-lawsuits-filed.html.

Catto, N.R. 2006. *Impacts of Climate Change and Variation on the Natural Areas of Newfoundland and Labrador.* Department of Environment and Conservation, Government of Newfoundland and Labrador.

– 2010. *A Review of Academic Literature Related to Climate Change Impacts and Adaptation in Newfoundland and Labrador.* Cabinet Secretariat, Government of Newfoundland and Labrador.

– 2011. *Coastal Erosion in Newfoundland.* Department of Environment and Conservation, Government of Newfoundland and Labrador.

– 2012. "Natural Hazard Identification, Mapping, and Risk Assessment in Atlantic Canada: Review, Progress, and Challenges." In *Disaster Risk and Vulnerability*, edited by C.E. Haque and D. Etkin, 235–74. Montreal and Kingston: McGill-Queen's University Press.

Catto, N.R., and M.J. Batterson. 2011. "Igor and Other Hurricane and Extratropical Transitions in Newfoundland: Geomorphologic and Landscape Impacts." *GeoHydro*, Proceedings of Joint Meeting of the Canadian Quaternary Association and the Canadian Chapter of the International Association of Hydrogeologists, Quebec City, QC, 28–31 August.

Catto, N.R., E. Edinger, D. Foote, D. Kearney, G. Lines, B. DeYoung, and W. Locke. 2006. *Storm and Wind Impacts on Transportation, SW Newfoundland.* Report to Natural Resources Canada, Climate Change Impacts and Adaptation Directorate.

Catto, N.R., and H. Hickman. 2004. *Flood Sensitivity Analysis for Newfoundland Communities*. Ottawa: Office of Critical Infrastructure Protection and Emergency Preparedness Canada.

Codnor, Robert, mayor of Torbay. 2012. Personal communication, Conception Bay South. "Conception Bay South Fire Department." http://firedept.conceptionbaysouth.ca/.

Conception Bay South. 2012. Conception Bay South Fire Department.

Conrad, M. 1988. "The Atlantic of the 1950s." In *Beyond Anger and Longing: Community and Development in Atlantic Canada*, edited by B. Flemming. Fredericton, NB: Acadiensis.

Dunn, C. 2002. *The Handbook of Canadian Public Administration*. Don Mills: Oxford University Press.

– 2004. "Urban Asymmetry and Provincial Mediation of Federal-Municipal Relations in Newfoundland and Labrador." In *Canada: The State of the Federation, 2004 – Municipal-Federal-Provincial Relations in Canada*, edited by R. Young and C. Leuprecht, 297–331. Montreal and Kingston: McGill-Queen's University Press.

Economic Council of Canada. 1980. *Newfoundland: From Dependency to Self-Reliance*. Ottawa: Economic Council of Canada.

Elkins, D., and R. Simeon. 1980. *Regional Political Cultures: Small Worlds*. Toronto: Methuen Press.

Hanrahan, M. 2004. *Tsunami: The Newfoundland Tidal Wave Disaster*. St John's: Flanker Press.

Hillier, J., and P. Neary. 1980. *Newfoundland in the Nineteenth and Twentieth Centuries*. Toronto: University of Toronto Press.

Howlett, M. 1996. "De-Mythologizing Provincial Political Economies: The Development of Service Sectors in the Provinces, 1911–1991." In *Provinces: Canadian Provincial Politics*, edited by C. Dunn, 423–48. Peterborough, ON: Broadview Press.

Hyndman, D., D. Hyndman, and N.R. Catto. 2008. *Natural Hazards and Disasters*. Toronto: Nelson.

Liverman, D. 2007. *Killer Snow*. St John's: Flanker Press.

Liverman, D.G.E., M.J. Batterson, and D. Taylor. 2003. *Geological Hazards and Disasters in Newfoundland: Recent Discoveries*. Geological Survey Report 03–1. St John's: Newfoundland and Labrador Department of Mines and Energy.

Liverman, D.G.E., N.R. Catto, and M.J. Batterson. 2006. "Geological Hazards in St John's." *Newfoundland and Labrador Studies* 21: 1719–26.

McMillan, A. 2006. *Channel-Port-aux-Basques: Exercise Dolphin. Community Profile, Emergency Response to Climate Change Impact on Atlantic Communities*. Ottawa: Health Canada.

Morrison, C. 2003. "In Crisis, under Control: 9/11 and Newfoundland's Emergency Procurement Response." *Summit* 6 (1): 3–6.

Noel, S.J.R. 1976. "Leadership and Clientelism." In *The Provincial Political Systems*, edited by D. Bellamy, 197–213. Toronto: Methuen Press.

Peddle, P. 2004. "When Ice Prevails: The Badger, Newfoundland, Flood, February 2003." Program with Abstracts. Paper presented at the First Annual Canadian Risks and Hazards Network Symposium, Winnipeg, June.

Picco, R., A.A. Khan, and K. Rollings. 2003. *Badger Flood 2003: Situation Report*. St John's: Department of Environment, Water Resources Management Division, Government of Newfoundland and Labrador.

Pierson, P. 1994. *Dismantling the Welfare State? Reagan, Thatcher, and the Politics of Retrenchment*. New York: Cambridge University Press.

PIEVC. 2008. *Engineering Protocol Assessment, Placentia*. Halifax: Report by Cameron Ells Consulting for Engineers Canada and the Ministry of Environment and Conservation, Government of Newfoundland and Labrador.

Power, Greg, Public Relations Officer, Torbay Volunteer Fire Department. 2012. Personal Communication.

Ruffman, A. 1995a. "Tsunami Runup Maps as an Emergency Preparedness Planning Tool: The November 18, 1929 Tsunami in St Lawrence, Newfoundland, as a Case Study." Report prepared for Emergency Preparedness Canada, Government of Canada. Halifax: Geomarine Associates Ltd.

– 1995b. "Comment on "The Great Newfoundland Storm of 12 September 1775" by Anne E. Stevens and Michael Staveley." *Bulletin of the Seismological Society of America* 85: 646–9.

Seguin, J., 2006. *Assessment of the Capacity of the Emergency Response and Public Health Systems in Atlantic Coastal Communities to Cope with and Adapt to Extreme Weather Events Exacerbated by a Changing Climate*. Ottawa: Health Canada and Natural Resources Canada, Canadian Climate Impacts and Adaptations Directorate.

Sinclair, P. 1988. *A Question of Survival*. St John's: Institute of Social and Economic Research, Memorial University of Newfoundland.

Sinclair, P., and R. Ommer. 2008. *Power and Restructuring: Canada's Coastal Society and Environment*. St John's: Institute of Social Economic Research, Memorial University of Newfoundland.

Stevens, A.E. 1995. "Reply to Comments on 'The Great Newfoundland Storm of 12 September 1775.'" *Bulletin of the Seismological Society of America* 85: 650–2.

Stevens, A.E., and M. Staveley. 1991. "The Great Newfoundland Storm of 12 September 1775." *Bulletin of the Seismological Society of America* 81: 1398–1402.

Tomblin, S. 2007. "Effecting Change and Transformation through Regionalization: Theory versus Practice." *Canadian Public Administration* 50 (1): 1–20.

Vasseur, L., and N.R. Catto. 2008. "Atlantic Canada." In *From Impacts to Adaptation: Canada in a Changing Climate 2007*, edited by D.S. Lemmen, F.J. Warren, J. Lacroix, and E. Bush, 119–70. Ottawa: Natural Resources Canada.

Wallace, L. 2006. "Responsibility for Natural Hazards." *Coping with Natural Hazards in Canada: Scientific, Government and Insurance Industry Perspectives*, edited by S.E. Brun, D. Etkin, D. Gesink Law, L. Wallace, and R. White. Toronto: Insurers Advisory Organization Inc.

Wilson, J. 1974. "The Canadian Political Cultures." *Canadian Journal of Political Science* 7: 438–83.

Young, R., and C. Leuprecht, eds. 2006. *Canada: The State of the Federation, 2004 – Municipal-Federal-Provincial Relations in Canada*. Montreal and Kingston: McGill-Queen's University Press.

5

Emergency Management in Alberta:
A Study in Multilevel Governance

GEOFFREY HALE

INTRODUCTION

On the surface, emergency management (EM) in Alberta municipalities is a natural by-product of municipalities' general responsibility to provide protective services and, more broadly, of all governments' responsibility to protect their citizens' lives and property against foreseeable calamities.

However, a series of policy shocks and "focusing events" regionally and across North America has resulted in the re-evaluation of provincial and municipal policies and processes. Increasingly, these "all-hazards" approaches link traditional emergency services such as fire, police, and emergency medical (ambulance) services to other policy fields, including public health and resource and industrial development, with greater emphasis on prevention (or "mitigation") and inter-sectoral cooperation. The result is a complex system of multilevel governance – the distribution of responsibility for a particular policy field over multiple jurisdictions and agencies among and outside governments.

Alberta has been exposed to relatively few major disasters in recent years. However, substantial, recurring natural hazards arise from periodic floods, forest fires and grassfires, hailstorms, and occasional tornadoes. Hazards posed by the province's major resource extraction and processing industries and related transportation systems, including pipelines, railroads, and major highways, have spawned a sizeable emergency response and hazardous-goods management industry.

This chapter examines the recent evolution of emergency management policies in five Alberta communities that are representative of the province's diverse municipal geography: the province's two major cities of Calgary and Edmonton and their surrounding regions; Lethbridge and area; the Town of Hinton, which straddles two major transcontinental transportation links; and Kneehill County, a rural municipality in Central Alberta. It summarizes major policies that shape EM functions in Alberta and, more specifically, in these municipalities. It outlines the complex networks of intergovernmental relations that influence their relative coherence and effectiveness and explores the interaction of policy-makers and front-line service providers with societal groups, including businesses and non-governmental organizations. Finally, it evaluates the relative effectiveness of these policies – based both on the assessments of senior policy-makers and on comparison to EM "best practices."

EMERGENCY MANAGEMENT IN PROVINCIAL AND MUNICIPAL CONTEXT

Contemporary theories of emergency management emphasize four dimensions of EM policy: mitigation, preparedness, response, and recovery (Haddow and Bullock 2003). Practitioners distinguish between this broad approach to "emergency management" and "the management of an emergency," which involves "crisis and consequence management" in response to a particular or threatened emergency (Lynch and Dauphinee 2005, 4). EM policies are further embedded in a wide range of policies, including public health, occupational health and safety, land use regulation, environmental protection, and the regulation of dangerous goods.

Emergency responders typically include four major sets of services: police, fire, ambulance or "emergency medical services" (EMS), and emergency social services (ESS), along with related support services such as emergency communications (9-1-1) providers and hazardous materials disposal firms. However, increasingly complex modern emergencies, reinforced by the complex, interactive character of modern technologies, can cut across a wide range of public, hybrid, private, commercial, and non-profit agencies.

The level of direct provision of these services by municipalities, rather than private or non-profit contractors or volunteers, generally increases with size – although internal response capacities are vital in major industries, especially those whose activities involve or generate significant hazards. Police services are provided by municipal forces in Calgary, Edmonton, the Lethbridge area, and some smaller municipalities and by the RCMP in most of the rest of the province. In larger communities, emergency social service teams provide additional support to individuals and families displaced from their homes. Many municipalities also have separate search-and-rescue functions.

For functional purposes, the most practical approach to emergency planning and response is to view "emergency management" or "disaster services" as a continuum. At one end of this continuum are routine incident responses by "tri-services" – police, fire, and EMS – as part of their normal duties. Such level 1 occurrences account for more than 95 percent of the activities of these agencies. Minor emergencies often require coordinated responses by tri-services (and possibly, emergency social services) within a limited time and a contained area – although possibly disrupting major transportation routes or other services. They often involve deployment of mobile command centres to coordinate incident response among key governmental and societal actors.

Major (level 3) emergencies or apprehended (level 2) emergencies, involving significant and/or widespread threats to public safety, often require the opening of municipal Emergency Operations Centres for more generalized response coordination. Level 3 emergencies may trigger the declaration of local states of emergency and in smaller communities, the activation of mutual-aid agreements. "Disasters" (level 4 emergencies in provincial operating code) involve widespread damage to life and/or property, requirements for significant and often extended intergovernmental coordination of response and recovery activities, and possibly the declaration of a local or provincial state of emergency invoking the use of emergency powers. Table 5.1 notes the major causes, number, and average duration of states of emergency declared by Alberta municipalities and First Nations in 2011–12. Table 5A1, in the appendix to this chapter, provides further details.

Most Albertans are fortunate not to have experienced level 3 or level 4 emergencies in recent years – although the province can expect to experience emergencies related to flooding or forest fires threatening population centres on a fairly predictable basis. The principal level 4 emergency in 2011 involved wildfires covering

Table 5.1
States of Local Emergency: Major Causes, Frequency, and Duration, 2011–12

	Number		Average Duration (days)	
	2011	2012	2011	2012
Forest fires	16	3	9.9	9.7
Flooding/flood risk	9	1	5.3	3
Water system breakdown	1	0	7	0
Fire at landfill (dump)	1	0	n/a	0
Grassfires, windstorms	1	8	1	1.3
Snowstorms	1	1	2	1
Total	26	13	8.4	3.3

Source: Alberta Emergency Management Agency.

much of Northern Alberta (including the Slave Lake fires), which accounted for 16 of the 39 states of local emergency declared in the province between January 2011 and December 2012.

Municipal responsibilities for EM and planning in Alberta are mandated by provincial legislation – including but not limited to the Emergency (formerly Disaster) Services Act. Some of these responsibilities overlap with those of the Energy Resources Conservation Board (ERCB), which oversees safety and health issues related to energy resource development, the Alberta Health Services Board (AHSB), which replaced nine regional health authorities (RHAS) in 2008, and several special-purpose agencies through the Public Health Act and other legislation. As a result, the AHSB has assumed responsibility for emergency dispatch and the provision of EMS services, usually in partnership with municipal, private, and non-profit agencies. Several other provincial ministries, most notably Environment and Sustainable Resources Development, merged in 2012. Health and Transportation have policy and operational responsibilities for EM that overlap with and sometimes supersede municipal functions.

HISTORICAL OVERVIEW

Alberta's formal legislative framework for the coordination of Emergency Management (or "Disaster Services," as it was labelled for many years) dates to 1950 and the concerns at the time for civil defence arising out of the Cold War. This framework has always coexisted somewhat uneasily with other provincial legislation governing municipalities, building standards, fire codes, public health, occupational health and safety, environmental protection, and public safety issues associated with the development of natural resources. The rapid growth of the provincial government during the 1970s and 1980s resulted in a proliferation of provincial agencies associated with these policy fields – but superimposed over a largely decentralized culture of municipal governance, as discussed below. The Klein government's aggressive deficit reduction program of 1992–95, which resulted in a 26 percent reduction in overall provincial spending (Bruce, Kneebone, and McKenzie 1997), resulted in a significant retrenchment in the province's disaster services capacity, including the closure of the provincial fire training college in Vegreville (Interview 1). Terrorist attacks on the United States in September 2001 provided a major focusing event that led to a renewed expansion of Emergency Management Alberta, the province's main coordinating agency. As discussed below, additional developments have often occurred in a haphazard fashion in response to particular focusing events or shifting provincial priorities.

GENERAL FINDINGS: INTERGOVERNMENTAL RELATIONS

The distribution of responsibilities for EM policies in Alberta is largely shaped by three institutional realities: provincial legislative and regulatory primacy, functional service delivery by relevant provincial ministries and agencies, and the exceptional decentralization of municipal governments.

The Alberta Emergency Management Agency (AEMA) was reorganized in 2007 to replace Emergency Management Alberta (EMA) as the province's horizontal coordinating EM agency. Reporting to the minister of municipal affairs and housing, AEMA is responsible for liaison with municipalities, facilitating the coordination of EM activities of other Alberta ministries and agencies when required by major emergencies, and developing a one-stop EM response system to enable improved coordination and response to emergencies (Interviews 1, 43, 64, and 76).

However, in practice, as demonstrated by Alberta Health's ill-coordinated response to the fall influenza scare of 2009, AEMA's coordination role appears to be somewhat conditional on the willingness of line ministries and agencies to "be coordinated," despite ongoing efforts to strengthen overall governance processes. These challenges, which prompted former AEMA managing director David Hodgins to "resign in frustration" in September 2010, are visible in the frequent turnover of agency leadership. AEMA has had three managing directors between 2009 and 2012 and six since 2001, with significant implications for policy continuity and adaptation (Interviews 83, 84, and 86).

Municipal roles vary significantly by policy field and the level of municipal capacity depends on the regulatory framework ("subject matter" legislation), the range of services provided directly or contracted for by individual municipalities, and the capacities and cultures of both provincial "subject matter" agencies, individual municipalities, and sub-provincial regions. These realities create a complex environment of multilevel governance for EM policies and operations in Alberta.

This complexity grows substantially in major cities. The Calgary Emergency Management Agency lists thirty-one member agencies, nineteen internal to city government, twelve external members (including six provincial ministries and agencies or their key operating units), major utilities, school boards, and Environment Canada, as well as a numerous "invited partners" ranging from the Calgary Airport Authority, the Calgary Stampede, and the Calgary Zoo to major volunteer-based agencies (Calgary Emergency Management Agency 2012, 28; Interview 86).

Particularly in smaller communities, this distribution of responsibilities shifts to the province (and through it, to industry) many responsibilities affecting local EM functions – suggesting the two-tier nature of provincial EM policies. Large and medium-sized cities – the so-called Municipal Group of 9[1] – function largely independently of the province (except on public health issues) and serve as EM anchors for their immediate regions. Policies towards smaller municipalities reflect varying degrees of municipal autonomy and provincial centralization by functional area of risk management, depending on broader assessments of public risk and political salience. This distribution of responsibilities reflects a fundamental trade-off: municipalities retain considerable autonomy in managing their EM functions, but they also bear most, if not all, of the responsibility for paying for these functions – unless, of course, the provincial government determines that public expectations or departmental priorities require them to take direct responsibility for them. A secondary trade-off is that most direct provincial EM support and service functions tend to be allocated towards smaller communities whose mitigation and response capacities are substantially less than those of larger cities.

Several persons interviewed suggest that, as noted above, the distribution of EM functions *within* the provincial government has contributed to the development of policy "silos," or "stovepipes," with widely varying degrees of information sharing and coordination with municipalities. These concerns have provoked the growth of informal coordination among senior EM officials within the Municipal Group of 9.

Large and medium-sized municipalities exercise considerable autonomy in developing local policies and procedures consistent with provincial legislation. Detailed interaction takes place primarily in the conduct of periodic EM exercises and through regular informal interaction between municipal EM coordinators and their provincial counterparts (Interviews 83, 84, and 88), although the extent of regional collaboration has grown considerably since 2005. Provincial and municipal officials interviewed for this study generally agree that municipal emergency service agencies have the responsibility, capacity, and expertise to carry out their functions and should be left to do so with minimal provincial interference. At the same time, the Alberta Fire Chiefs Association has been promoting greater standardization of training programs and processes, along with the consistent application of the Incident Command System (ICS) approach to EM training across the province (Interviews 84 and 88).

Smaller municipalities rely on AEMA's seven field officers to provide regular support to municipal emergency services coordinators and first responders. AEMA provides similar services to Alberta's seventy-two First Nations' communities under a memorandum of understanding (MOU) with Aboriginal Affairs and Northern Development Canada. Field officers facilitate training and the preparation of exercises and workshops. They encourage inter-municipal coordination and help to familiarize newly elected or appointed officials with their EM-related responsibilities under provincial legislation. They also assisted municipalities with applications for small-scale capital funding before the elimination of the Joint Emergency Preparedness Program (JEPP) in the 2012 federal budget.

Most municipal governments in Alberta have a minimal relationship with the federal government, although senior fire and police officials in large and medium-sized cities are deeply engaged with their national organizations. A 2004 Senate committee report suggested that federal officials are seen to have very limited capacity to extend support to their municipal counterparts and very limited credibility as a result (Senate of Canada 2004). Most municipal (and local health) officials interviewed for this study reiterated this outlook with varying degrees of bluntness, even before the 2012 federal budget eviscerated federal EM training programs and transfers to municipalities in support of capacity building (Cohen 2012; Kenny 2012).

Two significant exceptions are federal regulation of airport safety and security, which is subject to highly detailed, regularly monitored regulations and risk audits, and the Canadian Food Inspection Agency's lead role on public health issues related to the animal health and export-oriented food processing sectors. In addition, the federal government does provide useful financial support for provincial disaster recovery programs.

Other federal involvement has been episodic and fragmented. For example, Ottawa supported the development of Heavy Urban Search and Rescue (HUSAR) and Chemical, Biological, Radiological, Nuclear, and Explosives (CBRNE) response systems, but without ongoing operational funding, which it views as primarily a provincial and/or municipal function (Interviews, 2, 23, 69). Indeed, both the provincial and the municipal officials interviewed perceive the federal government as having largely withdrawn from the EM field outside its own direct areas of responsibility. Canada Task Force 2, created in 2005 as Calgary's HUSAR team, has evolved into a mobile all-hazards response team capable of drawing on the resources of a wide range of provincial and other municipal agencies (Interview 86). However, its mandate remains less than transparent for many EM officials, even those in larger municipalities, reflecting the tendency of both federal and provincial policies to reinforce existing silos and create new ones when it suits their interests.

Alberta's diverse and highly decentralized municipal structures, often reinforced by entrenched cultures of local autonomy, greatly increase the importance of processes for managing inter-municipal cooperation among municipal EM coordinators. Alberta has 348 municipalities serving a population of 3.6 million (Alberta

Municipal Affairs 2011). About 51 percent of Albertans live in Calgary and Edmonton, and about 64 percent in their combined metropolitan areas – including St Albert and heavily urbanized Strathcona County. Another 11 percent live in five regional centres with populations of fifty to one hundred thousand: Red Deer, Lethbridge, Fort McMurray (formally, part of the Regional Municipality (RM) of Wood Buffalo), Medicine Hat, and Grande Prairie. By comparison, Ontario's 12.9 million people are served by 445 municipalities (Statistics Canada 2012).

Calgary and Edmonton have totally different urban dynamics, with corresponding effects on the coordination of regional EM policies. Calgary, a uni-city of 1.1 million, which has grown through annexation from neighbouring rural municipal districts (MDs), towers above its surrounding region. By contrast, the twenty-four counties and municipalities around Edmonton are home to about 30 percent of the Capital Region's population of 1.1 million, its international airport, and the bulk of its heavy industry, including its oil refining and petrochemical sectors.

Most MDs and counties are organizationally separate from "urban" municipalities within their boundaries, if often interdependent in delivering emergency services. Strathcona County, Edmonton's heavily industrialized eastern neighbour, and the RM of Wood Buffalo, which contains Fort McMurray, are exceptions to this rule. The widely varying sizes, political cultures, and emergency response capacities of smaller communities and the rural MDs or counties around them vastly increase the complexity of inter-municipal cooperation in the organization and delivery of emergency services. As a result, the interpersonal skills and qualities of senior municipal administrators and directors or coordinators of emergency management are vital to EM effectiveness and related issues of inter-municipal cooperation.

MDs and counties close to Calgary, Edmonton, Lethbridge, and Red Deer generally have significant, though usually volunteer-based, emergency response capacities. However, volunteerism in ex-urban areas is coming under growing pressure with the spread of suburbanization, related expectations for the professionalization of emergency services, and the provincialization of EMS services previously run or contracted for by municipalities (Alberta Municipal Affairs 2010, 208; O'Brien 2011; Smith 2012; Interviews 81, 82, 85, and 87). Major cities also provide a significant reserve capacity for their surrounding communities, both for emergency response and as sources of trained personnel, including "two-hatters" who work for more than one fire department, although Alberta health regulations now prohibit EMS staff under contract with the province from serving as volunteer firefighters (Interview 87).

However, region-wide emergencies such as the floods of June 2005 across south-central Alberta, the forest fire emergency of 2011, or a genuine influenza pandemic (as opposed to the 'flu "scare" of 2009) may require assistance from outside the immediate region. The result is a complex, multi-layered, multi-directional set of intergovernmental relationships, reflecting widely varying circumstances, cultures, and capacities – mediated by the shared professional outlooks of local first responders. A common theme of municipal and provincial officials interviewed for this study is that "one size cannot fit all." Provincial policies must be tailored to acknowledge and accommodate the varying circumstances and capacities of local communities, while attempting to build capacity through effective collaboration and communication with other governments and stakeholders.

MAJOR FACTORS SHAPING PROVINCIAL AND MUNICIPAL POLICIES

Both US and Canadian studies suggest that EM policies at all levels of government are driven by "focusing events" that draw attention to the adequacy of public services that might otherwise be taken for granted (Haddow and Bullock 2003; Henstra 2003). Extensive interviews with policy-makers suggest that the attacks of September 11, 2001, and subsequent emergencies – most recently the 2011 fire that destroyed much of the town of Slave Lake – have increased official awareness of the importance of effective EM, prompting the allocation of greater resources to bolster EM capacities.

Provincial budget reductions during the 1990s largely removed Alberta from delivering emergency preparedness or training services. However, September 11 provided the political impetus for Emergency Management Alberta (EMA) officials to revitalize that agency as an "EM coordinating" organization (Interview 1). EMA responded by developing an "all-hazards" capacity as advocated by leading theorists of emergency management. The agency built a new Emergency Operations Centre capable of coordinating emergency response functions across the province, and its staff grew from eight to forty-one by mid-2005 and to fifty-five by mid-2012. It acquired and developed databases to enable its staff to identify and contact local officials in the event of particular emergencies; it also invested in sophisticated geographic information (GIS) systems to provide highly detailed site and neighbourhood information to incident command centres. Its successor agency, AEMA, has expanded training programs for smaller municipalities. It also operates Alberta Emergency Alerts – a public warning system using radio, the internet, and targeted e-mail feeds to inform the public and local officials of significant public risks and imminent emergencies. Municipal officials may initiate local emergency alerts as required.

Five major sets of emergencies inside and outside Alberta have identified areas of vulnerability in federal and provincial policies and prompted responses of varying degrees of vigour. The Pine Lake tornado of 2001 drew attention to major shortcomings in the interoperability of emergency responders' radio and other communications systems. The RCMP and "local" and "out-of-town" fire and EMS services could not communicate with one another on different radio frequencies – reflecting a widespread problem across North America. After prolonged discussions, the US and Canadian governments have allocated part of the 700 MZ band made available by the shift from analog to digital TV broadcasting for emergency responders – although some policy details remain to be finalized at time of writing (Industry Canada 2012a; Industry Canada 2012b; Jackson 2012). However, the substantial costs of converting radio systems suggest that it may be some time before this process is complete, particularly in smaller municipalities (Interview 82).[2]

Toronto's SARS epidemic of 2003 drew attention to the need for increased intergovernmental cooperation and preparedness to combat and respond to the transmission of infectious diseases. The SARS outbreak prompted senior governments to prepare for a possible avian influenza pandemic as an emergency cutting across all EM functions. The province's decision in 2008 to replace the health regions with a province-wide authority visibly contributed to organizational confusion and communications problems during the fall 2009 influenza season (Braid 2009; Bell 2010; Health Quality Council of Alberta 2010). Policy learning is evident in subsequent provincial decisions to decentralize the annual distribution of flu vaccines through a cross-section of community-based and private-sector health professionals.

Major floods across southern and central Alberta in June 2005, which resulted in recovery payments of at least $155 million, prompted a provincial review of land use planning policies, but otherwise minimal action in the face of this persistent hazard (Fekete 2010; Braid 2010). Municipal officials continue to express concerns that existing legislation makes it too easy for developers to overturn local restrictions on flood plain development through the Municipal Government Board (Braid 2012).

Following a train derailment at Wabamun Lake that resulted in a serious spill of toxic pollutants in 2005, a provincial review commission recommended major changes to the organization of the province's emergency services. In response, Alberta Environment created a rapid response force capable of responding to environmental emergencies and negotiated an agreement with Transport Canada that enabled provincial officials to provide prompt responses to such incidents on federally regulated railway lands, as well as in areas within provincial jurisdiction. Most recently, in May 2011 wildfires burned more than five hundred homes and other buildings in Slave Lake and neighbouring communities, forcing the evacuation of about eighty-five hundred people, and inflicting losses exceeding $700 million (Alberta Flat Top Complex Wildfire Review Committee 2012, 3; Alberta Emergency Management Agency 2011).

Four of the five communities studied have experienced major "focusing events" of their own in recent years that have influenced policy changes, with multiple events in Calgary and the Lethbridge area. The events and the reactions to them demonstrate the diversity of municipal (and regional) political and administrative cultures, the often informal nature of inter-municipal coordination, and its dependence on the quality of inter-personal relations among municipal politicians and senior officials.

Calgary has experienced the widest range of focusing events: major floods in 2005 and 2007 (and flash floods in 2011), several major public events requiring prolonged crowd control activities, and proposed sour-gas drilling near a planned new hospital site in 2005–06 that triggered a vigorous public debate.[3] Major condominium fires have also raised concerns over building standards (Massinon 2010).[4] These events led to several major personnel and structural changes – including the hiring of current fire chief Bruce Burrill, the creation of the Calgary Emergency Management Agency in 2007, and subsequent changes to stormwater management policies.

Edmonton's most traumatic focusing event – a tornado that killed twenty-seven people in 1987 – is distant enough to have a limited impact on current EM policies and practices. A riot by inebriated sports fans in 2001 resulted in some changes to policing and crowd-control practices. Municipal officials have invested considerable effort in crowd management (including the monitoring of social media) in recent years with a view to becoming more proactive in ensuring that major public events do not get "out of hand" (Interview 83).

Neighbouring Strathcona County, which combines the large suburban community of Sherwood Park with extensive stretches of heavy industry surrounded by rural areas on three sides, faced major wildfires in 2008 and 2009. Strathcona also has several major "dangerous goods" corridors, including three highways, railways, and pipelines, requiring close cooperation with large and small industry and ongoing investments in municipal infrastructure, training, and preparedness.

Some observers have suggested that the absence of a major industrial accident has resulted in a degree of official complacency in managing development and land use policies near major industrial facilities, especially "refinery row" located outside Edmonton's boundaries. The salience of these issues has increased with pressures for expanded refinery and upgrading capacity in Strathcona and Sturgeon Counties, rapidly growing residential development, and apparent differences in regulatory philosophies among area jurisdictions (Doug McCutcheon and Associates 2003; Interviews 13 and 84). These issues – and steps taken to address them – are discussed in the section on regionalization below.

Strathcona has a highly institutionalized EM culture characterized by strict planning rules, the close integration of firefighting and emergency medical services, and close cooperation between local emergency services and industrial groups. Sturgeon County, whose emergency services are primarily volunteer-based, has adopted development buffer zones based on Major Industrial Accident Council of Canada guidelines.[5] However, officials in neighbouring jurisdictions express concerns about their capacity to monitor industry compliance with provincial EM regulations, as well as their capacity to finance additional emergency services during the construction of major projects in "Upgrader Alley." Increased risk levels generally precede the availability of new property tax revenues as major energy processing facilities become operational (Interview 77).

Lethbridge, a municipality of eighty-eight thousand people strad-
dling the Oldman River in southern Alberta, experienced four "one-
hundred-year rain events" – levels of rainfall that trigger flooding
to the highest levels experienced in a hundred years – between 1995
and 2007. These events, reinforced by insurance industry pressures,
prompted municipal officials to make significant investments in
infrastructure improvements to take pressure off city storm and sanitary sewer systems. The city is organizationally separate from surrounding Lethbridge County, and the six other municipalities within
the latter's boundaries. Lethbridge has expanded its police coverage to include the Town of Coaldale, thirteen kilometres to the east.
Major wildfires driven by hurricane force winds, which threatened
parts of the city and surrounding communities in November 2011
and September 2012, have been significant recent focusing events,
although the city's position on major highway and railway corridors
make hazardous goods incidents an ongoing focus for preparedness
and training (Interview 88).

Hinton, a town of ninety-eight hundred people located two and
a half hours west of Edmonton and eighty kilometres from its nearest neighbours along the Trans-Canada Highway, Edson and Jasper,
has developed a sophisticated culture of partnerships with local and
regional industries and provincial agencies to leverage its capacity
to provide both basic services and an effective EM program. Most
major municipal buildings and services have been built or developed
as joint ventures with provincial governments or agencies, private
firms, and non-profit groups. The town's fire response zone covers
more than six thousand square kilometres of neighbouring Yellow-
head County, covering an area up of to ninety kilometres outside
the town. The town's fresh water and water treatment systems are
provided by its largest employer, Weldwood Canada Ltd, with oversight from municipal engineering and utilities staff. The paper mill,
whose construction in 1958 led to Hinton's municipal incorporation, accounts for 93 percent of local water consumption. Extensive
resource industry activity in the surrounding area provides Hinton
with an extensive reserve of trained emergency response personnel –
but also with incentives for higher staff turnover, which have led the
town to adopt a "paid, on-call volunteer" fire and rescue response
capacity (Interview 89).

As in the case of Edmonton, Hinton's major focusing event –
a 1986 derailment on the Canadian National (CN) main line – is

a distant memory, particularly with the 2005 retirement of the town's long-serving director of disaster services. However, the 2005 Wabamun train derailment renewed concerns about the adequacy of existing systems for allowing municipal officials to engage CN in the event of another major accident. The natural gas boom of 2004–08 also raised substantial concerns over dangerous goods shipments through town and the trade-offs associated with potential responses. Wildfire risks remain an ongoing focus, reinforced by the proximity of a major Ministry of Environment and Sustainable Resources Development (ESRD) fire training centre.

Kneehill County – whose population of about eleven thousand includes five organizationally separate municipalities in a fifty by seventy kilometre area of Central Alberta, about fifty kilometres east of Alberta's main north-south highway – also depends on partnership-building for effective EM, but in a very different geographic, organizational, and cultural context. Kneehill has not had a severe focusing event in recent years, although the 2001 Pine Lake tornado took place just north of the county, and tornadoes occur sporadically through southern and central Alberta. Rising oil and gas activity has contributed to the rapid growth of hazardous materials traffic on area roads, prompting greater attention to environmental concerns. Although extensive coalbed methane development has not affected local well-water supplies, the county is about to complete a four-year project, with substantial provincial assistance, extending municipal water lines to about two-thirds of county households (Interview 82).

Serious flooding risk provided an effective "live" exercise for county emergency personnel in 2005, and overland flooding remains an ongoing seasonal concern. However, despite extensive oil and gas activity, county officials have not had to deal with major pipeline spills that have affected local drinking water supplies twice in 2011–12 in parts of neighbouring Red Deer County.

ORGANIZATIONAL FACTORS: WHO MAKES POLICY AND HOW?

Municipal EM policies typically fall into four areas: the range of emergency services provided directly by or under contract to particular municipalities, the assignment of functional responsibilities for designing and implementing EM policies, cooperation with, or dependence on, other municipalities and/or external agencies, and the integration of EM with other functional areas of municipal governments. This section examines the first two areas. The other two will be addressed in subsequent sections.

Administrative Responsibility for Emergency Management

The organization and distribution of EM responsibilities among governments and emergency services agencies are central to policy development. Effective EM typically begins with a planning process that includes the identification of potential hazards, the resources to anticipate or respond to them, managers and specialists in municipal departments and external agencies capable of mobilizing and deploying those resources, and the processes for ensuring their effective coordination in an emergency. These processes, which are often extensions of normal departmental responsibilities, require effective inter-agency and, in some cases, intergovernmental coordination.

Provincial law requires that each municipality "shall maintain an emergency management agency," and appoint a director "who shall (a) prepare and co-ordinate emergency plans and programs for the municipality, (b) act as director of emergency operations on behalf of the emergency management agency, (c) co-ordinate all emergency services and other resources used in an emergency, and (d) perform other duties as prescribed by the local authority" (Alberta 2011, s. 11.2). In most municipalities studied, this responsibility is held either by the city (or county) manager (chief administrative officer, or CAO) or the fire chief. Formal responsibility for policy-making usually rests with senior municipal staff – often the fire chief – who tend to have "regular day-jobs." When asked about constraints on EM, one CAO interviewed commented, "time would be the biggest one by a mile. That would be 95 percent of it. I'm busy ... with the economic activity in the province and the shortage of staff, this sort of thing gets pushed to the backburner. Even if the province came up with a whole bunch of money, that's nice, but if people don't have the time to put towards it ..." (Interview 55).

The same challenges typically face municipal department heads, for whom issues related to emergency management – including business continuity planning – tend to be viewed as secondary priorities unless identified as a substantial and ongoing risk to their operations (Interviews 86 and 88). To manage these trade-offs, some larger

municipalities (including Calgary, Lethbridge, and Strathcona) have
created deputy chief positions responsible for the coordination of
emergency management and for providing policy advice to senior
decision makers.

Emergency services functions in Kneehill County are coordinated
with those of area municipalities through an integrated regional plan,
with the regional fire chief also serving as the director of emergency
management. To compensate for periodic staff turnover, municipalities frequently task incoming fire chiefs (or other EM coordinators)
to review and update the municipal emergency plan. This process
was noted in Hinton, Kneehill, Rocky View, Mountain View, Sturgeon, and Lethbridge Counties. In Edmonton and Calgary, municipal transit services maintain their own emergency management
functions, which are integrated with those of the tri-services when it
becomes necessary to set up unified command centres to deal with
major incidents or events.

Both Calgary and Edmonton have established formal Emergency
Social Service (ESS) functions with full-time ESS planners working
within their EM agencies. ESS functions include the setting up and
staffing of evacuation centres, using a mix of city staff "borrowed"
from their regular positions, contract staff provided by agencies like
the Canadian Red Cross, and volunteers provided by area community groups and businesses. Other functions include organizing supplies, housing, and emotional support for persons displaced from
their homes and following up with victims of disasters. These functions require highly creative individuals capable of identifying and
mobilizing resources both inside and outside the organization, as
well as responding to local or out-of-area emergencies. For example,
Edmonton had to support at least five thousand evacuees from the
2011 Slave Lake fire, while Calgary has been asked to assist people
displaced by earthquakes in Haiti (Interviews 83 and 86). Calgary's
ESS network includes more than one hundred volunteers in other
municipal agencies, area businesses, and non-profit and faith-based
agencies. Lethbridge's ESS functions are managed by the city's manager of community and social services, with the support of a contract
staff person, and they are delivered by local community agencies –
notably the Canadian Red Cross (Interview 72). Such functions
are generally rudimentary or absent in smaller communities, and
displaced residents are likely to depend on family and informal
community networks. The cultivation of community networks to

provide municipal officials in larger centres with "surge capacity" in the event of serious emergencies differs significantly from the largely professionalized, unionized environments for mutual assistance in other emergency response sectors.

Who Makes Policy?

The EM "doctrine" entrenched in Alberta's Emergency Management Act anticipates that major decisions relating to emergency planning and response will be made by elected officials based on bylaws passed by local councils. These bylaws typically provide for the creation of an Emergency Services Committee of Council and the development of a municipal emergency plan, under the direction of the municipality's director of emergency management. The Emergency Management Act enables the minister of municipal affairs to mandate inter-municipal cooperation if necessary (Alberta 2011, s. 10(1)), although Alberta has often preferred the use of guidelines to firm province-wide standards, in contrast with some other provinces such as British Columbia. As a result, municipalities may draw on provincial guidelines for land use and mitigation policies, regional and inter-municipal cooperation, and more technical rules such as emergency dispatch protocols (before the 2009 provincial takeover), or provisions to standardize rural addresses and signage.[6] Some municipal officials interviewed have expressed a willingness to accept greater standardization in various areas – as long as the province provides the resources to implement them. A March 2013 Health Quality Council report was highly critical of the "patchwork" of standards for emergency (911) call centres and has recommended their consolidation under provincial control (Henton 2013b).

The principle of municipal autonomy also applies to the declaration of states of local emergency (SOLE) by designated elected officials (usually, but not always, the mayor). Municipal officials may exercise the exceptional powers conferred on them by the Emergency Management Act to enforce evacuations, commandeer property for public purposes, and take other measures necessary for public safety. One official notes that "in BC, you have to apply to have a declaration approved. In Alberta, the minister can veto but he doesn't have to approve it. That goes along with the idea of municipal autonomy" (Interview 2). In larger cities, the activation of the Municipal Emergency Plan is an effective substitute for declaring a SOLE in coordinating actions across municipal agencies and with external partners – as well as signalling to the public that municipal officials are "on the job."

However, under normal circumstances, municipal EM policy-making is largely delegated to senior administrative officials. Local EM coordinators enjoy extensive discretion on technical matters of inter-agency coordination, except for those requiring major budget expenditures. However, the exercise of this discretion depends heavily on their interpersonal skills rather than on formal positional power. One official comments, "I don't have positional authority over anyone ... until you institute a State of Local Emergency under the Municipal Emergency Plan. But I work hard to make people want to work with me. But the second you start quoting the Act or the Municipal Emergency Plan, you've lost, because it's all about relationships. People will work with you because they want to work with you" (Interview 86).

In general terms, the more technical, specialized, and amenable to regulation the issues in question, the greater becomes the likelihood of policy leadership from technical staff experts in emergency service and relevant line departments. In an emergency, the mayor serves as a focal point for public communications but is encouraged to follow the guidance of the senior administrative official responsible for EM. Failure to do so – as seen from conflicting comments made by Premier Ed Stelmach and Health Minister Ron Liepert during the rollout of mass vaccination programs in late 2009 – can undermine effective service delivery and contribute to mass confusion (*Calgary Herald* 2009). Careless use of social media tools such as Twitter can also contributed to mixed messages, public confusion, and potential recriminations.

The greater the direct financial impact on municipal resources (or related issues of economic development), the more likely municipal councils are to play a major role, as in perennial debates over snow removal costs following major storms (e.g., Markusoff 2009; CBC News 2010). EM decisions are often driven by competition between staffing and capital budgeting priorities and efforts at mitigation. Central issues related to mitigation relate to land use planning, to the development and renewal of municipal infrastructure, and in some cases to major capital investments related to the EM function itself.

Decision-making processes – and relationships between "formal" and "expert" authority – vary significantly in smaller communities. CAOs and senior department heads typically dominate decision-making processes as long as they retain the confidence of their elected councils. None of the smaller municipalities studied during this project dedicated any senior staff function exclusively to EM. The shared responsibility for financing and providing emergency services typical of municipal districts (MDs), counties, and the small municipalities within their boundaries (which can range in size from populations of several thousand to a few hundred), are heavily mediated through the personalities of CAOs and to a lesser extent through those of mayors and reeves, whose willingness to collaborate with neighbouring jurisdictions often reflects the advice of their officials. The impression derived from interviews conducted in Hinton, Kneehill, Mountain View, Rocky View, and Sturgeon Counties and the County of Lethbridge and neighbouring municipalities is of diverse, almost individualized decision-making processes.

Organization of Municipal Emergency Services

Municipalities do not require direct operational control over "tri-service" agencies to deliver effective services, although such control is the norm in larger centres. Contractual arrangements and mutual-aid agreements allow smaller communities to access timely and generally reliable service beyond their immediate borders, particularly if the practice is reinforced by regular training and good interpersonal communications among senior agency personnel.

Organizational structures and cultures play a substantial role in the integration and coordination of different emergency functions and agencies. Before the provincial reorganization of EMS services in 2008–09, Calgary and Edmonton managed their own fire and EMS services but organized them as separate departments, or business units, with separate collective agreements. Lethbridge, Strathcona County, and the City of Red Deer fully integrate fire and ambulance services, so that all fire personnel hired are cross-trained as paramedics or EMS technicians trained to serve in ALS-equipped ambulances.[7] Ongoing changes to EMS services remain controversial in these (and other) communities, given widespread perceptions of declining levels of service, diminished local control, and ongoing provincial demands on local fire services for incident response, especially in smaller communities.

Fire service in small communities is usually provided by volunteer firefighters, often under the supervision of a full-time professional. In Kneehill, virtually all of the 154 local fire and rescue staff (across six municipal detachments) are volunteers, with the full-time county fire chief serving a coordinating role. Hinton's 34 paid, on-call volunteers are paid on a "per incident" basis when responding to fire or rescue calls, an approach that has been adopted by a growing number of communities (Interview 89). The STARS Society, a nonprofit organization, provides contract air-ambulance transfers with Alberta Health Services throughout the province – a vital service to link seriously ill or injured patients with specialized medical services in Calgary and Edmonton. Larger cities, including Calgary, Edmonton, Lethbridge, and a handful of smaller communities provide their own police services. Most other communities rely on RCMP services provided under contract with the provincial government.

Planning and Inter-Agency Coordination

Effective EM planning usually requires a capacity for inter-agency (and often, inter-municipal) coordination, as well as the periodic testing (or "exercise") of emergency plans to determine their effectiveness and build relationships among participating managers and agencies. Coordination activities take different forms in different communities, reflecting different corporate and regional cultures. Amendments to the Emergency Management Act introduced in 2010 formally provided for both the creation of Regional EM Partnerships among municipalities and the delegation of decision-making authority under specified conditions. However, provincial officials still express a preference for voluntary collaboration over prescriptive approaches, and they encourage it (Interview 81).

Calgary and Edmonton have mature, well-developed planning systems for the coordination of municipal departments and the mobilization of resources in the event of major emergencies across a wide range of hazards. The Calgary Emergency Management Agency brings together working-level officials responsible for relevant functions from nineteen municipal and twelve external agencies, including Police, Fire, Water Services, Community and Neighbourhood Services, Roads, Transit, and other functions. There is also representation from different elements of Alberta Health, public and separate schools, major utilities, AEMA, and other provincial agencies (Calgary Emergency Management Agency 2012, 28). Edmonton centralizes responsibility for planning, training, and response in the hands of a director of emergency preparedness with a small dedicated staff of support professionals. The director meets monthly with representatives of city departments, including police, fire, transit, EMS, ESS, public works, and information technology to share information.

Lethbridge's system appears to provide effective cooperation among first responders, benefiting from strong support from the city's senior administration. Calgary, Edmonton, and smaller cities provide significant reserve capacity for neighbouring municipalities through a variety of mutual aid agreements. Separate master mutual aid agreements have been negotiated covering the twenty-four municipalities in the Edmonton Capital Region, seven contiguous municipalities in the Calgary region,[8] and thirty-seven southern Alberta municipalities centred on Lethbridge (Interviews 84, 85 and 86). The latter is a comprehensive agreement that applies to any municipal service – although some officials comment that its potential remains largely unexplored.

Capacities in smaller and rural municipalities vary widely. Decision making and coordination in Kneehill County have been addressed by the development of a formal inter-municipal partnership coordinating each municipality's emergency plan and services. Kneehill's fire chief/director of emergency management is responsible for joint planning and training with area municipalities.

A key element of emergency planning involves the periodic exercise (or practice in application) of the plan. Municipalities are expected to exercise their plans at least every four years, although incidents serious enough to warrant the opening of local emergency operations centres fulfill this responsibility. Larger municipalities do so significantly more often. Such meetings are considered vital to build personal relationships across departmental and organizational boundaries, familiarize participants with different agencies' capacities and possible gaps, and break down organizational "silos," or "stovepipes," that can hinder effective responses in an emergency. However, local application of this non-legislated standard declined from 94 percent in 2008–09 and 91 percent in 2009–10 to 80.8 percent in 2010–11 (Alberta Municipal Affairs 2011).

Exercises take three major forms: scheduled "live" exercises involving a cross-section of participants in a simulated disaster exercise involving the actual deployment of resources; "tabletop" exercises involving small-scale simulation and discussion of plan activation in particular circumstances; and unscheduled "live" exercises involving actual preparations for an event that may or may not materialize. Larger cities usually attempt to schedule "live" exercises annually, unless preempted by a real or apprehended emergency that swallows the amount budgeted for live training. Resource limitations in smaller communities often result in two- or three-year gaps between live exercises, although officials may seek to compensate by scheduling regular training programs and tabletop exercises. Tabletop exercises are typically conducted monthly in Calgary, quarterly (or more often) in Edmonton and Lethbridge, and semi-annually in smaller communities. These exercises also benefit municipalities by increasing awareness of provincial standards and of the administrative practices that are necessary to establish that local officials have met their responsibilities if they are subsequently challenged in court.

One observer has noted that federal environmental legislation that requires major industry facilities to carry out a live exercise annually in cooperation with municipal partners can pose major resource problems for communities with significant concentrations of industry (Interview 66). One response to this approach is to conduct joint exercises.

Intergovernmental and Inter-sectoral Relations: The Challenge of Coordination

A major shortcoming in Alberta's EM system is the frequent absence of effective mechanisms for inter-sectoral coordination among the functional "silos," or "stovepipes," for emergency planning and the delivery of emergency services. This section examines the interaction between municipalities and provincial agencies other than AEMA that are responsible for sector-specific EM policies.

The extent to which the provincial government assigns or delegates responsibilities to municipalities (or other local/regional authorities) in EM-related areas is directly related to perceptions of available resources and professional capacity, mediated by overriding provincial priorities. Calgary, Edmonton, and most medium-sized municipalities retain considerable policy-making autonomy, except for critical infrastructure protection. EM policies and decision making in smaller municipalities are frequently constrained by limited resources and the fact that they are often "policy-takers" in areas dominated by other orders of government. Four other major constraints arise from the province's responsibility for Crown lands, for resource ownership and development, and for environmental protection, and from the federal government's regulatory responsibility for railroads and related transportation safety issues. Another factor sometimes raised is the lack of effective local planning capacity, which was reinforced by the abolition of regional planning commissions in the 1990s (Interviews 18, 38.)

As a result, rural and small urban municipalities have limited influence over conditions for resource development or related EM issues. Provincial legislation assigns operational responsibility for emergency preparedness and response by resource industries to companies themselves, subject to regulations by the ERCB and the Ministry of Environment and Sustainable Resources Development.[9] Federal environment and/or fisheries regulations may also apply in particular cases. In June 2012, Energy Minister Ken Hughes announced plans to introduce new provincial regulations governing oil and gas developments in urban areas, although it is far from clear how these rules will address "suburban" developments outside city boundaries (Vanderklippe 2012).

Fighting forest fires is the responsibility of the Ministry of Environment and Sustainable Resources Development (ESRD), in cooperation with the forest industry and local governments. ESRD's training centre in Hinton provides both research and training for forest and land managers and firefighting personnel. Some municipal officials have suggested the need for improved "cross-training" to assist smaller municipal fire departments in dealing with major grassfires that are a recurring safety hazard in much of southern and central Alberta (Interview 85). They have also suggested that ESRD's "fire-weather" index, an effective predictor of fire hazards, be extended to "white zones" of cropland and grassland to reinforce fire prevention in rural southern and central Alberta[10] and that the definition of "fire protection season" in the province's Forest and Prairie Protection Act be amended to recognize the greater risk of grassland fires during the winter dry season (November-March) (Interview 85).[11]

The ministry's FireSmart program, which is most useful for smaller municipalities, provides assistance of up to $50,000 to communities for mitigation efforts and capital equipment in heavily forested areas of the Rocky Mountain foothills and Northern Alberta to reduce risks of wildfires within municipal boundaries. Program funding was expanded significantly following the 2011 Slave Lake fire, although municipal take-up of the program, which remains voluntary, varies widely, often depending on how long it has been since the last major fire scare (Ibrahim 2012; Henton 2012).

Municipal officials in Hinton expressed little expectation that CN, whose main line passes through the town, would respond effectively to municipal concerns in the event of another major train derailment; they cited examples from British Columbia and the poorly coordinated intergovernmental response to the 2005 Wabamun incident. In response to such concerns, the federal and Alberta governments signed an MOU in early 2007 to facilitate provincial enforcement of federal (and relevant provincial) environmental and emergency response rules in the event of accidents in federally regulated rail corridors. Following the report of a provincial task force, Alberta Environment also established a Special Emergency Response Team (ASERT) that provides technical and logistical support to municipalities, industry, and agency incident commanders in the event of environmental emergencies.

Cooperation and Coordination among Municipalities

Alberta's highly decentralized municipalities make regional EM coordination a major challenge. Neighbouring municipalities typically have mutual aid agreements of varying levels of formality with one another for sharing services and the associated costs arising from out-of-area response calls. Coordination typically takes place on an informal, often hazard-specific basis, based on the shared professional training and outlook and personal relationships among EM coordinators. However, the frequent absence of more formal arrangements carries inherent risks in the event of a major region-wide emergency.

This problem has been recognized by AEMA officials, who are actively promoting greater regional coordination through a combination of incentives, persuasion, and examples, especially in rural areas. Training applications to support inter-municipal cooperation have a significantly higher probability of funding (Interview 85). Although provincial officials are more nuanced, one local official notes that "if we go to the province for funding, regional partnerships are higher on the list. You either work together or go without" (Interview 23). AEMA district officers have actively encouraged and facilitated the development of municipal networks, including First Nations communities, to exchange information and encourage greater cooperation among municipalities. The benefits of greater EM policy and planning cooperation are recognized by most local officials interviewed for this study. One comments that "there is a finite number of people. You can't have four EOCs here. You can only have one. You can't say: 'you're going to have the ATCO guy and I'm going to have the gas guy'" (Interview 55). Some officials interviewed have expressed a desire for stronger provincial mandating of regional partnerships to overcome the inertia sometimes caused by local rivalries and parochialism.

Regional coordination among municipalities is much more politically sensitive when the province's major cities are involved, leading to the appearance of a more hands-off approach by AEMA officials. As a result, EM coordination in metropolitan areas is heavily dependent on local leadership, as seen by the evolution of the Capital Region Emergency Preparedness Partnership (C-REPP). C-REPP was formed in 1997 to facilitate cooperation and information sharing among more than twenty Edmonton-area municipalities and as many as twenty other significant stakeholders, including educational institutions, utilities, industrial associations, and the local health region. Subsequent attempts to secure ongoing budgeted funding from member municipalities received a "dismal" response, resulting in the suspension of operations in 2006 (Interview 61). Renewed cooperation between Edmonton and Strathcona led to C-REPP's revitalization in 2008–09 with stable pro-rated funding based on municipal populations and participation by all twenty-four Edmonton-area municipalities by 2011. Municipal officials interviewed describe C-REPP as an important vehicle for joint planning and training initiatives, broadening capacity for most communities, and strengthening the networks and interpersonal relations necessary for effective EM collaboration (Interviews 81, 83, and 84). Inter-municipal cooperation in the Calgary Region takes place through the South Central Emergency Management Committee, comprising Calgary and six "contiguous" municipalities – although this group has experienced growing pains similar to those of C-REPP in its early stages (Interview 86).

Edmonton's relations with its neighbours tend to be cyclical, depending on local political conditions and the broader environment for development. As with Calgary, periodic tensions have resulted from the absence of an effective framework for land use planning and coordinating economic development. Edmonton's policy of allowing the encroachment of residential developments on major industrial facilities, including those in neighbouring communities, is an ongoing source of controversy (Interviews 2, 28, 30, and 33). These issues have been addressed to some extent by the formation in 2011 of a Joint Planning Study for Edmonton and Strathcona, in order to "achieve compatibility of land uses (and) common understanding of approaches to risk management/mitigation," among other things, along their shared 40-kilometre border (Planning Alliance 2011). However, Strathcona County continues to enforce a three-kilometre development setback requirement near major refineries and petrochemical facilities, compared with about three hundred metres in neighbouring Edmonton (Interview 84).

In response to these and other challenges, former premier Ed Stelmach mandated the creation of a region-wide land-use planning process in 2007 (Markusoff and Kent 2007). The formation in 2008 of the Capital Region Board facilitated a more coherent policy framework for regional cooperation through the Capital Region growth plan of 2009. It also appears to have enabled the development of a comprehensive, region-wide mutual-aid agreement among the region's twenty-four municipalities through C-REPP between 2009 and 2011.

An alternative approach oriented to cooperation among rural municipalities and small towns has been taken by Mountain View County, in central Alberta. The area's six municipalities have developed an integrated regional emergency response plan, using the services of an external consultant. The six directors of emergency services meet quarterly to review current issues and identify EM-related areas in which closer cooperation is necessary. These arrangements, which have been paralleled by several other MDs and counties in different parts of the province, are seen to increase flexibility in responding to local emergencies.

These regional plans reflect cultures of cooperation among area municipalities nurtured over more than a decade by long-serving municipal officials that have encouraged the development of a variety of shared services. Other shared services in Mountain View include a common HUB radio system that links all emergency service responders in the county, excluding the RCMP but including county constables responsible for enforcing traffic laws, county bylaws, and provincial environmental and dangerous-goods transportation regulations. Fire department costs are shared on a population ratio (percentage rural vs percentage urban) serviced by area municipalities. The county also has access to advanced GIS systems that facilitate rapid location and response to rural sites. Local energy industry groups have played a catalytic role in this process (Interview 59).

Industry Engagement with Emergency Management: Proactive and Reactive

The oil and gas industry plays a significant and substantial role in the development of EM policies within the province, most notably within the context of its engagement with the ERCB on standards for sour-gas production, the development of Directive 71 governing oil patch EM activities, and active collaboration with regional EM partnerships.

Major industrial stakeholders often seem to influence local government policies and policy coordination. One prominent stakeholder is the Sundre Petroleum Operators Group (SPOG), a consortium of twenty-six oil and gas firms active in West Central Alberta's Mountain View and Clearwater Counties. Others include Northeast Region Community Awareness Emergency Response (NR-CAER), an EM cooperative of working-level officials from the petrochemical industry and local government officials in Strathcona and Sturgeon Counties, east and north of Edmonton; the Strathcona Industrial Association, representing oil refineries and petrochemical plants in Strathcona County; and the Strathcona District Mutual Aid Partnership (SDMAP), noted above. Industry groups around Calgary have set up several groups, including the Cochrane Pipeline Operators Committee and the Balzac Community Advisory Panel. Municipal officials dealing with these groups report that they have taken a strong and constructive approach to EM. SPOG regularly conducts preparedness exercises in cooperation with local first responders. It has also financed the acquisition of advanced geographic information

(GIS) systems to facilitate area first responders' capacity to respond to local emergency calls (Interview 59).

EM officials and first responders work closely with industry officials in Strathcona County and the "industrial heartland" surrounding Edmonton. Industrial officials have sought to maximize transparency and proactive public communications in order to address actual and potential public concerns over the risks to public safety of extensive industrial developments. Most of northern Strathcona and eastern Sturgeon Counties have been designated for specific industrial developments in the massive expansion of oil, gas, and petrochemical industries within the region, resulting in large-scale land purchases by major companies, a process facilitated by Strathcona's requirement for a three kilometre buffer zone around such developments.

Major activities include regular exercises (and incident management in support of occasional spills or fires), land use planning to facilitate industry expansion, and ongoing public consultations, and for NR-CAER, the installation of an extensive call-out network to be available in the event of any incidents at local petrochemical plants. After several years, the Canadian Radio-Television and Telecommunications Commission (CRTC) allowed NR-CAER to access the area 9-1-1 system, in order to allow for automated access to unlisted as well as listed numbers so that it could alert a wider public of any incident. Strathcona County is currently working towards implementing its own reverse 9-1-1 system, enabling EM officials to access cell phone towers within the county to provide more timely and extensive coverage (Interview 84), as are other municipalities, including Lethbridge (Interview 88). In January 2013, acknowledging that cellphone traffic accounts for about one-quarter of incoming 9-1-1 calls, the Alberta government indicated that it would be introducing a 44-cent monthly levy on all cellphone accounts within the province to help fund these services, including call centres operated by municipal governments (Henton 2013a).

Some industry and municipal officials have expressed a desire for the provincial government to take over the financing of such activities as part of a broader process of extending the province's existing emergency alert system. However, industry officials acknowledge that these activities are seen as a necessary investment in public trust, given the industry's huge public footprint, especially in the Edmonton Capital region, and the inherent hazards of major energy and petrochemical plants adjoining populated areas. The large scale of industry land acquisitions provides effective buffer zones for such developments, allowing for future potential expansion while offsetting public criticism of their effect on other land uses.

Social Forces Influencing Emergency Management

Social forces – broadly defined to include individual corporations and business groups, advocacy and assorted interest groups, along with the expanding role of otherwise unorganized individuals networking through the internet and social media – are exerting growing, if still largely indirect, influence on EM policy-making in Alberta.

Emergency services agencies, particularly in the tri-services, have historically enjoyed high levels of public trust. However, both provincial and municipal officials note that the rapid spread of technologies, including cellphones, related camera applications, and social media such as Facebook and YouTube create significant opportunities for public comment and challenges to the performance of these groups. They emphasize that these trends have changed the context for many forms of emergency management and response, increasing challenges for accountability and responsibility, along with the potential for disseminating fragmented and inaccurate information to a wider public (Interviews 81, 82, 83, and 84).[12]

Traditionally, the technical and administrative-level details of emergency planning, response, and recovery management have attracted little public attention in the absence of major foul-ups or the exposure of systemic problems. Today, EM policy-makers, decision makers and front-line law enforcement officials and other first responders must contend with competing sources of public information that can challenge official narratives, call the actions or inaction of public officials into question, and in emergency response settings, serve as complementary, competing, or confusing sources of public information. Provincial and municipal officials state that these realities have complicated already challenging EM responses in managing local fire emergencies and evacuations in Slave Lake and Lethbridge County in 2011 (Interviews 81, 84, and 86). One official comments that "everybody wants to be the first to get things out. Social media has made things so much faster ... People may learn information in an appropriate way or inappropriately – and misinterpret it. So you have to be smoking fast" (Interview 86).

Monitoring Facebook and Twitter are now important elements of EM processes in larger cities, which can create generational challenges for some EM staff (Interview 83). Calgary officials can post alerts and updates in real time to the city's widely used 3-1-1 municipal information line, allowing prompt dissemination by radio and internet (Interview 86). The absence of major catastrophes and the general capacities of local and provincial officials to manage larger ones have defused most issues capable of generating a sustained public outcry, although a series of pipeline spills in Alberta, while not catastrophic individually, may have longer-term effects either on public confidence or policy responses, as noted below. Failing that, the provincial government's routine creation of internal or multi-stakeholder groups to investigate and make recommendations on perceived problems usually has been sufficient to contain and manage substantive problems. However, recent governments have generally avoided public inquiries, which are more difficult to "manage." When pressures for such inquiries become too great to resist, they generally impose relatively narrow terms of reference.

The general view is summarized by one official who notes that the public's "attention is fleeting and very contextual ... A lot of the public trust that we're taking care of them. They're not particularly worried if something happens" (Interview 2). An October 2012 nationwide opinion survey conducted for the Canadian Red Cross reinforces this observation. One-third of respondents expected that emergency responders would answer distress calls posted on social media; 63 percent suggested that emergency responders *should* be prepared to do so (Babineau 2012).

Such attitudes can contribute to public complacency. EM officials privately express concerns that only a tiny fraction of the public responds to annual calls during Emergency Preparedness Week to prepare the seventy-two-hour emergency kits recommended in case of major power outages or other emergencies (Alberta Emergency Management Agency n.d.). A 2011 survey in Strathcona County noted than only 17 percent of persons surveyed understood the concept of "shelter in place," the standard EM response to airborne toxic discharges until they have a chance to dissipate (Interview 84). The 2012 Red Cross survey referenced above noted that two-thirds of respondents "have not taken steps to prepare" for a disaster (Babineau 2012).

One major exception to the prevalence of public complacency has been the emergence of a strong landowner rights movement in rural Alberta, partly in response to intensified resource development and partly as a reaction against heavy-handed provincial legislation governing land-use planning related to resource development and electricity transmission corridors. These issues influence the context for EM policies and practices and have prompted a substantive response by the province's upstream and midstream oil and gas industries,[13] as discussed in the next section.

DEMOGRAPHIC ISSUES AND SOCIAL FORCES: CHALLENGES TO VOLUNTEERISM

A second major social trend of concern to both provincial and municipal officials is growing pressure on volunteerism, which has been the backbone of local emergency response capacities for many years in small-town and rural Alberta. Recruitment and retention has become a central preoccupation for EM coordinators and fire chiefs in small communities, although some officials suggest that "R and R" issues are only a symptom of demand overload on volunteer-based emergency services (Interviews, 81, 82, and 85).

Pressures on the volunteer EM sector result from broader societal trends, conflicting public expectations, and provincial policy changes. Many rural areas, particularly those at some distance from major transportation corridors, face pressures from aging populations, depopulation, and migration to larger cities and the Calgary-Edmonton corridor region. First responders along major corridors face growing demands, which must be balanced not only with family time but with frequent demands for extended commuting time to their primary jobs and limited flexibility in accommodating response calls by primary employers (Volunteer Alberta 2010; O'Brien 2011). Local EM officials suggest that with local fire departments typically scheduling weekly training sessions during most of the year, local forces risk burnout if required to respond to an average of more than two calls per week (Interview 85). For example, the Wandering River Fire Department, two hundred kilometres south of Fort McMurray, suspended highway service in June 2010 because of volunteer burnout from the high volume of serious accidents along Highway 63, forcing the province to supply full-time professional staffing (Pierse 2010; King 2010; Wingrove 2011).

The integration of dispatch, internet, and cellphone technologies also expands the capacity to place volunteers on call almost indefinitely, increasing related stresses and creating disincentives to recruitment (Interview 85). Measures such as the introduction of a 15 percent federal tax credit for volunteer firefighters who perform at least two hundred hours of annual service for their communities provide both recognition and a modest benefit. However, effective policies require effective and systematic local leadership (Volunteer Alberta 2010).

Rural and ex-urban municipalities face significant trade-offs in dealing with their residents' expectations of emergency services. Volunteer emergency services are significantly less costly than those staffed by full-time professionals, but they are not able to provide major urban levels of service, a not insignificant factor for rural municipalities with a limited property tax base. However, growing suburbanization can increase public expectations for emergency services, particularly for municipalities close enough to major urban centres to leverage their locations to promote larger-scale economic development (Smith 2012). Mutual-aid agreements with larger municipalities may provide support in case of serious emergencies. However, clarity of and accountability for service standards are important elements for local councils in evaluating the policy trade-offs associated with making sustainable commitments to emergency services.

SUBSTANTIVE POLICIES: DESCRIPTION AND EVALUATION

The multi-dimensional nature of EM policies – and substantial differences in the extent and effectiveness of their application – greatly complicates the process of policy evaluation in studying a cross-section of municipalities. This section assesses development in municipal and related provincial policies in several areas, including land use and stormwater management; resource and sour-gas development and related inspections; preparedness policies related to CBRN equipment, training, and operations; and provincial engagement with emergency social services.

Planning and Mitigation: Land Use and Stormwater Management

The principle of municipal autonomy shaped by provincial guidelines rather than "directive" policies, remains central to provincial land use and mitigation relating to EM. Municipal governments retain considerable autonomy in establishing rules and principles governing development within their communities, which allows both for the accommodation of local conditions and for innovation in the development of new technologies and "best practices." However, spillovers between wastewater and stormwater systems have led Alberta Environment to make the development of municipal stormwater control strategies consistent with provincial standards a condition for providing municipal wastewater systems with their ten-year Approval-to-Operate (Alberta Environment 2006; Edmonton 2008; Calgary 2011). Moreover, new or "replacement" stormwater drainage systems installed by developers "must be constructed according to the applicable design standard" and certified by a professional engineer in order to receive provincial approval (Alberta Environment 2003, ss. 5–6). Larger municipalities have moved aggressively to apply and extend these guidelines to fit local circumstances. Guidelines appear to be less effective in regulating development within floodplains (Braid 2012).

The biggest engineering challenge involves retrofitting infrastructure to address deterioration and improvements to environmental standards, along with changes to zoning rules to address development in flood plains or adjoining major industrial areas. Edmonton has addressed the former issue by building more than thirty underground storage caverns under older areas of the city. Calgary took similar steps after major floods in 2005, and Lethbridge also undertook a series of remedial measures after significant overland flooding in 2002, including the construction of surge caverns and sewer expansion. Since 2000, Lethbridge has dedicated funding for the rehabilitation and upgrading of sanitary sewers, helping to reduce incidents of sewer backup and related flooding based on detailed planning conducted in previous years (Interview 46; Lethbridge 2012).

Also problematic are the challenges of past construction in flood plains. After major floods in 1951, Lethbridge banned new development in the Oldman River valley and began a process of buying out private landowners that was finally completed in 2001. Some older Edmonton neighbourhoods remain in the North Saskatchewan River valley, while Calgary had to evacuate about fifteen hundred people from downtown areas of the Elbow River valley in June 2005 (Calgary 2005). Similar "legacy" problems exist in Medicine Hat.

Rural stormwater management issues also raise issues of multi-level governance. Provincial environmental regulations require that all new developments be designed to retain 100 percent of storm-water on-site unless municipal districts are able to negotiate a "con-veyance agreement" with the province and, where relevant, with regional irrigation districts. Such agreements require an operational plan for implementation (Interview 85). Drainage systems for most Southern Alberta irrigation districts were built during periods of lower rainfall and run-off than are typical now. As noted earlier, overland flooding has been a significant issue in large parts of south-ern Alberta – most recently in 2010 and 2011. These events have prompted municipal and county officials in Lethbridge County and Coaldale, its largest municipality, with seventy-five hundred people, to pursue an integrated development strategy with widespread pub-lic participation to address flooding issues in a broader planning context (Coaldale and County of Lethbridge 2012).

These issues suggest that while smaller municipalities may face challenges from limited municipal planning resources, strong local leadership can mobilize the resources necessary for effective inter-municipal collaboration when action is taken shortly after major focusing events. Kneehill County has addressed these concerns by retaining full-time planning staff, although turnover remains a prob-lem. Landowners seeking planning approvals and development per-mits are required to build dams to control water run-off, including provisions to manage downstream risk – a key factor in overland flooding issues noted above (Interviews 23, 48, and 71). These con-cerns increase the importance of drainage issues when approving rural developments and subdivisions.

Alberta Environment designated fourteen flood risk areas across the province between 1991 and 1996. In these areas, development was "discouraged" in "floodways," based on hundred-year flood risk mapping conducted by the ministry, and it was allowed, subject to "flood-proofing," in "flood fringe" areas. After the 2005 floods, the Alberta government set up the Flood Risk Management Com-mittee (FRMC) to assess the need for policy changes to reduce the impact (and related costs) of property damage from periodic floods. The committee was led by a government MLA and supported by an inter-ministry task force with representatives from the Ministries of Environment, Municipal Affairs, Transportation, Infrastructure, and EMA, among others. Municipal presentations to the FRMC suggest that municipal councils continue to prefer this non-prescriptive approach by the province, although this outlook is far from universal (Interview 44). One official contends that "they could ... mandate certain things to put on our bylaws ... If the province deems it to be that important, give us a set of rules. Like building in a 1 in 10 [year flood return zone] – are you kidding me? If they want to build there, they should get no compensation. Put a caveat on every single one of those properties. That's easy, and it protects future [buyers]. Just like those houses on a cliff in Edmonton. Now you can't touch them with insurance. If you ... go for it, you shouldn't be eligible for a single cent in government funding" (Interview 55).

However, the FRMC recommendation that flood plain locations be registered on property titles for purposes of consumer protection has never been implemented, and the report itself was released only in July 2012, six years after its initial preparation.

Mitigation and Preparedness: Resource, Sour Gas, and Pipeline Development and Inspections

Municipalities play a secondary role, as noted previously, in regulatory issues concerning the development of energy resources, which are governed by the ERCB. Oil and gas exploration and production involve potential health and safety hazards that have become the subject of intensified provincial regulation in recent years, spurred in part by the spread of residential development in rural, resource-intensive areas. This has resulted in growing landowner and environmental concerns over land use regulation and resource development.

The numerous oil and gas wells (and some gas plants) located near the boundaries of major cities raise significant municipal EM issues. In 2005, Compton Petroleum's proposal to drill sour-gas wells within several kilometres of a proposed new hospital and many proposed residential developments in southeast Calgary created a major controversy spearheaded by Calgary's medical officer of health and several residents' groups (Interview 37; Ebner 2005; Ebner and Walton 2006). Similar problems have occurred from time to time around Edmonton (Henton 2008).

The principal area of dispute was the alleged inadequacy of new provincial regulations governing the creation of Emergency Planning Zones (EPZs) in which residents would be encouraged to "shelter in place" following a sour-gas leak until its plume had a chance to disperse. Senior scientists interviewed suggest that the ERCB's draft guidelines may have been reasonable, based on existing levels of scientific knowledge, but that they were certainly open to dispute, depending on the degree to which policies were based on "risk management" or "precautionary" principles (Interview 31). The "precautionary" principle of regulation stresses minimizing risks to human health and safety to the lowest achievable levels, while "risk management" principles tend to focus on assessing and managing "relative risk" in a cost-benefit context involving other policy objectives. The Calgary Health Region's threat of litigation may have affected the Alberta Energy and Utilities Board's decision to order Compton to make major revisions to its emergency response plan. Compton's application was ultimately rejected in January 2006 after two months of hearings (Ebner and Walton 2006).

With industry activity growing in Southern Alberta, Lethbridge officials have persuaded the ERCB to provide wider EPZs than are normally provided for drilling activity within the city limits, suggesting that the provincial government is willing to accommodate persistent municipal lobbying on such issues. As noted above, the issue of "urban" oil and gas development remains under active consideration by the province (Vanderklippe 2012). As a result, the oil and gas industry has become much more proactive in dealing with EM issues. In addition to its extensive hazard management and response activities, it has also provided a major impetus for the expansion of technological capacities for emergency response in several areas of the province, especially in areas of rural and suburban population growth. Typically, major local industries have the primary responsibility for the initial response to incidents involving fires, explosions, or the discharge of hazardous materials. Energy firms in populated areas will typically notify local first responders, who provide "backup" functions to industry response teams. ERCB regional staff are empowered to take control of emergency response situations if company or local response capacities are judged inadequate (Interview 67). Table 5A.2, in the appendix to this chapter, notes ERCB enforcement actions taken in 2008–10.

A different approach, taken by municipal governments like Red Deer, is to conduct longer-term land use planning exercises. These signal to the oil and gas industry their plans for residential and industrial expansion over an extended period, perhaps fifteen years, to encourage the depletion of oil and gas wells within or adjoining that expansion zone. However, the effects of new technologies in expanding the capacity of extractive industries to recover oil and gas in formations previously thought un-economic complicate the best efforts of city planners to take such approaches. Another senior official comments that the location of active oil and gas wells is "a major input into land use policies ... Why would we annex a piece of land that would be on our books for sixty years but isn't developable ... It's like inviting a headache" (Interview 38).

Municipal Preparedness and Intergovernmental Relations

This section examines four major elements in municipal EM preparedness: the adequacy of federal and provincial assistance, training policies and programs, the problem of dealing with "non-standard emergencies," and harmonization of technical equipment.

Provincial and/or federal assistance to municipalities can take several forms, including technical advice and financial and training support. AEMA provides considerable assistance to smaller municipalities in designing municipal emergency plans. AEMA district officers are seen as helpful in facilitating the periodic exercise of municipal emergency plans to test response capacities and the effectiveness of inter-agency cooperation. However, smaller communities are inherently constrained from taking first responders out of the field, particularly the overburdened members of rural RCMP detachments. Similar problems are reported in supporting industry EM exercises required by federal environmental regulations, except where these can be coordinated regionally.

Officials in larger municipalities have different views of the adequacy of provincial assistance. Some prefer to be left alone, especially in the absence of expanded financial assistance. Others have expressed a desire for a more "hands-on" provincial approach, as in British Columbia. One suggested that "it's nice to say, 'have your own way,' but it would be nice to have more coordination" (Interview 2). Others call for the province-wide standardization of risk assessment tools and training standards, particularly the mandating of Incident Command System (ICS) processes for responding to incidents involving multiple agencies (Interview 88).

An almost universal refrain is the inadequacy of federal or provincial funding to maintain CBRNE response capacities or to provide adequate training to operationalize the substantial amounts of CBRNE equipment funded by federal capital grants since 2000. Much of this equipment is seen as having been "left to rot" in the absence of adequate training, operational funding, or integration with existing emergency service functions – an observation noted by the Senate Standing Committee on National Security and Defence (Senate of Canada 2004, 46).

All large and medium-sized municipalities studied perform extensive internal EM training activities as part of their normal activities. Some, like Lethbridge and Strathcona, make these programs available to first responders from neighbouring municipalities and local industries. Municipal officials interviewed expressed varied opinions on the quality of training provided by the Canadian Emergency Management College (CEMC) in Ottawa before its closure following the 2012 federal budget, noting its failure to follow the broader fire sector's adoption of the ICS systems for managing emergency response.[14] However, CEMC was valued for its related opportunities for networking and learning from peers in other provinces. Officials in smaller communities speak highly of the cooperative training programs conducted by municipal officials within their regions, often coordinated by AEMA officials.

Working-level officials suggest that the counter-terrorism approach taken by the Ministry of Justice and Solicitor General (JSG), which tends to communicate with local EM officials on issues of critical infrastructure protection only on a "need-to-know" basis, is rarely oriented towards the concerns of municipal emergency services. Some officials suggest that this "difference of cultures" is rooted in the former's counter-terrorism emphasis, as contrasted with the "all-hazards" approach typical of EM policies at AEMA and in municipal governments (Interviews 81 and 84).

Officials in larger and medium-sized cities suggest that one way of dealing with the training problem – and the related costs of taking staff off duty for up to a week, transporting them to Ottawa, and paying related travel costs – is to develop a "train the trainer" approach to conducting local or regional training sessions. (There is some evidence of a growing application of this principle in Alberta in recent years.) Others are more far-reaching, suggesting that the design of the CBRNE program is seriously flawed and that a more effective approach would be to integrate primary CBRNE training with existing "hazmat" training to deal with dangerous-goods spills or emissions in their own communities or regions of Alberta. One official commented that "the first ones we send off (to intermediate and advanced courses) are our hazmats paramedics. The techniques are linked so incredibly close that you can't separate them. It also has to be a multi-disciplinary approach. There isn't one service that can respond to a CBRN event independently of other services within your community" (Interview 25).

Others suggest that training levels be linked to response capacities, with first responders in all communities receiving level 1 training, enabling them to contain particular incidents, level 2 providing backup and response capacity to specified levels, and level 3 providing the most advanced training to selected departments with top-of-the-line response capacities (Interviews 47 and 86).

However, one challenge to designing *effective* regional response capacities will be to address labour-management issues that impose constraints on the timely deployment of CBRNE and HUSAR units from major cities in support of colleagues in other areas. Some municipal officials interviewed stress the importance of establishing formal protocols in advance for the deployment of municipal first responders based on federal or provincial mandates, as opposed to traditional inter-municipal mutual aid agreements (Interview 84). AEMA has addressed this problem to some extent by creating a protocol with the City of Calgary to pay all salaries and deployment costs of municipal first responders deployed through Canada Task Force (CTF) 2, which was set up after 2005 as one of five Heavy Urban Search and Rescue (HUSAR) units across the country (Interview 86).

However, training alone, without adequate operational funding for dedicated CBRNE equipment, will address only part of this problem of maintaining capacity in this area. One significant problem addressed by several municipal officials, as well as the provincial task force set up after the 2005 Wabamun incident, is the problem of specialized capacity to deal with "non-standard emergencies." Such emergencies include CBRNE incidents, Heavy Urban Search and Rescue (for example, a major building or bridge collapse), and hazardous goods spills or discharges in rural or remote areas where local officials may lack effective technical response capacities.

CTF-2 appears to be evolving in this direction as an integrated, multi-disciplinary force that can draw on a variety of EM resources in response to major emergencies inside and outside the province. It remains to be seen how this process, which to date has not involved other large and medium-sized municipalities, will evolve following discussions with the provincial government and the Municipal Group of 9.

Emergency Social Services

The concept of Emergency Social Services (ESS) – the provision of housing and medical and other social services to citizens forced to evacuate their homes, particularly those without access to alternative forms of shelter – has achieved a much higher profile since the fiasco following the 2005 US hurricane season (especially Hurricanes Katrina and Rita). Large and medium-sized municipalities typically contract with the Canadian Red Cross and other non-profit agencies to staff local evacuation and relief centres in the event of a mandatory evacuation.

Calgary and Edmonton have established full-time ESS planners. Calgary's ESS functions have been particularly active owing to evacuations as a result of a series of major fires and the floods of 2005, which saw the evacuation of fifteen hundred people from downtown Calgary. Several major fires and other local events since the late 1990s have also provided regular opportunities to test and evaluate local services and the effectiveness of their integration with other city services. As noted above, Edmonton's ESS network took responsibility for more than half the people evacuated from the Slave Lake fires in 2011.

ESS are sometimes seen as the "orphaned stepchild" of EM, particularly given the relatively hierarchical, insular character of tri-services agencies. Both federal and provincial EM doctrines anticipate that citizens will take responsibility for their own well-being and that of their families for the first seventy-two hours of an emergency to allow first responders to allocate their resources to those areas of greatest need.

This approach is probably realistic in areas with widely dispersed populations, particularly in dealing with natural emergencies such as widespread flooding and snow or ice storms. Interviews with emergency managers in Hinton and Kneehill County suggest that community spirit in Alberta is alive and well and that the biggest challenge facing local managers is often how to manage the large numbers of volunteers effectively in such circumstances. However, it may be less realistic in dealing with serious, prolonged emergencies affecting major metropolitan areas – especially since it relates to the growing populations of the most vulnerable citizens: the homeless, people with chronic medical conditions, and single parents and older seniors, especially those without close family members nearby.

Both Calgary and Edmonton have creative, highly professional ESS teams with the capacity to mobilize significant networks of non-profit agency providers and business organizations and other resources in case of need. However, unlike most other specialized areas of emergency services, there is no "line ministry" within the Alberta government responsible for oversight or support of mutual social service agencies. AEMA has responded to these concerns since 2007 by expanding staff support for ESS preparedness in municipalities.

CONCLUSION

Alberta's EM system has proven generally effective in meeting the broad criteria used to evaluate EM policies in other jurisdictions, particularly in areas within municipal jurisdiction. EM professionals across the province generally view current standards for risk-based emergency planning as effective in enabling municipal officials and first responders to identify and carry out their responsibilities in a consistent fashion, while providing sufficient flexibility to accommodate differences in municipal circumstances.

The largely technical character of EM policies, AEMA's flexible and largely decentralized approach to policy implementation, and senior municipal officials' tendency to avoid politicizing disagreements with the province tend to minimize overt conflicts. Even when frictions emerge as a result of different management styles or priorities, working-level officials are generally instructed to work within normal bureaucratic channels (Interviews 2, 7, 17, and 68). Interpersonal, rather than partisan, relationships are the critical factors in getting things done.

AEMA policies and programs are seen to provide effective assistance – especially to smaller municipalities – in designing municipal emergency plans and facilitating their periodic exercise to test response capacities. Some technical gaps remain, notably the harmonization of procedures to facilitate inter-service cooperation, although this issue is being addressed, if slowly, through the gradual adoption of ICS procedures across the province, as recommended by successive provincial inquiries (Alberta Environmental Protection Commission 2006; Alberta Flat Top Complex Wildfire Review

Committee 2012). In the absence of federal leadership (or the funding necessary for its effectiveness), the adoption of a national standard by the inter-provincial body of Senior Officials Responsible for Emergency Management (SOREM) could accelerate this process.

Municipal and provincial policies have been most effective in mitigating risk in areas of recurring natural hazards. The stormwater policies of larger cities are generally effective in mitigating property and environmental damage – although Calgary, in particular, faces significant challenges in retrofitting older neighbourhoods. Municipalities generally have the planning authority necessary to limit flooding risks – as demonstrated by Lethbridge, its neighbouring municipalities, and Kneehill – subject to their continuing willingness to invest in adequate planning capacity and support these decisions.

Mitigation activities related to human-induced hazards are most advanced in the mid-stream oil and gas industry – especially in high-density industrial regions in Strathcona County – although the ERCB has been scrambling to catch up with the growth of oil and gas drilling and processing activities around the province, as well as with ongoing issues of pipeline integrity. Upstream operators in some areas have worked effectively to enhance coordination with municipal emergency services, although anecdotal evidence suggests that such cooperation depends on strong industry leaders and the recognition of higher levels of risk. However, a recent spate of highly publicized failures suggests that the pipeline industry may need to take steps to restore public confidence in its safety measures (not just its response capacity) or face corrective government action. Table 5A3, in the appendix at the end of this chapter, summarizes the number, type, and intensity of spills occurring between 2005 and 2010.

Small and rural municipalities mentioned in this study, including Hinton, Kneehill, and Mountain View, among others, have demonstrated high levels of creativity in mobilizing resources and coordinating activities with other governments and community groups in providing higher than average levels of service, given the size of their municipalities. However, observers caution that these approaches suggest what is possible in smaller communities, given effective leadership, rather than what is typical, in light of the limited resources available to most small communities.

The greatest strength of Alberta's EM system lies in the dedication and professionalism of its emergency management professionals and first responders – whether at the provincial, regional, or municipal level. Proposed changes should build on these strengths and maintain the flexibility that enables local EM leaders to adapt plans and processes to Alberta's diverse municipal geography and conditions, while fostering increased cooperation in the identification and application of best practices across the province's municipalities.

Officials interviewed for this study suggest two complementary approaches in pursuing this objective. First, the province should encourage the extension and increasing formalization of emergency management education and training within the province, possibly through the expansion of existing programs, such as that at Lakeland College. Second, it should work with the interprovincial Senior Officials Responsible for Emergency Management (SOREM) group to fill the gap created by the closure of the Canadian Emergency Management College. This could be done in part by formalizing interprovincial training standards and programs and in part by utilizing the expertise of major municipalities to develop joint training and learning facilities comparable to the specialized training available through groups such as the Emergency Management Institute in the United States (Interviews 84, 86, and 88). The first approach would address the need for effective in-province training, especially for municipal officials and emergency responders from small communities; the second would facilitate the ongoing development and dissemination of best practices between provinces and among larger municipalities.

The AEMA has sought to respond to the Alberta EM system's greatest weakness – the relative decentralization of municipal governments – by actively encouraging increased cooperation among municipalities and, with it, greater capacity based on shared services. The result has been a growing number of Regional Emergency Partnerships since 2007, partnerships institutionalizing the professionalism and interpersonal skills of emergency services coordinators and AEMA field staff. However, under current political circumstances, the success of this approach depends entirely on the quality of local leadership.

To further systematize this process, the Alberta government should mandate the development of regional emergency plans, initially between rural and neighbouring small urban municipalities, but ultimately across regional planning districts aligned with the boundaries of relevant provincial agencies. However, the sizeable difference in the population densities and economic capacities of different parts of the province, as well as major differences in urban, small-town, and rural relations, tends to mitigate against a "one-size-fits-all" approach – as demonstrated by the challenges of centralizing Alberta's ambulance and emergency dispatch services since 2008. Further study is necessary to determine the extent to which the geographical dispersion of populations may limit the communities of interest (or shared risk) that would make this approach to EM effective.

APPENDIX

Table 5A.1
States of Local Emergency, Alberta, 2011–12

2011		
Date	Location	Emergency
Jan. 8–10	Town of Strathmore	Snowstorm, road closures, and stranded travellers
Apr. 4–10	Leduc County	Water-main break/Boil water advisory
Apr. 11–14*	Cypress County	Risk of dam collapse
Apr. 12–19	City of Medicine Hat	Risk of upstream dam collapse
Apr. 14–27	Siksika First Nation	Ice jam, flooding, road washouts
May 14–31*	M.D. Lesser Slave Lake	Out-of-control wildfires
May 14–31*	Town of Slave Lake	Out-of-control wildfires
May 14–29*	Driftpile First Nation	Out-of-control wildfires
May 15–21*	Loon River First Nation	Out-of-control wildfires
May 15–21*	Northern Sunrise County	Out-of-control wildfires Little Buffalo pipeline spill
May 15–21	M.D. of Big Lakes	Out-of-control wildfires
May 15–26*	M.D. of Opportunity	Out-of-control wildfires
May 15–29	Town of High Prairie	Out-of-control wildfires
May 15–21	Lubicon Lake First Nation	Out-of-control wildfires
May 15–21*	Martin Lake Metis Community	Out-of-control wildfires
May 15–29*	Gift Lake Metis Settlement	Out-of-control wildfires
May 15–31*	Whitefish Lake First Nation	Out-of-control wildfires
May 16–22*	Whitefish Atigameg First Nation	Out-of-control wildfires
May 17–20*	Woodland Cree First Nation	Out-of-control wildfires
May 18–29*	Sawridge First Nation	Out-of-control wildfires
May 21–27	Swan River First Nation	Out-of-control wildfires
May 26–30*	Town of High River	Overland, river flooding
May 27–28	M.D. of Foothills	Flooding
June 24–30	Town of Falher (Peace River)	Flooding
June 24–30	Sucker Lake First Nation	Flooding
June 24–30	Driftpile First Nation	Flooding

Table 5A.1 continued

July 12–15*	Mackenzie County	Flooding
July 17	M.D. of Bighorn (Exshaw)	Major dump fire
Nov. 27–28*	County of Lethbridge	Grassfires

2012		
Date	Location	Emergency
Jan. 4–5	M.D. of Willow Creek	Grassfires
March 20	Town of Oyen	Snowstorm, road closures, and stranded travellers
May 16–18*	M.D. of Bonnyville	Forest fires
July 6–20*	Mackenzie County	Forest fires
July 10–23*	Dene Tha First Nation	Forest fires
July 25–28*	Town of Whitecourt	Flooding
Sept. 10–13*	Blood Tribe	Grassfire, windstorm
Sept. 10*	Town of Coalhurst	Grassfire, windstorm
Sept. 10–11	Town of Hanna	Windstorm
Sept. 10–11*	City of Lethbridge	Wildfire alert, windstorm
Sept. 10–11*	County of Lethbridge	Grassfire, windstorm
Sept. 10–12*	Town of Milk River	Grassfire, windstorm
Sept. 10–12*	Warner County	Grassfire, windstorm

Source: Alberta Emergency Management Agency, "Daily Situation Reports." Edmonton: 1 January 2011 – 31 December 2012.
* Mandatory evacuation order imposed for some or all residents during part or all of state of local emergency period.

Table 5A.2
ERCB Compliance and Enforcement: Facilities and Operations Shut Down by Field Surveillance Request, 2008–10

	2008	2009	2010
Total shutdowns	143	127	62
Drilling operations	25	28	12
Average duration (hrs)	3.08	5.14	5.75
Well servicing	5	5	4
Average duration (hrs)	0.6	5.4	7
Gas facilities	16	12	3
Average duration (days)	15	11.3	29.3
Oil production facilities	34	27	3
Average duration (days)	30	15	30
Pipelines	53	45	30
Average duration (days)	41	29.5	36.7
Well site inspections	10	10	10
Average duration (days)	23	30.1	7.9

Source: Alberta Energy Resources Conservation Board 2008, 2010, 2011.

Table 5A.3
Alberta Pipeline Failures and Spills: 2005–10

	2005	2006	2007	2008	2009	2010	Avg.
Pipeline releases/hits	888	895	880	865	734	687	825
Priority 1 (serious)	32	38	36	45	33	33	36.2
Priority 2 (moderate)	117	115	97	108	81	103	103
Failures per 1,000 km	2.3	2.2	2.1	2.1	1.7	1.6	2.0
Spills – liquid hydrocarbon*	5.0	9.7	3.9	3.9	6.8	3.4	5.5
Spills – produced water*	13.2	27.3	22.0	26.2	23.3	24.6	22.8

Source: Alberta Energy Resources Conservation Board, 2010, 2011 (author's calculations).
* x 1,000 cubic meters; 1 barrel = 1 cubic meter or 1,000 litres.

NOTES

1 The Municipal Group of 9 – Calgary, Edmonton, Grande Prairie, Lethbridge, Medicine Hat, Red Deer, St Albert, Strathcona County, Regional Municipality of Wood Buffalo.
2 Media reports indicate that Calgary spent at least $3.5 million on replacing its fifteen-year-old emergency radio system in 2011–12, financed mainly from tickets revenues from red (traffic) light cameras, and a 37-cent monthly charge to telephone subscribers to pay for 9-1-1 services (Cuthbertson 2011).
3 Six years after the resolution of the Compton dispute, with routine industry consultation and mitigation practices substantially exceeding existing regulatory norms, provincial energy minister Ken Hughes has announced plans for an "urban oil and gas strategy" to expand regulatory protections for homeowners outside major cities (Vanderklippe 2012).
4 Calgary's costliest local event in recent years, a hailstorm in July 2010, triggered more than $400 million in private insurance claims (Gignac 2010). CEMA's 2011 annual report identifies six major events with a net cost to the city (not including individual citizens or businesses) of $456,000 (Calgary Emergency Management Agency 2012, 33). Province-wide damage from major hailstorms in 2012 is estimated at close to $500 million – mainly in Southern Alberta.
5 The Major Industrial Accident Council of Canada (MIACC) was a collaborative partnership involving the federal government, provincial and municipal governments, and industrial stakeholders, which was formed in

1986 to promote industrial safety and emergency planning for hazardous substances. It was dissolved in 1999 owing to insufficient funding, but many of its guidelines and standards remain in use today.

6 The evolution of rural addresses and signage stems from a provincial decision in 2007 to promote digitization of rural addresses to facilitate the identification of rural properties by emergency responders, following the practice in Ontario and some other provinces.

7 ALS – advanced life support

8 The cities of Calgary and Airdrie; the MDs of Foothills and Rocky View; and the Towns of Chestermere, Cochrane, High River, and Okotoks.

9 This division of responsibility has raised questions among some municipal officials interviewed on who has legal authority to take the lead on incidents related to pipeline spills. The answer appears to depend on relative capacity and established EM planning arrangements in particular legal and geographic jurisdictions.

10 "White zones": daily fire hazard maps omit data on most of central and southern Alberta. Alberta Environment and Sustainable Resources Development, "Fire Danger Forecasts," Edmonton, 3 May 2012; http://www.srd.alberta.ca/Wildfire/FireDangerForecasts/Default.aspx.

11 The fire-weather index is a general index of fire danger in forested areas. See also Canadian Wildland Fire Information System at http://cwfis.cfs.nrcan.gc.ca/background/summary/fwi. The *Forest and Prairie Protection Act*, F–19 RSA 2000, empowers municipal districts to regulate and control fire hazards on public and private land (sec. 10), as well as issuing fire permits under the Act (sec. 19–21). Sec. 17 designates the period between 1 April 1 and 31 October as the "fire season," except as otherwise designated (e.g., 2012: March 1).

12 Electronic technologies have multiple uses capable of disrupting traditional relationships, both in employment and in various forms of internal and external accountability. For example, *internal* GPS use is not uncommon among Alberta municipalities. However, in June 2012 members of Kneehill Council instructed staff to mount an LCD display in the lobby of the county building in Three Hills that uses GPS technology to indicate the location on county roads or works yards of every single county vehicle, e.g., vehicles of by-law officers, fire trucks, and road-repair vehicles. Although such a display may have value in demonstrating residents' tax dollars at work, it certainly creates other opportunities for public observation and comment!

13 "Upstream": oil and gas exploration and production; "midstream": energy upgraders, refineries, gas plants, and pipelines.

14 Both the provincial and the municipal officials interviewed noted the proactive approach of the provincial and national police, fire, EM, and EMS
organizations in promoting dissemination of Incident Command System
(ICS) training across Canada, based on materials adapted from the US
Federal Emergency Management Agency (FEMA) (Interviews 81 and 83).
AEMA appears to be strongly supportive of the diffusion of ICS training,
but based on recommended guidelines rather than a legislative mandate.

INTERVIEWS

Between mid-2005 and mid-2012, the author conducted ninety semi-structured interviews, primarily with provincial, municipal, and health region
officials and first responders; business and industry representatives; and
academic experts. Interviews were conducted on the basis of confidentiality
to encourage greater frankness in the discussions. The following provides a
summary of persons interviewed during this period.

1   Senior official, Alberta government, Edmonton, 16 June 2005.
2   Municipal official, Edmonton capital region, 17 June 2005.
3   Business representative, Lethbridge area, 20 July 2005.
4   Senior municipal official, Lethbridge area, 26 July 2005
5   Elected official #1, Lethbridge, 27 July 2005.
6   Emergency Services official #1, Lethbridge area, 27 July 2005.
7   Emergency Services official #2, Lethbridge area, 28 July 2005.
8   Health region official #1, Lethbridge, 28 July 2005.
9   Elected officials #2 and #3, Lethbridge, 29 July 2005.
10 Alberta cabinet minister, by telephone, 29 July 2005
11 Senior official, Emergency Management Alberta, Edmonton, 4 August
    2005.
12 Senior official, Public Safety and Emergence Preparedness Canada,
    Edmonton, 4 August 2005.
13 Emergency services official #1, Edmonton capital region, 4 August 2005.
14 Local business representative, Hinton, 5 August 2005.
15 Municipal councillor, Hinton, 5 August 2005.
16 Senior municipal official, Hinton, 5 August 2005.
17 Emergency services official, Calgary, 9 August 2005.
18 Senior municipal official, Calgary, 15 August 2005.
19 Emergency services official #2, Calgary, 18 August 2005.
20 Emergency services official #3, Calgary, 18 August 2005.
21 Senior official, Calgary Airport Authority, 18 August 2005.

22 Health region official #2, Lethbridge, by telephone, 22 August 2005.

23 Emergency services official #4, Calgary, by telephone, 23 August 2005.

24 Alberta cabinet minister, 12 August 2005.

25 Emergency Services official #1, Central Alberta, Three Hills, 19 August 2005.

26 Elected official #1, Central Alberta, by telephone, 23 September 2005.

27 Municipal official, Edmonton capital region, 21 November 2005.

28 Emergency services official #2, Edmonton capital region, 21 November 2005.

29 Senior municipal official #1, Edmonton capital region, 21 November 2005.

30 Emergency services official #3, Edmonton capital region, 22 November 2005.

31 Senior academic, University of Alberta, Edmonton, 22 November 2005.

32 Responsible officer, Royal Canadian Mounted Police, Edmonton, 23 November 2005.

33 Senior municipal official #2, Edmonton capital region, 23 November 2005.

34 Specialist official, Alberta Energy Utilities Board, Calgary, 24 November 2005.

35 Specialist official, Alberta Energy Utilities Board, Calgary, 24 November 2005.

36 Specialist official, Canadian Association of Petroleum Producers, 24 November 2005.

37 Senior official, Calgary Health Region, 24 November 2005.

38 Senior municipal official, Calgary, 25 November 2005.

39 Senior municipal official #2, Calgary, 25 November 2005.

40 Alberta cabinet minister, by telephone, 29 November 2005.

41 Alberta cabinet minister, 18 July 2006.

42 Mid-ranking official, Emergency Management Alberta, Edmonton, 20 July 2006.

43 Senior official, Emergency Management Alberta, Edmonton, by telephone, 24 July 2006.

44 Alberta MLA, 2 August 2006.

45 Emergency services officials #5 and #6, Calgary, 2 August 2006.

46 Municipal officials #3 and #4, Lethbridge, 4 August 2006.

47 Emergency services official #2, Lethbridge, 4 August 2006.

48 Municipal officials #2, #3, and #4, Lethbridge County, Lethbridge, 11 August 2006.

49 RCMP detachment commander, small Alberta municipality, 18 August 2006 (exchange of correspondence).

50 Senior municipal official #2, Hinton, 28 August 2006.
51 Senior municipal official #3, Hinton, 28 August 2006.
52 Emergency services official, Hinton, 28 August 2006.
53 Senior official, Alberta Municipal Affairs, Edmonton, 29 August 2006.
54 Elected official #2, senior municipal officials #1 and #2, Central Alberta, Three Hills, 30 August 2006.
55 Senior municipal official #3, Central Alberta, Three Hills, 30 August 2006.
56 Emergency services official #2, Central Alberta, Three Hills, 30 August 2006.
57 Senior official, MD of Rocky View, 19 September 2006.
58 Responsible official, Calgary Health Region, 19 September 2006.
59 Senior municipal official #4, Central Alberta, Didsbury, AB, 24 November 2006.
60 Emergency services official #7, Calgary, 12 April 2007.
61 Municipal official, Edmonton capital region, 25 May 2007.
62 Regional official, Public Health Agency of Canada, Edmonton, 19 June 2007.
63 Senior public health official, Alberta Health and Wellness, Edmonton, 16 July 2007.
64 Senior official, Alberta Emergency Management Agency, Edmonton, 18 July 2007.
65 Emergency services official, Edmonton, 18 July 2007.
66 Industry representative, emergency services, Edmonton capital region, 19 July 2007.
67 Emergency services official, Energy Resources Conservation Board, 9 August 2007.
68 Responsible official, Alberta Energy and Utilities Board, Calgary, 9 August 2007.
69 Senior emergency services official #7, Calgary, 9 August 2007.
70 Mid-ranking official, Alberta Environment, Red Deer, 24 August 2007.
71 Emergency services official #3, Central Alberta, Three Hills, 24 August 2007.
72 Senior public health and emergency services officials #1, #2, and #3, Red Deer, 24 August 2007.
73 Municipal official #5, Lethbridge, 27 August 2007.
74 Senior municipal official #3, Three Hills, by telephone, 29 August 2007.
75 Health region officials #3 and #4, Lethbridge, 19 September 2007.
76 Senior official, Alberta Emergency Management Agency, Lethbridge, AB, 27 October 2007.

77 Senior official, Fire Commissioner's Office, Alberta Emergency Management Agency, 27 October 2007.
78 Senior municipal official #3, emergency services official #5, Edmonton capital region, 24 June 2008.
79 Municipal official, Edmonton capital region, 25 June 2008.
80 Emergency services official #4, Edmonton capital region, 25 June 2008.
81 Senior officials, Alberta Emergency Management Agency, 12 June 2012.
82 Senior municipal official #3, Three Hills, 20 June 2012.
83 Emergency services official #5, Edmonton capital region, 21 June 2012.
84 Emergency services official #6, Edmonton Capital Region, 3 July 2012.
85 Municipal officials #4 and #5, Lethbridge area, 3 July 2012.
86 Emergency services officials #9 and #10, Calgary, 10 July 2012.
87 Emergency services official #3, Central Alberta, Three Hills, AB, 10 July 2012.
88 Emergency services officials #3 and #4, Lethbridge area, 11 July 2012.
89 Senior municipal official #4, Hinton, by telephone, 16 July 2012.
90 Emergency services official #3, Lethbridge area, by telephone, 1 August 2012.

REFERENCES

Alberta. 2011. *Emergency Management Act*. RSA 2000, chapter E–6.8. Edmonton: Queen's Printer.
Alberta Emergency Management Agency. 2011. *Daily Situation Reports*. Edmonton: Alberta Emergency Management Agency.
– n.d. "72-hour Emergency Kit." http://www.aema.alberta.ca/AB-72 Hour Kit.cfm.
Alberta Energy Resources Conservation Board. 2008. ERCB *Provincial Surveillance and Compliance Summary: 2007*. Calgary: Alberta Energy Resources Conservation Board.
– 2010. ERCB *Field Surveillance and Operations Branch Provincial Summary, 2009*. Calgary: Alberta Energy Resources Conservation Board.
– 2011. ERCB *Field Surveillance and Operations Branch Provincial Summary, 2010*. http://www.ercb.docs.products/STS/ST5allan7–2011.pdf.
Alberta Environment. n.d. *Canada-Alberta Flood Damage Reduction Program*. http://www3.gov.ab.ca/env/water/flood/FDRP.pdf.
– 2003. "Wastewater and Storm Drainage Regulation, Environmental Protection and Enhancement Act." *Alberta Regulation 119/1993*. Edmonton: Queen's Printer. http://qp.alberta.ca/documents/1993_119.pdf.

– 2006. *Standards and Guidelines for Municipal Waterworks, Waste-water and Storm Drainage Systems.* http://environment.gov.ab.ca/info/library/6979.pdf.

Alberta Environmental Protection Commission. 2006. *A Review of Alberta's Environmental Protection and Emergency Response Capacity.* http://www.environment.gov.ab.ca/info/library/7584.pdf.

Alberta Flat Top Complex Wildfire Review Committee. 2012. *Final Report.* Edmonton: Alberta Environment and Sustainable Resource Development.

Alberta Municipal Affairs. 2010. *Business Plan 2010–13.* http://www.finance.alberta.ca/publications/budget/budget2010/municipal-affairs.pdf.

– 2011. *Municipal Profiles.* http://www.municipalaffairs.gov.ab.ca/mc_municipal_profiles.cfm.

Babineau, Janice. 2012. "Tech Talk: Canadian Survey on Social Media in Emergencies," 9 October. http://redcrosstalks.wordpress.com/2012/10/09/tech-talk-canadian-survey-on-social-media-in-emergencies.htm.

Bell, Rick. 2010. "Flu Fiasco Unmasked." *Calgary Sun,* 17 December.

Braid, Don. 2009. "Province's Vaccination Plan a True Soviet-style Debacle." *Calgary Herald,* 3 November, A5.

– 2010. "Was Provincial Response Report Washed Out by Political Change?" *Calgary Herald,* 5 June, A1.

– 2012. "Little Action from the Top as Flood Waters Surge Again." *Calgary Herald,* 27 June, A4.

Bruce, Christopher J., Ronald D. Kneebone, and Kenneth J. McKenzie, eds. 1997. *A Government Reinvented: A Study of Alberta's Deficit Elimination Program.* Toronto: Oxford University Press.

Calgary, City of. 2005. *2005 Flood Report: The City of Calgary's Report on the 2005 June Flooding in the Elbow and Bow River Watersheds.* Calgary: City of Calgary.

– 2011. *Stormwater Management and Design Manual.* http://www.calgary.ca/PDA/DBA/Documents/urban_development/bulletins/2011-stormwater- management-and-Design.pdf.

Calgary Emergency Management Agency. 2012. CEMA *2011 Annual Report.* Calgary: City of Calgary.

Calgary Herald. 2009. "Who Should Get the H1N1 Vaccine in Alberta?" 31 October, A5.

CBC News. 2010. "$10 million Added to Calgary's Snow Plowing Budget." Calgary: 1 February.

Coaldale, Town of, and County of Lethbridge. 2012. *Water, Water, Every-where: Integrated Development Strategy: Coaldale, County of Leth-bridge*. Lethbridge: County of Lethbridge.

Cohen, Tobi. 2012. "Critics Decry Emergency Preparedness Cutbacks." *Ottawa Citizen*, 21 June, A3.

Cuthbertson, Richard. 2011. "Radio System Upgrade Urged." *Calgary Herald*, 25 July, B1.

Doug McCutcheon and Associates and Armin A. Preiksatis and Associ-ates Ltd. 2003. "Review of Land Use Policies and Regulations Affecting Heavy Industrial and Residential Separation and Transition Uses." Final Report prepared for Strathcona County, January.

Ebner, Dave. 2005. "Small Firm to Drill for Sour Gas outside Calgary." *Globe and Mail*, 23 June, B7.

Ebner, Dave, and Dawn Walton. 2006. "Alberta Rejects Sour Gas Wells Request." *Globe and Mail*, 5 January, B1.

Edmonton, City of. 2008. "City of Edmonton Stormwater Quality Control Strategy and Action Plan." http://www.edmonton.ca/environmenta/ documents/swQStrategyActionPlan.pdf.

Fekete, Jason. 2010. "Alberta Wasting Flood Lessons." *Calgary Herald*, 5 June, A1.

Gignac, Tamara. 2010. "Record $400M in Claims after July 12 Hail-storm." *Calgary Herald*, 12 August, A1.

Haddow, George D., and Jane A. Bullock. 2003. *Introduction to Emer-gency Management*. Burlington, MA: Butterworth-Heinemann.

Health Quality Council of Alberta. 2010. *Review of Alberta's Response to the 2009 HINI Influenza Pandemic*. http://www.health.ablberta.ca/ documents/HQCA-Review-Pandemic-2009.pdf.

Henstra, Daniel. 2003. "Federal Emergency Management in Canada and the United States after 11 September 2001." *Canadian Public Adminis-tration* 46 (1): 103–16.

Henton, Darcy. 2008. "Rage, Tears as Small-town Alberta Pleads Its Case." *Edmonton Journal*, 24 June, A3.

– 2012. "Provincial Election Delayed Fire Probe Report, NDP Alleges." *Calgary Herald*, 15 May, A3.

– 2013a. "Cellphone Users to Help Pay 911 Costs." *Calgary Herald*, 5 January, A6.

– 2013b. "Alberta Told to Fix EMS Jumble." *Calgary Herald*, 5 March, A1.

Hodgins, David. 2007. "The Agency." Edmonton: Alberta Emergency Management Agency.

Ibrahim, Mariam. 2012. "Alberta Boosts Spending on Fire Prevention in Wake of Slave Lake Disaster." *Edmonton Journal*, 11 May.

Industry Canada. 2012a. "Consultation on a Policy, Technical and Licencing Framework for Use of the Public Safety Broadband Spectrum in the Bands 758–763 MHZ and 788–793 MHZ (D Block) and 763–768 MHZ and 793–798 MHZ (PSBB Block)." Ottawa: Spectrum Management and Telecommunications, Industry Canada, 24 August. http://www.ic.gc.ca/eic/site/smt-gst.nsf/eng/sf10459.html.

– 2012b. "Policy and Technical Framework: Mobile Broadband Services (MBS) – 700 MHZ Band; Broadband Radio Service (BRS) – 2500 MHZ Band. Ottawa: Spectrum Management and Telecommunications, Industry Canada, 1 November. http://www.ic.gc.ca/eic/site/smt-gst.nsf/eng/sf10127.html.

Jackson, Donny. 2012. "Obama Makes It Official, Signs D Block Legislation." *Urgent Communications*, 23 February. http://www.urgentcomm.com/policy_and_law/news/obama-signs-dblock-law-29129223.

Kenny, Colin. 2012. "Disaster in the Making." *Globe and Mail*, 27 June, A11.

King, Laura. 2010. "Facing Facts." *Firefighting in Canada*. http://www.firefightingincanada.com/content/view/7914/213/.

Lethbridge, City of. 2012. *Wastewater Utility and Stormwater Business Plan 2012–2014*. http://www.lethbridge.ca/City-Government/city-administration/Documents/2012–2014-Wastewater-Stormwater-Bus%20Plan.pdf.

Lynch, Tim, and Wayne Dauphinee. 2005. "Quality Management Case Studies in Health Service Emergencies: SARS and Wildland-Urban Interface Fires." *Quality Management in Health Care* 14 (1): 2–17.

Markusoff, Jason. 2009. "Calgary Snow Removal Budget Boosted by $1M." *Calgary Herald*, 24 November.

Markusoff, Jason, and Gordon Kent. 2007. "Cooperate or Else: Stelmach Tells Region." *Edmonton Journal*, 13 June, A2.

Massinon, Stephane. 2010. "Safety Rules Year Too Late for Condos." *Calgary Herald*, 20 March, A1.

O'Brien, Stacy. 2011. "Community Fire Departments Stretched Thin, While Demand for Service Grows." *Red Deer Advocate*, 29 December.

Pierse, Conal. 2010. "Emergency Services at Risk along Highway 63." *Edmonton Journal*, 5 June.

Planning Alliance. 2011. "Edmonton/Strathcona Joint Planning Study." http://www.planningalliance.ca/project/edmontonstrathcona-joint-planning-study.

Senate of Canada. 2004. *National Emergencies: Canada's Fragile Front Lines*. Third Report. Ottawa: Standing Senate Committee on National Security and Defence.

Smith, Dawn. 2012. "Fire Chief Responds to Concern about Fire Services." *Rocky View Weekly,* 12 March.

Statistics Canada. 2012. "Focus on Geography Series, 2011 Census." Catalogue # 98-310-XWE 2011004. Ottawa: October.

Vanderklippe, Nathan. 2012. "The Oil Well Next Door? Even in Calgary, It's Too Close." *Globe and Mail,* 28 June, A1.

Volunteer Alberta. 2010. *Volunteer Firefighter Recruitment and Retention Strategy*. Final report prepared for Alberta Fire Chiefs' Association. http://www.afca.ab.ca/images/stories/PDFs/final_report_rr_may_15_2010.pdf.

Wingrove, Josh. 2011. "Alberta to Hire Responders to Work Oil Sands Highway." *Globe and Mail,* 12 April, A12.

6

Conclusion

ROBERT YOUNG AND DANIEL HENSTRA

As the chapters in this collection indicate, Canadian communities are vulnerable to a wide range of hazards that occasionally trigger serious emergencies that threaten people and property. Whether it is an ice storm that collapses power lines, a train derailment that releases poisonous chemicals, or a virulent, highly contagious strain of influenza, governments must be prepared to respond swiftly to the needs of victims and be equipped to mount a successful recovery. Municipal governments clearly have a central role in formulating and implementing policies in this field, and past experience demonstrates that the quality of local plans and protocols significantly influences the effectiveness of response efforts when disaster strikes. But experts assert that effective emergency management policy also requires coordination between officials at all levels of government and collaboration among governments and stakeholders from the private and voluntary sectors (Kapucu and Garayev 2011; Waugh and Streib 2006). The policy field of emergency management is therefore one of multilevel governance, whereby policy-making involves interaction among multiple levels of government and various social forces.

As noted in the introductory chapter, the studies in this volume are part of a larger research project about multilevel governance and public policy in Canadian municipalities. Consistent with the project's objectives, the authors have sought to document emergency management policies and to analyze how intergovernmental interaction and public participation influence policies and policy-making in this field. The chapters examined the government of Canada, as well as three Canadian provinces that differ significantly in geography, hazard exposure, political culture, settlement patterns, economy, and municipal structure.

Luc Juillet and Junichiro Koji described the federal role in this policy field. Although federal emergency management policy has evolved over time, largely in response to high-profile emergency events, an enduring characteristic is its traditional intergovernmental structure, whereby federal, provincial, and territorial officials develop policy agreements, and municipal governments are regarded as implementation agents, rather than full partners. Despite major emergency events that have highlighted the importance of preparedness and response capacity in cities (such as 9/11), jealous defence of the constitutional division of powers has prevented the incorporation of municipal officials into policy discussions about national emergency management. As the authors explain, a review of federal legislation and policies initiated in the wake of high-profile emergencies and crises in the early 2000s sparked debate between two coalitions of actors, one arguing the priority of policy effectiveness over jurisdictional considerations and the other seeking policy legitimacy by preserving historical divisions of authority. In the end, the latter view prevailed, perpetuating the virtual exclusion of municipalities from intergovernmental policy-making in this field.

In their study of Nova Scotia, Malcolm Grieve and Lori Turnbull find that municipal emergency planning is generally perceived to be adequate. Focusing on four municipalities of various sizes and located in different parts of the province, the authors demonstrate that local officials are actively engaged in emergency planning and report that policies in this field appear to be improving because of the provincial government's efforts to standardize municipal preparedness plans and training for local personnel. However, emergency planning is largely regarded as an appendage to other responsibilities: with the exception of Halifax and Cape Breton Regional Municipalities, which employ full-time emergency managers, local governments generally assign responsibility for emergency planning to officials with a range of other duties. This practice is reflected at the provincial level as well, where the minister of emergency management is also the attorney general and minister of justice and is responsible for overseeing roughly half a dozen other important pieces of legislation. Nevertheless, the authors find a general consensus among both local and provincial officials that Nova Scotia communities are sufficiently prepared for the emergencies the province faces. There is still room for improvement, though, particularly in mitigating the impacts of hazards before emergencies occur, and the authors offer various recommendations in this regard.

Norm Catto and Stephen Tomblin identify dozens of hazards facing communities in Newfoundland and Labrador and document an extensive history of emergencies and disasters in the province. These experiences have forged a strong tradition of informal, community-based emergency response, which has proven resistant to efforts by provincial officials to standardize and formalize local emergency management. Moreover, the authors report significant disparities in emergency management capacity between larger, urban municipalities and smaller, rural communities. The provincial government has attempted to correct this by encouraging the regionalization of emergency services but has faced significant barriers owing in part to the isolated, insular nature of many communities. Despite these formidable challenges, there is a general recognition among public officials that improving local emergency response capacity is necessary and desirable. Emergency management policy in Newfoundland and Labrador is therefore in a period of transition, which suggests that a more formalized system of preparedness and response will emerge in the future.

Drawing on a great deal of documentary evidence and ninety interviews, Geoffrey Hale presents a comprehensive analysis of emergency management policy in Alberta. He finds that policy formulation in this field is largely technical, rarely involving political conflict or intergovernmental friction, and that it is little influenced by partisanship. Alberta municipalities appear to possess sufficient legal authority to develop emergency plans and initiate response operations. Provincial officials typically focus their efforts on advising and supporting smaller municipalities, while granting larger cities considerable autonomy to design and implement emergency management policies provided that they are consistent with legislative parameters. Hale reports evidence of inter-municipal cooperation and collaboration in emergency planning but notes that it is largely informal, uneven throughout the province, and difficult to replicate in all areas: it depends a great deal on trust relationships developed over time between municipal administrators. One unique finding discovered by Hale is the prominent role played by the oil and gas industry in local emergency management. Particularly in rural Alberta and in areas with a high concentration of oil and gas firms, such as Strathcona County, municipal emergency planners rely on close cooperation with industry, which brings resources to the table, including trained emergency response personnel, warning systems, and funds to pay for joint exercises and shared equipment. Hale concludes that policy-makers and stakeholders generally regard emergency management in Alberta as effective, but further improvements in areas such as training and regional coordination are warranted.

THE POLICY FIELD

One objective of this volume has been to examine how emergency management in Canada is structured – to describe the organization of this policy field at the various levels of government. As illustrated in the provincial chapters, municipal governments organize the emergency management function in different ways, depending largely on the size of the community. In smaller municipalities, the responsibility for coordinating emergency planning is typically assigned to an administrator with other duties who is usually located in the police or fire department. In larger communities, an individual is often assigned specifically to serve this role, and in very large cities there is commonly a team of emergency management officials. Most emergency management work involves routine processes of consultation, networking, plan updating, and public education.

Policy formulation occurs largely in the administrative sphere. Ideas arise out of a small, specialized network of policy actors, including representatives from first-responder agencies (police, firefighters, and emergency medical services), provincial and municipal emergency planners, business risk managers, and nongovernmental organizations that perform emergency functions. Municipal emergency managers typically develop specific proposals in conjunction with a committee, which normally includes representatives of other departments and agencies that play a role in emergency response, including certain private firms and nongovernmental organizations.

The extent to which elected officials are involved in local emergency planning appears to depend on their personal or professional interest in the issue. In Lethbridge, Alberta, for example, some councillors are familiar and experienced with emergency management and therefore adopt a more "hands-on" management style in this policy field. Perhaps the most striking example of political involvement uncovered by the researchers is that of Halifax mayor Peter Kelly, who was an active champion of emergency management and a vocal advocate of integrating municipal views and interests into federal policy (perhaps because he was chair of the Big Cities Mayors' Caucus). However, the cases generally illustrated that emergency planning takes place without close scrutiny by elected officials. Although political approval is required for significant program changes, politicians typically entrust policy design to administrators with training and experience and apparent mastery of the subject matter of emergency management.

Emergency management is generally a low-salience policy issue, and public and political interest is sporadic and event-driven. Emergencies serve as occasional "focusing events," in that they temporarily direct attention to a community's vulnerability and raise questions about emergency preparedness. In Nova Scotia, for instance, the media coverage of Hurricane Juan in 2003 focused attention on emergency planning and contributed to a general sense among policy-makers that it illustrated the potential for greater losses from disaster in the future. Skillful emergency managers capitalize on these windows of opportunity to secure authority or resources to support their work, but these moments are rare and short-lived. Although attention spikes in the immediate aftermath of an emergency, it then wanes as the memory of the event begins to fade and other issues jostle for attention and resources.

One of the current challenges facing policy-makers in this field is the regionalization of emergency planning and response. In all provinces, the authors observed efforts by provincial officials to encourage inter-municipal partnerships for emergency planning as a means to coordinate plans and share response resources. But the extent to which these partnerships have been developed has varied. In Alberta, for example, several large cities provide reserve response capacity for smaller, neighbouring communities, and there are a number of long-standing mutual aid agreements among municipalities in different parts of the province. In Newfoundland and Labrador, by contrast, the provincial government has faced challenges in implementing regional partnerships, in part because there is no history of regional governance in the province. Nova Scotia has had much more success in this regard.

Another important challenge observed by the authors of the provincial chapters is a weakening of the volunteer base that has traditionally been the bedrock of response capacity in rural areas. Rural-urban migration, out-of-province commuting, shrinking tax bases, and concerns about liability are some of the factors that have eroded the supply of volunteers that rural communities have historically depended on to perform services such as firefighting, search and rescue, social services, and emergency medical response. Regionalizing emergency services may be part of the solution to this problem, but it seems clear that policy intervention by higher-level governments is required to ensure that rural areas have sufficient capacity to respond to emergencies.

MULTILEVEL GOVERNANCE AND PUBLIC POLICY IN MUNICIPALITIES

Intergovernmental Relations

Emergency management is clearly important for municipalities, but protecting citizens and communities from hazards is a responsibility shared by all levels of government. Emergencies can quickly escalate in scope and severity, and their impacts can often exceed the coping capacity of a single jurisdiction, so intergovernmental collaboration is essential to an effective emergency management system. In light of this, it is crucial to examine the structure and dynamics of intergovernmental relations, the roles and responsibilities of federal, provincial, and municipal authorities, and patterns of interaction between officials based at different levels of the state.

With superior resources and a vast national network of assets and personnel, the government of Canada could reasonably be expected to be an important actor in this policy field. Indeed, a number of Canadian federal departments manage information and deliver services that are valuable inputs for municipal emergency planning. For instance, Environment Canada's weather service – the Meteorological Service of Canada – provides information about past, current, and future weather conditions and issues warnings of severe weather. Similarly, Public Safety Canada maintains the Canadian Disaster Database, which contains information on more than nine hundred disasters that have affected Canadians since the year 1900 (Public Safety Canada 2012a). In analyzing emergency management in various provinces, the authors sought to assess the extent and nature of federal-municipal relations in this field.

In all of the provinces examined in this volume, local officials perceive the government of Canada as a distant, remote actor with little influence over the scope and substance of emergency management policy. Although local officials appear familiar with key federal programs in this field – particularly the Joint Emergency Preparedness Program and the Disaster Financial Assistance Arrangements, which operated until very recently – they are virtually unanimous in their ambivalence toward these contributions, and report little contact with federal officials in this area. The general perception is that, particularly since the terrorist attacks of 9/11, the federal government is preoccupied with narrow aspects of emergency management, such as counter-terrorism and border security, which seem only marginally relevant to municipal emergency planning. As Hale reports from Alberta, federal intervention is "episodic," involving occasional investments in ephemeral policy priorities such as specialized training for chemical, biological, radiological, and nuclear (CBRN) response but failing to provide adequate funding to maintain these capabilities over time.

This distant attitude is not common in other countries. Ottawa's role in Canada's emergency management system appears to differ significantly from that in the United States, for example, where the federal government has long provided central leadership by offering policy direction, expertise, and financial support to state and local governments through the Federal Emergency Management Agency (FEMA) (McEntire and Dawson 2007). There simply is no Canadian agency analogous to FEMA, and the structure and focus of the federal emergency management portfolio has changed so often that many local officials are unable to identify what role they can expect from the national government. Public Safety Canada, the department currently responsible for coordinating the federal government's emergency management activities, has no mandate to direct other departments in a united effort and has been plagued by chronic understaffing and frequent employee turnover (Auditor General of Canada 2009).

Furthermore, the government of Canada's financial contribution to emergency management lags well behind other federal states. The Joint Emergency Preparedness Program, which was effectively the only source of federal funding for municipalities to finance emergency management, had an annual budget of approximately $8 million, and the program committed about $170 million since its

inception in 1980 (Public Safety Canada 2012b). To put these fig-
ures into comparative perspective, in fiscal year 2011, under the
Urban Areas Security Initiative, one of eight funding programs of the
United States Department of Homeland Security designed to support
state and local emergency preparedness, $8 million was allocated to
Seattle, Washington, alone, and the total program budget was more
than $650 million (U.S. Department of Homeland Security 2011).
Australia's Natural Disaster Resilience Program, initiated in 2009,
provides approximately $27 million per year in grants to enhance
the resilience of communities against the impact of disasters (Government of Australia 2011).

What explains the federal government's disengagement from local
emergency planning in Canada? Perhaps this is a product of Canadian federalism, which generally involves limited formal engagement between the federal government and municipalities. Some
provincial governments have long resisted direct federal involvement
with municipalities, and their position is buttressed by the constitutional division of powers, which allocates to the provinces exclusive
jurisdictional responsibility over municipal institutions. As in many
other policy fields, Ottawa's relationship with municipal governments in emergency management is indirect, mediated by the provinces. For instance, provincial approval is required for municipal
proposals to the Joint Emergency Preparedness Program, and local
administrators must apply through provincial channels in order to
enrol in courses at the Canadian Emergency Management College.
Disaster mitigation funding under the Building Canada program is
allocated only to municipal projects that have been approved by
provincial departments. Relief funds available under the Disaster
Financial Assistance Arrangements are paid to provincial governments, which allocate the money directly to individuals who have
experienced losses, rather than to local governments.

Limited federal-municipal engagement in emergency management
is also consistent with the Harper Conservative government's doctrine of "open federalism," which espouses respect for the division of
federal and provincial constitutional responsibilities and envisions
"a strong central government that focuses on genuine national priorities like national defence and the economic union, while fully
respecting the exclusive jurisdiction of the provinces" (Harper
2004). As Young (2006, 9) explains, open federalism implies a strict
reading of the constitution, whereby provincial governments have

exclusive constitutional jurisdiction over municipal institutions and are thus "the principal actors vis-à-vis municipal governments." Only the provinces have authority to pass legislation and issue regulations governing local emergency planning. There are other tools that Ottawa could use to support emergency management, such as insurance reform to encourage hazard mitigation, but these avenues have not been taken, which is testimony to a lack of interest in this policy field. This only reinforces the general resistance to engaging municipalities, a characteristic reflected in recent program cuts.

Relative to the federal government, the provinces have a much more direct relationship with municipalities in this policy field. In all the provinces studied in this volume, there is legislation that authorizes or instructs municipal governments to undertake emergency planning, and all the provinces have a department or agency that is tasked with overseeing and supporting municipal emergency management. In Nova Scotia, the Emergency Management Act requires all municipalities to pass an emergency by-law, appoint an emergency management coordinator, establish a municipal emergency management organization, appoint an advisory committee, and prepare emergency management plans. The Nova Scotia Emergency Management Office, a division of the Department of Justice, coordinates municipal emergency planning and reviews local plans every two years.

In Newfoundland and Labrador, the Emergency Services Act was passed in 2008, requiring all municipal governments to adopt a formal emergency plan and appoint an emergency management coordinator. The act is administered by Fire and Emergency Services, an agency that reports to the minister of municipal affairs, who is also designated the minister responsible for emergency preparedness. Through its central headquarters and four regional offices, the agency collects and approves municipal emergency plans, provides information and resources to local emergency planners, and offers training programs for municipal staff.

Alberta's Emergency Management Act, adopted in 2006, mandates municipal authorities to establish a local emergency management agency, appoint a director, put in place an emergency advisory committee, and prepare and approve emergency plans and programs. The Alberta Emergency Management Agency (AEMA), which reports to the minister of municipal affairs, has chief responsibility for overseeing municipal emergency planning. Through its seven regional offices,

AEMA works to facilitate collaboration and coordination among all organizations involved in emergency preparedness and response.

Provincial-municipal interaction in this field occurs almost exclusively at the administrative level and involves frequent contact between representatives of the various provincial emergency management agencies and municipal officials responsible for emergency planning. Relying primarily on exhortation and persuasion, but supported by legislation, the provincial officials promote emergency planning among communities and offer information and expertise to support local programs. Much of their attention is devoted to smaller communities, which typically lack the human and financial resources to undertake comprehensive emergency planning, while larger communities are granted considerable autonomy in designing emergency management programs to suit their needs. Municipal informants generally express a positive impression of provincial efforts and the working relationship in this policy field appears amicable and productive.

Social Forces

The second broad set of issues that the researchers in this volume sought to address is the role of "social forces" in policy-making and implementation. Analyzing how organized interests participate in the agenda-setting, policy-formulation, decision-making, and implementation stages of the policy process is important for understanding policy scope and content. Of particular interest for the authors was the role of business in shaping municipal public policy, in light of the robust scholarly literature on this issue and long-standing debates about business influence in local government.

In the field of emergency management, policy design appears to be little influenced by organized interests. Local emergency managers typically engage like-minded actors in the private and nonprofit sectors in their planning activities, but none of the authors discovered evidence of a dense community of active interests seeking to influence the scope or direction of public policy, as is often characteristic of other policy fields. In Nova Scotia, for example, representatives from the Canadian Red Cross participate in local emergency planning discussions and exercises and offer information and expertise that support policy formulation, but they refrain from advocating specific policy choices.

Similarly, members of the business community, such as electricity, gas, and telecommunications firms, are frequently incorporated into local and regional emergency planning, because the services and infrastructure under their control are critical to community well-being and represent key points of vulnerability in an emergency. However, there is no evidence that municipal governments face pressure from the chamber of commerce or other business associations to adopt a specific course of action or focus more resources on emergency management. One important exception is the insurance industry which, through research and public education, advocates more proactive efforts to prevent disasters or mitigate their impacts. The insurance industry has a huge stake in this policy area. It works through the Insurance Bureau of Canada (IBC) to educate the public and lobby governments about emergency preparedness, and it has had some success in achieving reform at the federal level. The industry also established the Institute for Catastrophic Loss Reduction, which conducts research and aims to educate the public and policy-makers about appropriate policies. But the IBC is a national organization, and its provincial arms seem to be relatively weak. Curiously, the industry seems to be quiescent at the local level. The researchers whose work is presented here found no evidence of local insurers pressing municipal governments for better emergency management.

Engagement with social forces is strongest at the implementation stage. It is very common for nongovernmental organizations to provide emergency-related services on behalf of municipal governments or the provincial government, either on a voluntary or a contractual basis. For instance, in Alberta the larger and medium-sized municipalities have contracts with the Canadian Red Cross to provide emergency social services to affected residents, and a similar arrangement exists with the provincial government in Nova Scotia. These cooperative arrangements are vital for effective emergency management at the local level, as is the involvement of major industrial actors. In recent years, firms have become more focused on the analysis of risk of all types. As the Alberta cases showed in particular, large companies bring their risk-mitigation strategies to the emergency planning table, and in implementation they can supply specialized equipment and personnel. In municipalities that have big plants or industrial clusters, in sectors like energy or chemicals, private-sector expertise and resources are essential for implementing emergency management.

EVALUATING MUNICIPAL EMERGENCY MANAGEMENT POLICY

A final area of analysis pertains to the quality of emergency management policy, which can be evaluated using various criteria. These criteria are standard in policy analysis: they are the benchmarks for determining how good the policies in place are.

One criterion is the speed of policy development: is policy formulated in a timely manner so as to capture changes in environmental conditions and respond to evolving needs? The research in this collection suggests that emergency management policy development is generally iterative and incremental, involving periodic tweaks and adjustments to objectives and instruments, usually in the aftermath of an emergency. With low public visibility and limited political interest, professional emergency managers have relative autonomy to make policy changes, provided they remain within the legislative parameters set by the province and the limits of their budgetary resources. However, some policy initiatives in this field have developed very slowly, despite nearly universal agreement that they are necessary and desirable. A specific example is the interoperability of communications equipment among members of the emergency management community, which has been a chief priority for local first responders for more than two decades but has only recently received serious attention from higher-level governments.

Another criterion to consider is whether the scale of policy is adequate to address the problem society confronts. Judging by the degree of effort expended by provincial agencies to impel municipalities to devote more time and resources to emergency planning, the scale of policy in this field is not as comprehensive as it could be at the local level. There is considerable variation in response and recovery capacity between larger, urban municipalities and smaller, rural ones, and agreements to coordinate resources between communities are lacking in many regions. However, emergency management capacity appears to be expanding, as evidenced through the growth in staff and resources among provincial agencies. Catto and Tomblin, for instance, report that the number of provincial personnel devoted to emergency management has grown significantly over the last decade in Newfoundland and Labrador.

Coherence is a third criterion for evaluating policy quality. The key question here is, do the various components that make up the overall course of action in this field complement and support each other, or do they leave gaps or work at cross-purposes? On the one hand, the government of Canada and all the provinces studied in this collection have adopted the doctrine of comprehensive emergency management, which includes prevention/mitigation, preparedness, response, and recovery. Experts in this field have long argued that attention to each of these components of emergency management policy is necessary in order to achieve the ultimate goal of safe, resilient communities (for example, McLoughlin 1985). On the other hand, the focus of emergency management in many communities remains largely confined to preparedness and response; less attention is devoted to preventing disaster losses (by, for example, limiting development along waterways and coastlines susceptible to flooding). Policy actors in this domain generally accept that preventative measures can reduce the impacts of emergencies on people and property, but such efforts are in their infant stages in Canada.

Another area of incoherence in emergency management policy stems from the potential perverse incentives attached to disaster financial aid. Government assistance to replace homes and belongings lost in a disaster is an essential element of recovery, but it can also undermine efforts to prevent disaster losses if it discourages behaviour that mitigates risk or encourages people to reinhabit hazardous areas. For example, some homes north of Winnipeg have been flooded and repaired multiple times, and after another flood in 2009 the Manitoba government faced a difficult choice between rebuilding the damaged properties or purchasing and demolishing them (CBC News 2009).

Effectiveness is a fourth consideration: how well does Canadian emergency management policy achieve its goals? The effectiveness of emergency management is hard to measure: although there are hazards in every community, municipal governments face difficulties in deciding how much response and recovery capacity is necessary and in assessing the quality of emergency planning (Waugh 1999). Indeed, O'Leary states that "one of the most formidable challenges facing local communities today is learning to apply the concepts and methods of performance measurement to disaster preparedness" (2004, 1). However, we found that policy-makers and stakeholders generally perceive community-level emergency preparedness to be adequate to address the risks municipal governments face, while recognizing that further effort is required to improve inter-organizational and intergovernmental coordination. Provincial agencies generally provide effective guidance and oversight to support and encourage municipal emergency planning, although local officials complain about the absence of funding to subsidize emergency management activities. But at a systemic level, Canada's emergency management policy appears ineffective in facilitating the kind of vertical intergovernmental collaboration that exists in other federal states, such as the United States and Australia, where the national government has a clear and robust role in emergency management and provides substantial support to state and local governments (McEntire and Lindsay 2012). As noted above, though the government of Canada contributes to emergency management in various ways, it continues to be perceived as a peripheral actor, rather than an important partner.

Efficiency – whether policy goals are achieved at a reasonable cost – is another measure of good public policy. Generally, emergency management programs appear to be efficient. At the local level, emergency planning requires remarkably little money and often represents one of the smallest items in a municipal government's budget. Municipal emergency managers rely heavily on personnel from other departments to participate in planning, training, and exercises, and these "in-kind" resources supplement the budget they have to work with. Planning, response, and recovery capacity is further enhanced through partnerships with outside stakeholders, such as non-profit humanitarian organizations, volunteer groups, and amateur radio operators, who shoulder some emergency functions. Provincial governments contribute to efficiency in this field by distributing templates, guidebooks, and advice to local emergency planners, in order to facilitate knowledge-sharing and diffuse good practices across communities.

Equity is another criterion of good public policy. In emergency management, one issue is the uneven preparedness and response capacity among municipalities, which is particularly pronounced between large urban centres and small rural communities. Whereas some municipalities have formulated comprehensive plans to manage emergencies and their impacts, others have drawn up only a basic course of action as required by provincial statute. Disparities in capacity mean that emergencies of similar scope and magnitude could impose a greater burden on residents in some communities than in others. Another equity issue pertains to the intergovernmental

division of responsibilities that has developed in this field, which
delegates much of the responsibility for emergency management to
municipalities. Municipal governments operate with tight resources and often lack the capacity to formulate comprehensive policies
and programs, so it is unfair to expect high-quality local emergency
management programs without robust support from higher-level
governments.

A final criterion for evaluating public policy is optimality, that is,
whether the policy is the best that can be achieved. The evidence in
this volume suggests that Canadian emergency management policy
is not as good as it could be. It is apparent that policy has improved
in recent years, spurred largely by high-profile emergencies that have
focused attention on this issue. At the federal level and in all provinces studied, policy goals have been revised to embrace principles
such as all-hazards planning, collaborative governance, and disaster risk reduction. These priorities expand the scope of emergency
management beyond the historical preoccupation with preparedness
and response and reflect international "best practices" in the field.
However, while the goals have expanded, the means to implement
them have not. Municipalities are mandated to prepare emergency
plans, but none of the provinces offers financial assistance to support expenses such as equipment purchases, exercises, training, or
salaries, leaving local emergency planners to compete with other
administrators for limited municipal resources. Federal money to
cover these expenses is scarce, and the government's apparent commitment to a strict interpretation of the constitutional division of
powers suggests that federal-municipal engagement in this domain
is unlikely to increase.

THE OVERALL PATTERN OF GOVERNANCE IN EMERGENCY PLANNING

Emergency planning is a fascinating policy field and an unusual
one. All levels of government bear some responsibility, providing
much opportunity for multilevel interaction. Further, there is a very
broad engagement of social forces in the field, primarily in the area
of implementation. Few organized interests are engaged in policy
formation and decision making at higher levels of government:
only the insurance industry and the Red Cross stand out as social
actors. At the local level, more are involved in consensual processes

as plans are made and tasks are allocated to cope with emergencies. For its part, the general public is largely unaware and quiescent until disasters strike, at which point citizens have high expectations of government, and they are prepared to attribute blame for inadequate performance. Public preoccupation with emergencies soon fades, however. Concern is not perennial, as with policies in fields like education or health. Finally, the effects of emergencies are in no way sectoral, affecting different segments of the population, but are purely geographic, since emergencies affect everyone within a certain locale or space. Whole areas and communities are affected by disasters of various kinds. This is unlike education, say, which has a much greater effect on children and parents than on others, and it is unlike health policy, which potentially concerns everyone but is of greatly disproportionate interest to the ill. This geographic universality is a very unusual policy characteristic: it means that all members of a community have a stake in emergency management.

This geographic dimension, fundamental to the field of emergency planning, is striking from an analytic viewpoint. It suggests that emergency management policy is classically "nested," the term used by Hooghe and Marks (2003) to describe Type I multilevel governance. In this pattern there is a limited number of levels of government, and the arrangement is stable. Each government bundles multiple functions. Finally, the membership boundaries do not intersect. (This contrasts with Type II multilevel governance, where special-purpose agencies deliver particular services at various scales, sometimes overlapping.) As Hooghe and Marks put it (236), "in Type I governance, every citizen is located in a Russian Doll set of nested jurisdictions, where there is one and only one relevant jurisdiction at any particular territorial scale." Now, the first part of this sentence nicely captures the nested character of the emergency management field. But the second half is misleading, because all the jurisdictions are relevant and operative in lower scales. The municipal space, clearly, is filled with municipal government policies about emergency management and many other things. But it is also penetrated by provincial policies, in this case the rules and guidelines about emergency planning established by provincial governments. And in the municipal – and provincial – space we also find federal government policies (as was shown by Juillet and Koji in chapter 2). The policies of the three levels come together in municipalities, where they intersect and interact with each other.

The nested character of Type I multilevel governance perfectly characterizes the field of emergency planning. All disasters are local. They affect a particular geographic area. But their severity and scale vary: some are confined to a small space, while more serious and widespread emergencies have provincial and national implications. This means that appropriate measures in terms of prevention/mitigation, preparedness, response, and recovery need to be coordinated across the levels of government. Second, at each tier of government, the multiple functions for which each government is responsible need to be coordinated. Municipal governments need to involve almost every department in emergency planning, while provincial governments need to coordinate functions like policing, transportation, natural resources, provincial utilities, and so on. Finally, the "governance" aspect of Type I multilevel governance fits this policy field, because effective planning and response to emergencies involve a very wide range of extra-governmental actors – social service agencies like the Red Cross, business groups, local utilities, and large firms.

The centrality of geography and the nesting of responsible governments in emergency planning play out in another important manner that is related to the probability of disasters and emergencies. At the national level, in any given period, the probability of an emergency occurring somewhere in Canadian space is very high. For every province, it is lower. For any individual municipality, it is much lower. This "intergovernmental paradox" has implications. All emergencies are local, and their costs can be enormous for municipalities and their citizens, but the incentives to mitigate and prepare are lowest at the local scale. The incentives are larger at higher orders in the nested governance system. "Senior" governments have a large stake in the efforts made at lower tiers.

In Canada, all provincial governments have invested in emergency planning systems and organizations that appear to be adequate, if not optimal. Provinces have spurred municipalities to engage in more systematic planning, and the situation on the ground, almost everywhere, is better than it was not long ago. Gaps remain in inter-municipal cooperation in many places, particularly in rural areas: regional organization is often weak. But the weakest part of the overall system is at the federal level of government. Responsibility has shifted between agencies and ministries. The federal emphasis is strongest on terrorism and national security threats, which are genuine but have lower probabilities than natural and industrial disasters. Recently, cuts have been made to the very weak supports that Ottawa provided for local efforts. The Joint Emergency Preparedness Program, which made small grants for gear for emergency preparedness and urban search and rescue operations, was eliminated in the 2012 federal budget, and the Canadian Emergency Management College, which provided some specialized training, is ceasing operations – though some training will continue through the Canada School of Public Service for a few years at least (*Calgary Herald* 2012). Given the distribution of disaster probabilities, the federal government is "missing in action."

It should be noted that Ottawa has very substantial emergency powers under the Emergencies Act. The successor to the War Measures Act, this act defines a "national emergency" as "an urgent and critical situation of a temporary nature that (a) seriously endangers the lives, health or safety of Canadians and is of such proportions or nature as to exceed the capacity or authority of a province to deal with it, or (b) seriously threatens the ability of the Government of Canada to preserve the sovereignty, security and territorial integrity of Canada and that cannot be effectively dealt with under any other law of Canada" (Canada 1985). The act covers four types of emergency, including Public Welfare Emergencies, which include natural disasters of various kinds, diseases, and accidents and pollution. The act provides for the declaration of an emergency by the federal government, which occurs after consultation with provincial governments if several are concerned, and only with the permission of the provincial government if just one is concerned. After a declaration, federal authorities can control travel, requisition property, require essential services to be provided, take over the distribution of goods, set up shelters and hospitals, and engage in the remediation of property and the environment. In all of this, federal power should not interfere with provincial governments' efforts; indeed, the act envisions "concerted action" with the provinces involved.

These powers are backed up, in the end, by the Canadian Forces. The authority is formidable. But the entire act is focused on response. It does not provide for mitigation or preparedness, and the role in recovery is secondary. In part, this is sensible. Mitigation is best undertaken at the local level, with provincial assistance and advice. Recovery is inevitably local, ideally with financial support from the provincial and federal governments. But there is room for a much greater federal presence in preparedness. Here, Ottawa could play an effective part.

In emergency preparedness, there are gaps where Canadian citizens are concerned. According to general doctrine, individuals and families are supposed to be prepared to endure emergency conditions for seventy-two hours. They should be in a position such that they do not have to count on assistance for three days. But few citizens are prepared: in a national survey conducted in 2009, for example, 42 percent of respondents admitted they were not prepared for the emergencies that they would be likely to face within the next ten years (Oulahen 2009). There is no clear and consistent message that has reinforced the need for Canadians to take responsibility for themselves in the early days of emergencies. In other policy areas, such as physical fitness, the federal government has shown its capacity to undertake sustained and effective public information campaigns. Conducting one about preparedness would fit into agendas focused on safety and security. Such a campaign is surely a legitimate federal government activity. Moreover the cost would be relatively small.

The federal government's decision to reduce its presence in preparedness is congruent with the current orientation about contacts with municipalities – they should be minimized (Young 2011). But there are no such strictures on relations with the provinces. Indeed, the federal government is involved in post-secondary education and research, infrastructure, and health. Emergency planning is a function that is not allocated to any order of government by the Constitution Act. De facto, it is an area of shared responsibility, and given the distribution of probabilities about emergencies, there is good reason for this. There is room, therefore, for new shared-cost programs in the area of preparedness. Such programs could usefully target equipment and facilities (and their updating) to be used for provincial or regional purposes, which would bolster provincial preparedness and, in practice, could be used to generate regional cooperation in planning. Again, such programs would be inexpensive and congruent with a security agenda.

Federal governments are always interested in direct contact with citizens. One group in the emergency planning field has already been targeted by Ottawa, but it needs more help. These people are voluntary firefighters. They are vital first responders in emergencies, and their organizational strength is unique in many small towns and rural areas. There are about eighty-five thousand of them, but demographic change in the places they serve is making it hard to find recruits of the appropriate age and fitness. In the 2011 budget, the federal government introduced a tax credit of 15 percent on $3,000 for those working more than 200 hours in a year (Canada 2012), which is enough to constitute some recognition of their importance to local communities. But it is unlikely to induce much change in behaviour among potential members of the forces. To help the preparedness agenda by actually stimulating recruitment, this tax expenditure should be increased very substantially.

CONCLUSION

Protecting citizens is a fundamental role of government, and planning for emergencies is a vital component of this public safety imperative. As the first line of response, municipal governments necessarily bear much of the responsibility for emergency management, but the scale and complexity of recent emergencies highlight the importance of effective intergovernmental and inter-sectoral collaboration in this policy field. In analyzing these relationships, the research in this volume suggests that the quality of Canadian emergency management policy has generally improved in recent years, but it also illuminates important shortcomings and challenges that demand further attention and resources.

Municipal emergency planning is generally adequate, in that communities have formulated response plans, organized themselves to deploy resources when required, and established lines of regular communication with provincial emergency management personnel. But response capacity varies considerably from one community to another, and there are marked disparities between larger, urban municipalities and smaller, rural municipalities. Regionalization – the development of collaborative regional arrangements in order to jointly plan and pool resources through mutual aid – seems to be a promising approach to equalizing capacity, but implementation faces many hurdles. Provincial governments are the key actors here, and they will need to draw on instruments ranging from financial incentives to legal mandates in order to effect regional emergency management collaboration.

Provincial governments have increased their engagement with municipalities, adopting or amending legislation to formalize local emergency planning and encouraging municipal governments to work together in emergency management. The provincial-municipal working relationship appears to be collegial, and provincial officials rely on persuasion and partnership, rather than command and control. The federal government's commitment to emergency management, meanwhile, remains unclear. On the one hand, as Juillet and Koji explain in chapter 2, Ottawa has adopted new legislation and entered into compacts with provincial and territorial governments, which suggests a deeper commitment to emergency management. On the other hand, the decision to phase out federal funding for preparedness and training appears to signal a withdrawal from the policy field. As noted here, there is much the government of Canada can do to support provinces and response agencies in preparing for emergencies. A national campaign to raise awareness about individual and family preparedness should be contemplated, as well as more help for the provinces and territories. A strong federal commitment is an important ingredient of a well-performing national emergency management system.

Although Canada has experienced many major emergencies in recent years, more serious disasters may be on the horizon. Climate change, population growth in hazardous areas, economic and technological interdependence, and environmental degradation are some of many converging factors that point to more frequent and severe disasters in years to come (Etkin 1999; Kettl 2006; McBean 2004). The risk of disaster demands high-quality emergency management policies, including efforts to mitigate hazards, reduce the vulnerability of people and property, and respond effectively to emergencies and their impacts. The research presented in this volume shows that Canadian governments have established the legal and organizational foundation on which to build a robust emergency management framework. Further efforts to equip first responders, coordinate response resources, and enhance vertical and horizontal collaboration will be required to meet the challenges ahead.

REFERENCES

Auditor General of Canada. 2009. *Fall 2009 Report of the Auditor General of Canada to the House of Commons*. Ottawa: Public Works and Government Services Canada.

Calgary Herald. 2012. "Stakeholders Cry Foul as Feds Cut Funding for Emergency Preparedness." 30 June.

Canada. 1985. *Emergencies Act*. R.S.C., 1985, c. 22.

– 2012. "Introducing a Volunteer Firefighters Tax Credit." Ottawa: Government of Canada. http://actionplan.gc.ca/initiative/introducing-volunteer-firefighters-tax-credit.

CBC News. 2009. "Government Might Buy, Not Rebuild, Some Flood-Prone Homes." 20 April. http://www.cbc.ca/news/canada/manitoba/story/2009/04/20/mb-flood-buyout.html.

Etkin, David. 1999. "Risk Transference and Related Trends: Driving Forces towards More Mega-Disasters." *Environmental Hazards* 1 (2): 69–75.

Government of Australia. 2011. "Natural Disaster Resilience Program." 14 October. http://www.em.gov.au/Fundinginitiatives/Pages/Natural DisasterResilienceProgram.aspx.

Harper, Stephen. 2004. "My Plan for 'Open Federalism.'" *National Post*, 27 October, A19.

Hooghe, Lisbet, and Gary Marks. 2003. "Unraveling the Central State, But How? Types of Multi-level Governance." *American Political Science Review* 97 (2): 233–43.

Kapucu, Naim, and Vener Garayev. 2011. "Collaborative Decision-Making in Emergency and Disaster Management." *International Journal of Public Administration* 34 (6): 366–75.

Kettl, Donald F. 2006. "Is the Worst Yet to Come?" *Annals of the American Academy of Political and Social Science* 604 (1): 273–87.

McBean, Gordon. 2004. "Climate Change and Extreme Weather: A Basis for Action." *Natural Hazards* 31 (1): 177–90.

McEntire, David A., and Gregg Dawson. 2007. "The Intergovernmental Context." In *Emergency Management: Principles and Practice for Local Government*. 2d ed. Edited by William L. Waugh, Jr, and Kathleen Tierney, 57–70. Washington, DC: International City/County Management Association.

McEntire, David A., and John R. Lindsay. 2012. "One Neighborhood, Two Families: A Comparison of Intergovernmental Emergency Management Relationships." *Journal of Emergency Management* 10 (2): 93–107.

McLoughlin, David. 1985. "A Framework for Integrated Emergency Management." *Public Administration Review* 45 (Special Issue): 165–72.

O'Leary, Margaret. 2004. *Measuring Disaster Preparedness: A Practical Guide to Indicator Development and Application*. Lincoln, NE: iUniverse.

Oulahen, Greg. 2009. "Be Ready for an Emergency: Results of a National Survey Reveal Opportunities for Canadians to Improve." *FrontLine Security* 4 (2): 28–30.

Public Safety Canada. 2012a. "Canadian Disaster Database." 20 February. http://www.publicsafety.gc.ca/prg/em/cdd/index-eng.aspx.

– 2012b. "Joint Emergency Preparedness Program." 20 February. http:// www.publicsafety.gc.ca/prg/em/jepp/index-eng.aspx.

U.S. Department of Homeland Security. 2011. "Grant Programs Directorate Information Bulletin No. 370." 23 August. http://www.fema.gov/pdf/ government/grant/bulletins/info370.pdf.

Waugh, William L., Jr. 1999. "Assessing Quality in Disaster Management." In *Performance and Quality Measurement in Government*, edited by Arie Halachmi, 65–82. Burke, VA: Chatelaine Press.

Waugh, William L., Jr, and Gregory Streib. 2006. "Collaboration and Leadership for Effective Emergency Management." *Public Administration Review* 66 (S1): 131–40.

Young, Robert. 2006. "Open Federalism and Canadian Municipalities." In *Open Federalism: Interpretations, Significance*, edited by Keith Banting et al., 7–24. Kingston, ON: Institute of Intergovernmental Relations.

– 2011. "The Federal Role in Canada's Cities: The Pendulum Swings Again." In *The Federal Idea: Essays in Honour of Ronald L. Watts*, edited by Thomas J. Courchene, John R. Allan, Christian Leuprecht, and Nadia Verelli, 313–22. Kingston, ON: Institute of Intergovernmental Relations.

Contributors

NORM CATTO is professor of geography and chair of environmental science at Memorial University. His research interests include natural hazards, coastal landforms, emergency measures, response of river systems to climate and weather events, mass movements, and the impacts of climate and weather events on transportation, fisheries, and communities.

MALCOLM GRIEVE retired as associate professor and head of political science at Acadia University in 2011. His writings include work on non-profit organizations and networks and emergency planning.

GEOFFREY HALE is professor of political science at the University of Lethbridge. He was worked on a wide range of public policy issues in the Canadian and North American contexts.

DANIEL HENSTRA is associate professor of political science at the University of Waterloo. His research interests include public administration, public policy, local government, and multilevel governance. His recent published work has focused on emergency management and climate change adaptation.

LUC JUILLET teaches at the Graduate School of Public and International Affairs of the University of Ottawa, where he also holds the Jean-Luc Pépin Chair in the Study of Canadian Government.

JUNICHIRO KOJI holds a PHD in political science (with specialization in Canadian Studies) from the University of Ottawa. His dissertation analyzes the evolution of Quebec's immigrant integration policy from 1976 to 1991, and his research interests include Canadian and Quebec politics, multilevel governance, immigration, and diversity management policy.

STEPHEN TOMBLIN is professor of political science at Memorial University, where he has taught since 1985. He has published widely on comparative policy issues.

LORI TURNBULL is associate professor of political science and Canadian studies at Dalhousie University. Her teaching and research focuses on institutions of politics and governance in Canada, the United States, and Westminster systems around the world.

ROBERT YOUNG is professor of political science at the University of Western Ontario, where he holds the Canada Research Chair in Multilevel Governance. He is the editor of the Fields of Governance Series.

Index